BORIS

Also by Andrew Gimson

THE DESIRED EFFECT

BORIS

The Rise of Boris Johnson

ANDREW GIMSON

SIMON &
SCHUSTER

London · New York · Sydney · Toronto

A CBS COMPANY

First published in Great Britain by Simon & Schuster UK Ltd in 2006
A CBS COMPANY

Copyright © 2006 by Andrew Gimson

1 3 5 7 9 10 8 6 4 2

Simon & Schuster UK Ltd
Africa House
64–78 Kingsway
London WC2B 6AH

www.simonsays.co.uk

Simon & Schuster Australia
Sydney

A CIP catalogue for this book is available
from the British Library.

ISBN: 0-7432-7584-5
EAN: 9780743275842

Typeset by M Rules
Printed and bound in Great Britain by
The Bath Press, Bath

For Sally

Contents

Introduction   xi

Acknowledgements   xix

1   The Birth of Boris   1
2   The Death of Ali Kemal   5
3   Small Blond Heads   11
4   Learning to be a Johnson   17
5   Greek Before Breakfast   29
6   An Etonian Performance   35
7   Genuine Bogusness   56
8   The Oxford Politician   68
9   Boris in Love   76
10   Troubled Times   85
11   Our Man in Brussels   97
12   Twelve Days a Bachelor   107
13   The Fall of Darius Guppy   117
14   A Telly Star is Born   124
15   Ape Gets Ming Vase   131
16   Member for Henley   141
17   Conrad Black's Indulgence   153
18   The Start of an Affair   162
19   Sellotaping Everything Together   174
20   The Calm Before the Storm   185
21   Operation Scouse-grovel   193
22   The Pyramid of Piffle   209

23 Toff Fired   219
24 Theatricals   226
25 Overtaken by Cameron   235
26 Roman Civilisation   247
27 Coming Up on the Outside   255

    Index   267

BORIS

Introduction

'It was at Rome, on the 15th of October 1764, as I sat musing
amidst the ruins of the Capitol, while the barefooted friars were
singing vespers in the Temple of Jupiter, that the idea of writing
the decline and fall of the city first started to my mind.'

—Edward Gibbon, *Autobiography*

It was at London, on the 4th of June 2004, as I sat musing amidst
the ruins of breakfast, while my wife said she supposed she
would not really mind if we all went barefoot, that the idea of
writing the life of Boris Johnson first started to my mind.

Like Gibbon, Boris is a historian of Rome, but that was not
why his name occurred to me. In the summer of 2004, Boris's
star shone with amazing brightness. Reputable judges predicted
he would be the next Conservative Prime Minister, and that
June morning he was all over the newspapers, which were
enthralled by a scoop he had gathered while waiting on his bike
at a traffic light.

An hour or two later I rang Boris and left a message on his
mobile, telling him that I'd had an idea. I have known Boris
since 1987, and in January 2000 he gave me the unpaid post of
Foreign Editor of the *Spectator*, but it was almost unprecedented
for me to ring him with an idea.

Two minutes later he rang back. Almost his first words were:

'Hang on, Andrew. A very beautiful girl has got to get off the train.'

Boris was at this time much bothered by girls who did not appreciate that he had editorial duties.

As soon as she had gone, Boris said, 'I met this rather beautiful singer. She just directed a coy, backward glance at me.'

I asked Boris if I could write his biography. He laughed for a long time before saying, 'Such is my colossal vanity that I have no intention of trying to forbid you.'

He said he would introduce me to the people I wanted to talk to, and provide photographs of himself as a child. He also declared, in the manner of a Victorian statesman, 'I will of course give you full access to my papers.'

Boris himself pointed out that the book could be 'the most fantastic piss-take'. Nobody is quicker than Boris to spot his own life's comic possibilities.

But then he asked: 'What about poor Allegra?' Allegra was Boris's first wife, and although for some years he omitted her from his entry in *Who's Who*, she is not omitted from this book. I wondered if he was worried what Allegra would say about him. I was already more worried about Marina, his present wife. It is one thing to write about a marriage that is over, quite another to intrude on a marriage which is still going.

Boris reminisced about our past: 'You introduced me to journalism. You gave me pork chops in your flat. We both got very drunk. Basically you introduced me to T. E. Utley, who introduced me to *The Times*, who gave me the traineeship.'

Boris has a remarkable memory and is one of the great flatterers of our times. It was delightful of him to say that I had introduced him to journalism, but the truth was that a number of people, all of them far more powerful than myself, helped Boris into journalism, and he has left each of them with the heart-warming impression that he or she was solely responsible for launching him. It is also true that Boris was more than capable of launching himself. His energy, ambition and talents were so remarkable that he could have pushed into almost any profession that attracted him, though it is true that he has failed to become a concert pianist.

For a time Boris continued kind. He loves reciting poetry, and when next we spoke he burst out into a great chunk of 'Lycidas', by John Milton:

> Alas! What boots it with uncessant care
> To tend the homely, slighted, shepherd's trade
> And strictly meditate the thankless Muse?
> Were it not better done, as others use,
> To sport with Amaryllis in the shade,
> Or with the tangles of Neaera's hair?
> Fame is the spur that the clear spirit doth raise
> (That last infirmity of noble mind)
> To scorn delights, and live laborious days:
> But the fair guerdon when we hope to find,
> And think to burst out into sudden blaze,
> Comes the blind Fury with the abhorred shears
> And slits the thin-spun life.

I put it to Boris that sporting with Amaryllis might be preferable to fame, but he made no reply. He was at this time doing so well that it seemed he could have everything he wanted. There was a risk, from my point of view, that others would hit on the idea of writing his life, but he said he would 'actively dissuade' anyone else who tried to do so before I had finished.

Boris also enquired, in the words of Sir Arthur Conan Doyle, whether his life was like 'the giant rat of Sumatra, a story for which the world is not yet prepared'. I took this as false modesty, but in retrospect it can be seen as his first note of caution.

During our third talk about the book Boris very sportingly gave me his father, mother and sister's telephone numbers. He also invited me to his fortieth birthday party, which was soon to take place, and to the cricket match between a _Spectator_ side, captained by himself, and the team of his friend Lord Spencer, brother of the late Princess of Wales. The game was to take place on the ground at Althorp, the Spencer estate near Northampton.

Boris again mentioned Allegra, his first wife. I said I was having lunch with her that very day.

'Oh no!' he said. There was a pause, after which he went on: 'My life is literally in your hands.'

A few days later I had lunch with a friend of Boris's mistress, Petronella Wyatt, who told me that in 2003 she had got pregnant by Boris, and had aborted the child, but that Boris had told her he would look after any child she had by him.

No word of any such pregnancy had yet appeared in the newspapers, but on 16 June 2004 I found, not altogether surprisingly, that Boris was getting cold feet about the book. I met him that evening outside the House of Commons, in New Palace Yard, having rung him on his mobile while he was voting at 7 p.m. As we walked out into Parliament Square and across the road into Whitehall, Boris pushing his bike, he said in a worried tone: 'If it's a piss-take that's OK.' But he also said, 'Anything that purported to tell the truth really would be intolerable.'

I contended that politicians almost always get into trouble not for telling the truth but for trying to conceal it. Painful episodes in Boris's past would lose their power to hurt him once they were known, and it would be much less dangerous to deal with this stuff now than when he became Prime Minister.

In George Otto Trevelyan's classic book about another brilliant Old Etonian politician, _The Early History of Charles James Fox_, we are reminded that 'the senatorial habit of regarding the daily press as a criminal organisation' was already fully developed in the eighteenth century. Trevelyan described why in 1770 the Prime Minister tried to suppress the reporting of Parliament:

'Conscious of belonging to the class with regard to whom truth
is the worst of libels, Lord North and his followers esteemed the
reporter an equally dangerous enemy with the pamphleteer.'

Boris is not a member of 'the class with regard to whom truth
is the worst of libels'. He is a man of immense energy, who was
no more brought up to be faithful to a single woman than
Charles James Fox was brought up to abstain from gambling.

As we sauntered into Whitehall, Boris gave his reluctant consent to the book, but it was becoming clear that his family were
worried. His mother, Charlotte, sounded wonderfully sympathetic on the telephone, but deferred by a month a meeting I
was to have with her.

His sister, Rachel, was the only one of his three siblings and
two half-siblings with whom I was already acquainted. A week
or two after I rang her, she sent me an e-mail, in which she
referred to Boris as 'Al', the name by which the Johnsons call
him, and said: 'There is little appetite among the siblings for
sharing, much as we love Al, which we really do, but these are
complicated issues and until Al has talked to us all about the
"grand projet" I don't think I can have our meeting. In fact, it's
because we love the bugger and regard our shared childhood as
so precious that there is reluctance to turn it, like so much else,
into public knowledge.'

Worst of all, I heard from a friend of mine that Marina,
Boris's wife, and her parents Charles and Dip Wheeler were
very worried about the book and had tried to enlist this friend's
help to stop it. Marina is loved by all who know her, while her
father is one of the most respected correspondents the BBC has
ever had.

Perhaps at this point I should have renounced the project.
This book may inflict some pain, especially since, in an attempt
to convey some flavour of Boris, I have quoted with impudent
freedom from private conversations I have had with him.

I might claim I owed it to history to leave my impressions of this great man. But that would be the most unutterable balls. Like Boris himself, I have been selfish. I found him too enjoyable to give up. There was too much laughter in him, and almost everyone to whom I mentioned the idea of the book responded by laughing, or at least by smiling. Boris is filled with a vitality which bursts the bounds of good taste. He is a figure from the eighteenth century, a magnanimous Merry England Conservative who has the gift, very unusual in a Member of Parliament, of cheering people up. Nobody could be less sanctimonious, or more anxious to win our love by telling jokes. He reaches far beyond the ranks of those who are interested in politics, and attracts support even among those who hate politicians.

I was attracted by the idea of writing about a politician before he had achieved high office. It is such a relief not to have to go into the details of Boris's sixth budget, or the third administration which he will form at the age of eighty-one. If you want that sort of thing, there are plenty of great works where you can find it. But where else can you find a sketch of a shadow Conservative spokesman on higher education (if that is what he still is when this book comes out)?

Boris is a celebrity, which is a bizarre thing for a man with his classical education at Eton and Balliol College, Oxford, to have become, or to want to become, and I wanted to see how he had done it. The celebrity living a life above the rules is the epitome of our tabloid culture, and to write about him in a completely sanitised way would be to misunderstand him. He or she appeals to our fantasies of effortless success, a sort of modern version of the effortless superiority once attributed to Balliol men.

The celebrity has sex without responsibility and is attractive enough never to be without a lover. As Boris himself once boasted to a woman: 'I haven't had to have a wank for twenty years.'

Some months after starting my research, I decided the time

had come to speak to Boris himself about his childhood. I went one morning to the *Spectator* and waited for him in his office.

Boris looked shocked to see me when he arrived. In what now strikes me as a rather gauche way, I said I wanted to talk to him about his childhood. Boris said, 'Oh my God,' and held his head in his hands. He went on to say, 'What I'm worried about is that stuff will come out, no matter how delicate and tactful you are . . . Other people will use the appearance of the book to fan old coals and heat up long-dead issues.'

When I remarked that I was writing the book anyhow, and urged him to have his say, he responded: 'As the *News of the World* would say' – and here he switched into a brutish accent – 'your name's going to be in this anyway. We'd just like you to put your side of the story.'

I reminded Boris that he had agreed to the book. He replied: 'I wasn't thinking straight then.'

Boris asked how large an advance Simon & Schuster were paying me for the book, which I refused to tell him. He offered to buy me out, and as the book progressed, his bids increased in size. I am inclined to think that all this must have been a protracted joke. At one of our last encounters before the book went to press, when I bumped into him in Trafalgar Square, he raised the amount in large jumps, as if bidding in an auction, and for a fleeting moment offered me £100,000 not to write the book. In a subsequent communication, he thought better of this approach and offered instead to give my children free Greek lessons.

Boris had moved from complete agreement with the book to total disagreement. He began by sounding utterly confident, and ended by sounding strangely vulnerable. It was a curious transformation, but also, as I was to discover, a rather characteristic one.

So this is not an authorised biography, nor can I pretend that it is exhaustive. I have tried to be fair to Boris and to those near to him, and if I have failed the fault is mine alone, but I have not attempted to monopolise this colossus of our times. In years to come, there will be any amount of work for younger, fitter Johnson scholars.

I sought the advice of other writers. Tony Blair's biographer, John Rentoul, warned: 'The sex is difficult.' Charles Moore, who is at work on Margaret Thatcher's authorised biography, said of Boris: 'You'll need 200 pages for his foreign policy.'

But time has given out, and those 200 pages remain unwritten. All I can offer is a sketch drawn from life, by one who was lucky enough to know Boris.

Acknowledgements

My greatest debt is to Boris, for providing such good subject matter, and for remaining generally good-tempered. I would like to thank his mother, Charlotte, and father, Stanley, for outlining the family background, and his sister, Rachel, for supplying a couple of anecdotes. Their cousin Sinan Kuneralp provided valuable information about the Johnsons' Turkish ancestry, as did Geoffrey Lewis, Andrew Mango and David Barchard.

Boris's first wife, Allegra Mostyn-Owen, was immensely helpful, and Marina Wheeler, his present wife, kindly broke her rule of not talking to journalists (apart from members of her own family) and corrected some inaccuracies. Max Benitz undertook some last-minute research. Among the many other people I must thank are Darius Guppy, Shusha Guppy, Conrad Black, Charles Moore, Frank Johnson, Ann Sindall, Nick Garland, Nigel Howard, Alan Davidson, Clive and Rowena Williams, Eric Anderson, John Lewis, Martin Hammond, Michael Meredith, Penny Hatfield, Chris Bayston, Andrew Gilmour, Jesse Norman, James Hughes-Onslow, Johnnie Boden, Joshua Neicho, Jasper Griffin, Jonathan Barnes, Anthony Kenny, Lloyd Evans, Justin Rushbrooke, Radek Sikorski, Frank Luntz, Patrick Hennessy, Gary Gibbon, Toby Young, Michael Gove, Jessica Pulay, David Ekserdjian, John and Sarah Biffen, Miriam Gross, Susanna Gross, Peter Stothard, Charles Wilson, George Brock, John Bryant, Simon Heffer, Paul Hill, Rory Watson, David Usborne, Michael Binyon, Sarah Helm, Charles Grant, John Kerr, Douglas Hurd,

Philippe Sands, James Landale, Max Hastings, Dominic Lawson, Trevor Grove, Marcus Scriven, Sue Lawley, Ian Hislop, Richard Ehrman, Stuart Reid, Mary Wakefield, Peter Oborne, Peter McKay, Olivia Walmsley, Henrietta Malcolm-Smith, Stephen Glover, Sarah Sands, Anne Jenkin, Tom Henry, Matthew Pencharz and Henry McCrory. Many other people helped but asked not to be quoted by name. I am acutely aware that there are yet others to whom it would have been desirable to talk, and would urge anyone with memories of Boris which he or she is willing to share with a wider audience to get in touch. I am grateful to those writers from whose articles I have quoted.

My agent, Rivers Scott, and Angela Herlihy and Andrew Gordon at Simon & Schuster all gave indispensable help. My wife Sally encouraged me in a way that nobody else could have done.

Andrew Gimson
Gospel Oak
July 2006

The Birth of Boris

BORIS WAS BORN TO BRITISH PARENTS IN NEW YORK City on 19 June 1964. His mother, Charlotte, who was only twenty-two years old, relates that even at birth he had the thick yellow hair for which he was later to become so celebrated: 'We didn't cut it, so it turned into ringlets.'

His father, Stanley, who was twenty-three, wrote a radio talk about the birth which was broadcast later that summer in Britain on the Light Programme. In it he recalled that Charlotte 'received a constant stream of letters and cables from England entreating her to go back and have the child there'. Their friends said it would be appallingly expensive to have the baby in America, and they also pointed out that the child would be a US citizen, 'eligible to be drafted and like as not dispatched into the jungles of Vietnam'. They must also have doubted whether Stanley would be able to look after Charlotte and the baby properly.

By Stanley's account, the most powerful argument 'was, of course, the financial one'. Doctors in New York were not cheap: when Charlotte broke her toe, her treatment cost $70. But then they heard of 'the Clinic', a place where you paid only what you could afford. Respectable New Yorkers did not go to the Clinic:

'Socialized, or as it is more sinisterly called, communistic medicine is in America evil almost by definition.' But as Stanley said in the radio talk, 'we were neither respectable nor New Yorkers'.

For five weeks, Stanley attended ante-natal classes, before asking himself: 'Did real men bother themselves with all this?'

One detail which he omitted from the talk, but mentioned in conversation to me, was that he had been 'doing my stuff', rubbing Charlotte's back and uttering words of encouragement during her labour, but had 'popped out for a pizza at the crucial moment'.

On his return, Stanley was surprised to see that the soles of their new-born baby were black. This was because his footprints had been taken, to ensure that no baby-swapping took place.

The boy's full name was Alexander Boris de Pfeffel Johnson. The name Boris was in honour of Boris Litwin, a White Russian in Mexico City. On leaving Oxford in 1963, Stanley had won a Harkness Fellowship to study in the United States. In the same year, he married Charlotte, who was herself an undergraduate at Lady Margaret Hall, Oxford. They met when he won the Newdigate Prize for poetry, which led to his being invited to dine at All Souls', where she too was dining, because her father, James Fawcett, was a fellow of that college. She deferred the final year of her degree, and they went together to America, where Stanley started by attending the State University of Iowa in Iowa City for one term.

From Iowa, where Boris was probably conceived, they moved to New York, where they lived in a loft on West 23rd Street, opposite the Chelsea Hotel and above a café called the Star Bar, where Stanley first heard the Beatles.

A condition of the Harkness award was that he must do at least three months' travel each summer, for which purpose he was given a brand new Chevrolet Bel Air.

At the end of May 1964, when Charlotte was eight months pregnant, they drove from New York to Laredo in Texas, a distance of 1,700 miles as the crow flies, which as Stanley says was 'quite a long haul'.

Stanley, it has been said by one who knew him over a long period, does not believe in comfort or sickness. He neither admitted to sickness himself, nor noticed it in others. The same is true of Boris, of whom this observer said: 'I'd never put him in charge of hospitals.'

The young couple were not allowed to take the car out of the country, so left it on the border and took the Greyhound bus to Mexico City, about 600 miles farther on, where they met Boris Litwin, whose daughter was a friend of a friend of Stanley's at Oxford.

When Litwin saw Charlotte's condition and heard that Stanley proposed to take her all the way back to Laredo on the bus, he was appalled, and the following exchange took place:

LITWIN: 'I want to give you a first-class ticket to New York.'
CHARLOTTE: 'Oh Mr Litwin . . .'
LITWIN: 'Call me Boris.'
CHARLOTTE: 'Oh Boris, whatever the baby is, I shall call it Boris.'

In the event, Charlotte and Stanley accepted two tickets from Litwin to get them back to the United States and then drove back to New York. Soon afterwards, Boris was born, and the next day Stanley typed a letter to Litwin:

I write at once to tell you that Alexander BORIS de Pfeffel Johnson was born at 2.00 p.m. yesterday and that both he and his mother, Charlotte, are very well and happy.

It is a source of immense satisfaction to me, sir, that we have thus been able to redeem the promise which we made to you in Mexico, so long ago, that, should it be possible, the child would be named after you in some small recognition of the kindnesses which you showed to us then.

Alexander BORIS weighed 9 pounds 1 ounce at birth and is a remarkably lusty child.

Litwin had unfortunately died, so never received this news. As for the lusty child, he is still known to the Johnsons as Al, and his first articles for *The Times* appeared under the byline Alexander Johnson, but we shall call him Boris, the name under which he was to become famous. As someone fated to devote so many of his prodigious energies to public performance, he was lucky to have been given such a simple and memorable stage name.

2

The Death of Ali Kemal

BORIS'S FOREBEARS WERE CLEVER AND COSMOPOLITAN. HIS father's family was notable for its recklessness, while his mother's family are distinguished for their learning. In the direct male line, Boris is descended from a Turkish polemicist who went into politics and was murdered after backing the wrong side. His great grandfather, Ali Kemal, was a handsome, brilliant and provocative Turkish journalist before and just after the First World War, during the last years of the Ottoman Empire. Ali Kemal's own father came from Kalfat, a village in north-west Anatolia where there were many children with blond hair, perhaps descended from the Goths. This is thought to be the origin of the remarkably fair hair, more white than gold, which is found to this day in the Johnson family and is one of Boris's most distinctive characteristics.

Ali Kemal's mother was a Circassian, reputedly of slave origin. The Circassians were an unruly, good-looking race of mountaineers from the western Caucasus. Their fighting spirit and willingness to risk life and limb are seen in Boris, but appeared with even greater force in Ali Kemal. He was first arrested in 1888, for setting up a students' society, and spent many years before the First World War in exile from Ottoman Turkey.

Ali Kemal was an educated man, a poet and novelist who

enjoyed living abroad. But even before he was murdered it was said of him that 'the life of a predatory bird tends to be short', and according to Andrew Mango, the foremost British authority on the period, 'his pen ran away with him. He was clearly a difficult man with an angry temperament. In Britain today he would be a vituperative journalist.'

At the end of the First World War, Ali Kemal became one of the most prominent advocates of co-operation with the victorious Allies, including the British, and the sworn enemy of the Turkish Nationalist movement which was emerging under the leadership of Kemal Atatürk.

Atatürk, who at this point was still known as Mustafa Kemal, was a senior army officer who had distinguished himself at Gallipoli. He was about to achieve worldwide renown as the founder of modern Turkey, but not before Ali Kemal tried to stop him.

In May 1919 Ali Kemal was made interior minister. On 16 June he instructed post offices to refuse the flood of protest telegrams being sent by Anti-Annexation Societies all over Aegean Turkey to the government in Istanbul and to the Allies. These telegrams contained demands for protection against Greek troops, who had landed with Allied help in Izmir and were driving out the Muslim population with heavy loss of life and wholesale destruction of Muslim property.

Ali Kemal immediately understood how vital the telegraph system was to the Nationalists. Boris shows a similar ability, both as a journalist and as a politician, to see how power works.

Atatürk, who was later to say that he won the War of Independence by using the telegraph wires, hit back on 20 June 1919 with a circular to post offices in which he threatened to court martial any official who obeyed Ali Kemal's ban on telegrams. Three days later, the government backed down and allowed the transmission of telegrams, on condition that these were approved by the local authorities.

On the same day, 23 June, Ali Kemal sent a circular to the provincial authorities ordering them to have nothing to do with Atatürk. But Ali Kemal was dangerously isolated. He was the only minister who was determined to get rid of Atatürk, and he became embroiled in a furious argument with the war minister, with the result that on 26 June they both resigned.

While Atatürk led the Nationalists to victory, attained in August 1922, Ali Kemal returned to journalism. He edited a newspaper called *Peyam-i Sabah*, or 'Morning Message', and attacked the Nationalists very violently in print, telling them that by opposing the British they would get a worse deal. In the view of the Nationalists, he was a traitor who wanted to turn Turkey into a British colony.

On 10 September 1922 Ali Kemal published an editorial in which he attempted to make his peace with the Nationalists, expressing his joy at their victory. This last editorial did not save him. On 4 November 1922, he was kidnapped by Nationalist agents outside the Cercle d'Orient club in Istanbul, bundled into a boat and taken across the Bosphorus to Izmit, where he was handed over to Nurettin Pasha, a brutal general who dealt with enemies by handing them over to a mob which could be relied upon to lynch them.

Nurettin had already disposed of Chrysostom, a Greek Archbishop, in this way, and he applied the same bloodthirsty method to Ali Kemal. The mob finished him off with sticks, stones and knives, before hanging him up in a tree in the square of Izmit. Atatürk was furious, declaring, 'We're not bandits operating in the mountains,' and sacked Nurettin.

Boris is a passionate defender of Turkish entry into the European Union. He refers quite often to Ali Kemal, usually getting some of the facts wrong, as in a disappointing television programme about the Turkish exhibition at the Royal Academy which he presented in February 2005.

It is usual on these occasions for the presenter to be filmed in the places from which the artefacts are drawn, but Boris had travelled no further than the RA in Piccadilly, where he made repeated use of the word 'magnificent' to describe the exhibits.

Boris has also related how, when accused at a meeting during the 2001 General Election of stoking up base feelings against asylum-seekers, he responded by announcing, 'I am the grand-son of an asylum-seeker.'

This too is incorrect. Ali Kemal's first wife, who was half-English and half-Swiss, gave birth in Bournemouth in September 1909 to a son, Osman Ali. It had been thought she would be safer in England than in Turkey, but she died in childbirth. Her son was brought up by her mother, Margaret Johnson, and was renamed Wilfred Johnson.

On 27 June 1919, Margaret Johnson wrote a formal letter from 15 Foxholes Road, Southbourne-on-Sea, just east of Bournemouth, to the British Delegation to the Versailles Peace Conference:

Sir,

I beg leave to inquire if you can inform me whether I should be able to have an interview with one of the Turkish Delegates at present in Paris, under the following circumstances:

(1) The Delegate referred to is ALI KEMAL BEY, who I am informed is at present staying at the Château de Monteclin, Jouy-en-Josas, near Paris.

(2) He was married to my daughter, who died in the year 1909, leaving two children, a girl now aged 12, and a boy now 10 years of age. By arrangement with their father, the above mentioned Delegate, these children were, on the death of their mother (my daughter), left in my care, and were both baptised into the Church of England. Both are now being educated here.

(3) Since the outbreak of war with Turkey the father has not contributed anything towards their maintenance.

(4) As I am, unfortunately, left without means, the support of these dear children has been a very great strain on my efforts.

(5) Knowing that their father is now in Paris in connection with the preparation of the Treaty of Peace with Turkey, I am very anxious to see him, if possible, in order to get money from him towards the support of his two children. That is my sole and only reason for seeking an interview with him, and I am most anxious not to take any steps that would not meet with the approval, and be in strict accordance with the permission, of the British Delegation.

This enquiry brought no joy: the British Delegation informed Mrs Johnson that Ali Kemal had already left Paris. But several things emerge from the letter. One is that Mrs Johnson was bringing her grandson up as an Englishman, and indeed as a member of the Church of England. Another is that Ali Kemal had made no attempt since the end of the war to see his English children, or to send them money, although money was certainly needed.

Ali Kemal contracted a brilliant second marriage in 1913, to Sabiha, daughter of Zeki Pasha, a distinguished soldier who was head of the Ottoman artillery. They had one son, Zeki Kuneralp, whom Sabiha brought up in exile in Switzerland after Ali Kemal's murder. Sabiha sold Ali Kemal's collection of oriental manuscripts to the British Library after his death and gave the proceeds to Mrs Johnson. Zeki, her son, was a man of great ability and charm. He entered the Turkish diplomatic service, in which he rose to become ambassador in London and then in Madrid, where in 1977 his wife and her brother, the Turkish ambassador in Oslo, were murdered by Armenian terrorists.

The Turkish and English sides of the family were by this time in friendly contact. But the panache with which Boris plays the part of stage Englishman can be traced to the determination of the Johnsons to be seen as English. It is a role they have perfected over three generations.

Wilfred Johnson, known as Johnny, did not care to be reminded of the Turkish father who had abandoned him. Boris's grandfather grew up in England, farmed in Canada and then went to Egypt, where he worked on the farms of various Swiss cousins. It was here that he met Boris's grandmother, Irène Williams, known as 'Buster' because of her kick-boxing prowess. Johnny saw her do a camel kick to get rid of a cheeky soldier who had molested her in a bar. They were married in 1936.

Buster was half-French and half-English. On the English side, she was descended from Sir George Williams, who in 1844 founded the YMCA, or Young Men's Christian Association. His grandson, Stanley Williams, married Marie-Louise de Pfeffel, daughter of the Baron de Pfeffel, who lived in a fine house in Versailles which is now the Chamber of Commerce. Boris's grandmother was born in that house, and wanted to keep the name 'de Pfeffel' in the family, which is why Boris bears it.

During the Second World War, Johnny served in Coastal Command in the RAF, and on one occasion, when Buster was watching from the ground, he tipped the wing of his plane to her and crashed, injuring himself quite severely. This was later spoken of by the family as a great joke. A mangled fragment of this wrecked plane – it looks like the joystick – is preserved at Nethercote, the 500-acre sheep farm on Exmoor which Johnny and Buster bought with her money after the war.

3

Small Blond Heads

SOON AFTER BORIS WAS BORN, HIS PARENTS CAME BACK WITH him to England so that Charlotte could return to Oxford and finish her English degree. She was the first married undergraduate her college, Lady Margaret Hall, had ever had, and during her final year she became pregnant for a second time: 'The Principal never spoke to me again when she learned that Miss Fawcett, as I continued to be known, was pregnant again.' In the autumn of 1964, the Johnsons took a modern flat in Summertown, Oxford. Here Charlotte looked after Boris with the aid of a woman next door, and studied for her exams. She remembers Boris as an 'incredibly good baby' who never cried. She would be writing an essay and he would sit on the floor at her feet, with a box or saucepan to amuse him. On looking down, she would sometimes find he had fallen asleep on his back. Once, when he was being looked after by her old nanny at her parents' large house in Cavendish Avenue in St John's Wood, London, Charlotte's mother and the nanny, Miss Reid, were having coffee downstairs and heard a crash. Boris's cot had broken and they found him lying fast asleep on the mattress on the floor.

Until the age of eight or nine he was very deaf, and had to undergo several operations to have grommets put in his ear.

According to his mother, 'I think that not hearing very well made him quite quiet.' Although he always had the gift of amusing people, he was not the rumbustious figure he later became.

Boris's aversion to eggs dates from early childhood, when he claims to have been fed too many of them. His rough and ready attitude to food reflects an upbringing where he was expected to eat pretty much anything. He has recalled with pride how he was able to eat the disgusting food which was served in one of his early primary schools.

Charlotte took her finals in June 1965, when Boris was a year old and she was about six months' pregnant with Rachel. At the end of her exams, when she was wearing subfusc – formal academic dress – made out of black-out curtains to accommodate her bump, Stanley and Miss Reid, the Fawcett family nanny, brought the one-year-old Boris to celebrate with her. The photograph of this occasion shows Boris with a magnificent head of fair, curly hair, attempting to drink some his mother's champagne, with Miss Reid looking on.

Charlotte's ancestors included Henry Fawcett, the Radical MP for Brighton, who was blinded by his own father in a shooting accident and became known as 'the blind Postmaster General', a position he was given by Gladstone in 1880. His wife, Millicent Garrett Fawcett, was one of the most famous campaigners for votes for women. Charlotte is herself one of the five children of Sir James Fawcett, an international lawyer who was described in his *Times* obituary as 'an intellectual colossus'. He was educated at Rugby and at New College, Oxford, where he obtained a double first in Mods and Greats before becoming a fellow of All Souls.

From his mother's family, Boris has inherited a tradition of humane and erudite liberalism. For twenty-two years, from 1962 to 1984, Sir James Fawcett was a member of the European Commission of Human Rights at Strasbourg. As a politician, Boris displays similar instincts to his grandfather. In an obituary piece for the *Independent* published on 1 July 1991, Lord Lester summarised some of the principles upheld by Sir James during his long period at the Commission, including the right to respect for family life of unmarried mothers and their children, the degrading nature of judicial corporal punishment, the right to free speech in a democratic society, the right to equal citizenship without racial discrimination, and the need for adequate safeguards against the misuse of necessary powers of clandestine surveillance.

In retirement Sir James pursued his interest in astronomy: 'Behind his house in Combe in the Berkshire hills was a telescope through which friends would share his love of the Heavens.' Lord Lester said of him: 'James was a gentle, considerate and private man, of extraordinary charm and dignity, and strikingly handsome. What mattered most to him were his marriage to his beloved Bice, and their delightful children and grandchildren. Bice was his constant and adored companion.'

The Fawcetts were great friends of the Pakenhams – Lord and Lady Longford – one of whose daughters, the novelist Rachel Billington, is Charlotte's best friend, and Boris's godmother. If Boris had taken his party allegiance from his mother's family, he would have joined Labour, and the Fawcetts were somewhat shocked when Charlotte married, in Stanley, a Tory.

Charlotte's mother, Beatrice Lowe, or Bice, was a Catholic convert of partly Jewish extraction. She was the daughter of Elias Lowe, né Loew, an immensely learned Lithuanian-born palaeographer of Latin manuscripts who worked at Oxford before becoming a professor at Princeton. His wife, Helen Lowe-Porter, was American, and for fifty years enjoyed the exclusive right to translate Thomas Mann's works into English. Mann had the highest opinion of her, but some rival scholars considered her translations to be stunningly inaccurate.

When I spoke to Charlotte, she was plainly thinking far more about the need to protect and help others, including her children, daughter-in-law and grandchildren, than about herself.

Stanley took a second degree, in agricultural economics, and in the spring of 1965 he also joined the Foreign Office, from which he resigned in the autumn of the same year, because 'by then the World Bank had come through with an offer for me to go to Washington'.

Charlotte, Stanley, Boris and Rachel spent the winter of 1965–66 on Exmoor, in a house they rented between Nethercote and Dulverton. Charlotte looked after the children while Stanley wrote his first novel, *Gold Dust*. On 22 February 1966 they flew to Washington. A year later, their third child, Leo, was born – a birth for which Charlotte returned to London. In 1968, when Stanley was already leaving the World Bank, he played a successful April Fool on its senior staff by putting forward a proposal to finance the building of three new pyramids in Egypt.

Charlotte was not keen to stay in America. According to Stanley, she was 'badly shaken by the riots in spring 1968' involving Martin Luther King. The Johnsons remained in Washington until the middle of 1968, when they moved to New York, where Stanley had got a job funded by John D. Rockefeller to look into the question of overpopulation. He had become convinced that the world was going to perish from this cause, and travelled 35,000 miles to research a book called *Life Without Birth*.

Stanley admitted in his first chapter that he had not himself practised the birth control which he had come to regard as an urgent necessity. It is one of the first references to Boris (still known as Alexander) in print, and also indicates one of the origins of Boris's style. Stanley is urging the need to do something now to save the world from overpopulation:

Act now. Act now. Oh God! I look at my guilty face in the shaving mirror as my children clatter down to breakfast –

it's too late to act. By all means bolt the stable door but the horses have gone. Where were you, *New York Times*, with your full-page advertisements [warning against over-population], when we added Rachel to Alexander? Where were you, conservationists of the world, at the getting of Leo? How can I face that row of small blond heads bobbing over the cornflakes knowing that I am statistically accountable for the burdens they will add to society?

We can be confident that Stanley could face the small blond heads with no trouble at all. He is immensely proud to have six children, four by Charlotte and two more by his present wife, Jenny.

Stanley had soaked up the progressive opinions of the day. He remarks that he has married a Catholic, but this does not stop him condemning the Pope (as did many Catholics too) for in July 1968 issuing *Humanae Vitae*, the encyclical forbidding birth control:

> If any single human being is to be brought to the bar of history for crimes against humanity in this last third of the twentieth century, it must be Pope Paul VI – for he has consigned countless millions to misery and anguish, mental and material. I believe that *Humanae Vitae* may come to be ranked as one of the most massive errors of judgment ever made . . . Paul VI, on the black day in July 1968, sacrificed the whole world to save the Church's soul.

This does not sound like Boris, who never denounces anyone in such harsh terms. But Stanley was only about twenty-seven when he wrote this, and his impetuousness, and urge to talk up the story he is telling, could be said to characterise some of the reports from Brussels which Boris was to write at the same age.

In May 1969 the Johnsons returned to London, where they

lived in Blomfield Road, Maida Vale. Stanley says he was 'actually quite rich – the Ford Foundation had given us rather a valuable scholarship to be in London studying demography'. He also had 'a variety of jobs', including one as the first environment desk officer in the Conservative Party's Research Department, where he shared an office with Chris Patten. Lord Patten, as he later became, remembers Stanley as 'absurd but harmless'.

There is a precarious feeling to all this. Nothing is solid or permanent. As Charlotte recalled: 'We moved thirty-two times when I was married to Stanley.' He was quick-witted and energetic, and had an eye to the main chance, but he had not hit the jackpot, and was not by birth a man of substance. The farm on Exmoor lost money and was subsidised out of Stanley's scholarships. Boris had a privileged upbringing, but also a rather rackety and hand-to-mouth one. As I worked on this book, I came to believe that he suffers to this day from a sense of insecurity, and a worry that he is about to be rumbled, which outsiders seldom detect. Along with his boundless optimism goes the fear that he and his family are only a couple of meals away from the poor house.

4

Learning to be a Johnson

FROM HIS EARLIEST YEARS, BORIS DEVELOPED A PASSION FOR coming top. His sister Rachel recalls that when asked as a small boy what he wanted to be, he would say 'the world king'. Nor has he ever grown out of this ambition. He has simply learned to conceal it. His manner is so shambolic and laid-back that, as with the insecurity mentioned at the end of the last chapter, this side of him can easily be overlooked. You will never find a more ferocious competitor than Boris, driven on by that sense of insecurity, but also by what he himself has called, with the intention that we should presume he is merely joking, his megalomania. He was not born to ease and comfort, but to wage a ceaseless struggle for supremacy. No Prussian militarist with a bankrupt estate in the barren depths of Brandenburg could be more single-minded than Boris in pursuit of knock-out victory.

In Boris's case, the estate which could never be made to pay, and which made it necessary for him to go out and win a place in the sun, was his grandparents' farm on Exmoor. Boris was almost five years old when the family left London and bought Nethercote Cottage, smallest of the three houses on the farm. It might be thought that in this remote spot, playing with his siblings rather than with other children, he would be sheltered from competitive pressure, but the Johnsons knew how to make their own competition. His grandmother would ask Rachel, a precocious four-year-old, to sit at the kitchen table and read the *Times* leader, and would tell her how well she had read it. This praise for his sister, who was just over a year younger than him, drove Boris mad with rage.

Another favourite family story has Boris playing table tennis with Rachel, losing a point to her during the knock-up, and kicking the wall so hard that he broke his toe. He is also supposed, when playing snooker with her, to have got so angry that he ripped the cloth and broke the cue, after she got a fluky shot in.

Julia Johnson, one of Stanley's two children by his second wife, Jenny, has described a Johnson upbringing:

> My father has six children, of which I am the last but one, and as long as I can remember there have been cut-throat mealtime quizzes, fearsome ping-pong matches, height, weight and blondness contests, and, of course, academic rivalry of mind-numbing magnitude. When my brother Jo gained a First from Oxford, Rachel rang Boris to tell him the 'terrible news'. If I came second in Latin, my father would instantly demand: 'Who came first?' It became a standard catchphrase in our household and a vigorous deterrent against being anything except top.

According to Julia, 'If anyone is coming top in the Johnson league table, it would be the one my father refers to as: "Boris, that great prodigious tree in the rainforest, in the shade of which the smaller trees must either perish or struggle to find their own place in the sun."' The comparison is comic, but also slightly chilling. We find ourselves watching a struggle for the survival of the fittest, though one should add that they all proved fit, with five of them going to Oxford while Julia herself went to Cambridge.

For a year after they came back from America, when they were living in her parents' house in Cavendish Avenue, Charlotte taught all three children – Boris, Rachel and their younger brother Leo – herself: 'Stanley was going round the world as usual – he used to leave me for periods of six months – so I got very close to the children.' She remembers this as 'one of the happiest times'. Each child had an exercise book, even Leo, who was too young to write, and each morning she would teach them many different subjects. They made lots of things and Boris was very artistic. Charlotte is a painter by profession, and Boris continues to paint with great enthusiasm, and with more ability than many amateurs.

Here was a gentler world, which still exists in Boris, but was overlaid by rivalries. Boris's sister Rachel told Julia: 'There was always tremendous competition to climb trees higher, or learn to read first. I think the last time I beat Boris at anything was when I won the Scottish dancing prize at the age of twelve. It's been a rapid ascent for him ever since. He planted his flag first on the summit of so many Mount Olympuses that we younger siblings have to content ourselves in tooling quietly around the foothills of our own careers.' The expression 'tooling quietly around' is a ridiculous way for Rachel to refer to her own immensely energetic attempts to become a top author.

Boris himself told Julia: 'As the oldest, I've always known that my position was basically unchallengeable. It is the fixed point about which my cosmos is organised. I smile indulgently on everybody else's attempts to compete with me. Bring it on, I say.'

Julia ended her account by commenting: 'I must e-mail this to my father, so he can check that there's more about him than anyone else.'

The Johnsons are very loyal to each other, but also compete like mad against each other. This is perhaps true, to some extent, of all families, but they present an extreme case. What can sometimes amount to deep hurt and bitter rivalries are covered up by jokes, and by laughing at the jokes we become complicit in the cover-up. But one reason why Boris attracts people is that this cover-up, though maintained with such heroic fortitude that it has become second nature to him, is never sufficient to hide his humanity. People love him because he makes them laugh, but also because they glimpse the hurt young kid behind the laughter. The English pretence that all is well is accompanied by an un-English depth of feeling, which survives even when he performs on television. Boris's vulnerability is akin to someone like Marilyn Monroe's: it is part of his attraction, and like her he can use it to seduce audiences pretty much at will.

Boris has described how he felt when a man was unexpectedly nasty to him on a plane: 'I quivered, like a puppy unexpectedly kicked.' Not everybody is prepared to tolerate a grown man who behaves like a puppy, but the English are exceptionally fond of animals and a lot of people find Boris refreshing, especially when they compare him to more mature and stilted politicians.

In August 2005 I visited Stanley at Nethercote. He arranged for Mr Whitley, the local taxi driver, to pick me up from Taunton station. For almost an hour Mr Whitley drove westwards past Combe Florey, where the journalist Auberon Waugh lived, into the Exmoor National Park and over the Brendon Hills, before descending into the deep valley of the River Exe, which rises on Exmoor and runs through the Johnsons' farm, between Exford and Winsford, before turning south on its way to Exeter and the sea.

In Winsford, where about 300 people live, we drove through a small ford and up to the old village school. This was where Boris went to school, a white building next to the church, with the headmistress living in a house next door. The school closed about ten years ago.

We drove out of Winsford, past the Old Vicarage, and turned up Stanley's drive. It was a perfect summer's day and as we came into the valley we seemed to be entering heaven upon earth. Two girls on bicycles, a young man and a labrador noted our arrival and raced off up the track ahead of us. The drive runs for a mile and three quarters under trees beside the River Exe. When Boris was young, this track was very rough, so that visitors would sometimes lose heart before they got to the farm buildings and turn back, but a new and smoother surface has recently been applied. The valley still has a shaggy, unimproved feeling, its sides a mixture of rough pasture, bracken and woodland.

There are three houses grouped together at the end of the drive, after a final bridge over the river. The welcome party had gone into the second house, which belongs to Rachel, Boris's sister. Stanley's is the last house you come to, beyond an empty farmyard. The patriarch was sitting outside drinking a glass of white wine, with a volume of Cavafy's poems in Greek and English. His farmhouse, where his parents used to live, is long, low, stone, an old and scruffy building, though also very clean, whereas visitors who went there when Boris was a lad remember it being very dirty. It has a huge open fireplace and smells of woodsmoke. It has not been tarted up, and none of the out-buildings has been turned into a house. There is nothing prissy about the set-up, or about Boris himself, which is yet another reason why people like him.

Stanley said Boris had rung the previous day, before taking Marina and the children on holiday in Uzbekistan, and was highly suspicious of my visit. I felt I had penetrated an Arcadian sanctuary, but one which – as Stanley's own mother found – could also be a prison.

Stanley walked me round to Nethercote Cottage, where he installed Charlotte with their three small children some time after their return from America. As we walked up to the cottage he said: 'Charlotte maintains I left her here for a year while I wrote a book called *The Green Revolution*. I've looked at my diaries. I did three longish trips but it doesn't add up to a year.' Charlotte remembers living at Nethercote without a car, washing machine or television, but having 'actually a wonderful time'.

A small wooden building to the left of the cottage served as the children's playroom, though now it is fitted up as a workshop. Here Stanley showed me 'Alexander's first known literary effort'. At the age of about five, Boris painted a message on the wall in clear blue letters: 'Boo to grown ups!'

Birdie, Stanley's sister, who lives here, had made herself scarce, but he led me inside and up the stairs. Near the top on the left, a small door, only a few feet high, opened into a kind of box room – a long, narrow space, with a sloping roof, and a small window at the far end.

A grown-up could not stand in here, but one could imagine that a small boy would love it, though he would need to climb on to the stairs with some care or he would tumble down. It is the room where Boris slept. Some childish pictures were still attached to the wall at the far end. We could make out a rainbow, a frog (or possibly a flying saucer) and some birds, and these two words in capitals:

MAMA
ANDER

The second of these words is short for Alexander, or it could also be that the first four letters of the name by which Boris was then known have been obscured.

It seemed extraordinary that these pictures should still be here. Stanley said later, when we were on our way back to Taunton: 'I had no idea they were still there. Like cave art.'

Hanging on the stairs is a framed poem by Buster, Stanley's mother, which starts:

We have come to the end of the track
And must part

For our journey together is ended
For the last time I pause and look back
Sick at heart
While my hand in farewell is extended.

The poem continues for about another twenty lines in the same vein. At the bottom of the stairs is a framed photograph of a man in RAF uniform – Stanley's father.

Stanley said: 'When my father came here he had no other thoughts but to farm it. It has turned out to be a wonderful place to have. I consider myself to be the son of a farmer. My mother was different. She read modern languages – French and Russian, I think – at Oxford, and had been at Cheltenham Ladies' College. She thought she might have married a diplomat. I think my mother did see Nethercote as a gilded prison. The high point of her life was often driving down to the bottom of the drive to see if someone had left a letter for her.'

Buster took great trouble with Stanley's education. Her money was sufficient to send him and his brother Peter to school at Sherborne. Stanley was head boy, played rugby for the school and won a scholarship in classics to Exeter College, Oxford.

Stanley did not seem to wish to linger any longer in his sister's cottage. This could be impatience on his part. He likes to get on with things, and had already waited while I transcribed the start of the poem.

On the way back we looked inside Rachel's house. Four children were there, two of them Rachel's and two friends who were visiting. A young man – an Australian – seemed to have the job of looking after them. Rachel was said to have gone for a very long walk.

Stanley asked the children if they wanted to come up to the top of the farm with us in the back of the Land Rover. This suggestion was met with wild enthusiasm. We got into an incredibly old, battered Land Rover, four children and two dogs in the back, and set off up the hill. Stanley has two of these vehicles, neither of which is licensed for use on the public road.

The children took it in turns to open gates, and to clamber back in as the Land Rover moved on.

'Look out for the brambles!' Stanley cried as we ground our way up a steep track between high banks. He could remember horse-drawn hay wagons coming down this way in the 1950s. In 1951, when he was ten and moved here with his parents, the farm had no electricity, and they used Tilley lamps and Aladdin stoves. They got a generator in the 1960s, and mains electricity in the early 1990s.

The farm is 960 feet above sea level, rising to about 1,200 feet. We emerged into a field of thistles. Stanley said: 'I'll have to tell my chap to cut some of these thistles.' There were screams of delight from the children, and marvellous views in all directions. To the north we could see Dunkery Beacon, which at 1,703 feet is the highest point on Exmoor.

When Stanley's father gave up active farming in the autumn of 1969, Stanley got the train down from London with Boris. They drove to the farm and saw all the stock penned in for auction. This, Stanley says, was the worst day of his father's life. The ashes of his parents were scattered on these fields above the farm.

When we returned to the cottage, Stanley left me in the garden with some wine and a pile of old photograph albums while he went inside to cook some pork chops.

The first pictures I saw were small, colour photographs taken when the Johnsons were living on an island in Norwalk, Connecticut, when Boris would have been about four years old and Stanley was working in New York. My host came by and said: 'An absolutely fabulous house – it really was.' He is a man with a great enthusiasm for houses and remembers many of the places he has lived with affectionate relish.

Charlotte, I thought to myself, looked lovely in the pictures – very attractive. I then realised that this young woman, perhaps only nineteen or twenty, who was kneeling with the children and smiling so happily, is not Charlotte, but the au pair girl. Stanley, who is himself only about twenty-seven, is stripped to the waist.

We come to Charlotte: she too is very young, and looks sweet and beautiful, but also vulnerable and unhappy. We see Charlotte breast-feeding – Leo perhaps – and Boris naked. Boris looking out of a train window. Boris in a beige sun hat. Boris up to the age of five or six does not look particularly happy.

There are also some pictures of a safari in East Africa. Boris stands on an ant hill, striking a pose.

We lunched in the garden and Stanley drove me at high speed in his little Subaru back to Taunton. As we descended into Taunton Vale, he remembered the very hot summer of 1976, when 'our au pairs wore nothing – I do remember them certainly parading down by the river – Oliver Walston says they wore nothing in the house too – he sent a card afterwards saying "Thanks for the mammaries".'

They usually had a pair of au pair girls, in the hope that they would not both leave at once, though on a couple of occasions they did. Stanley mentioned that Vreni, a Swiss girl who came to live with them in America, had looked after Boris. She must be the girl in the photographs.

Once the au pairs refused to cook lunch because it coincided with the arrival of the stag's heart, borne by Stanley and Charlotte's fourth child, Jo. Boris has written a fine description of this scene, at the start of an article in which he defends hunting, reprinted in his book *Lend Me Your Ears*:

All the warning we had was a crackling of the alder branches that bend over the Exe, and then the stag was upon us. I can see it now, stepping high in the water, eyes rolling, tongue protruding, foaming, antlers streaming bracken and leaves like the hat of some demented old woman, and behind it the sexual, high-pitched yipping of the dogs. You never saw such a piteous or terrible sight.

In that instant we would have done anything to help the stag get away. I think we vaguely shouted and flapped our arms, but too late. In a trice, the stag had been brought to bay by the hounds, almost at our feet in the meadow. And then a man with an ancient-looking pistol, a bit like a starting gun, blammed it in the head and they cut it open in a kind of laparotomy.

I can remember the guts steaming, and stag turds spilling out on to the grass from within the ventral cavity. Then they cut out the heart and gave it to my six-year-old brother, still beating, he claimed ever afterwards, or still twitching, and he went dancing home singing: 'We've got the heart! We've got the heart!' So we cooked it up with a bit of flour, and the German au pair girl left the next day.

In the winter of 1970 the family moved to London, first back to Blomfield Road, then to Princess Road in Primrose Hill, and in about November 1972 round the corner to Regent's Park Road, where they occupied a house they later sold to the journalist Simon Jenkins. Boris went to Primrose Hill primary school until April 1973, when Stanley took the family to Brussels, where he had secured a job as one of the first Britons to join the European Commission. Stanley became the first head of the Prevention of Pollution and Nuisance Division. It might not be a glamorous title, but he was and is an ardent environmentalist, and had secured a post at the most wide-ranging and least accountable bureaucracy in Europe.

Boris went to the European School in Uccle in Brussels, where he met a girl of exactly his own age called Marina Wheeler. She arrived in Brussels from Washington wearing an 'Impeach Nixon' badge and taught Boris the meaning of the word 'impeach' – a process he tried, many years later, to apply to

Tony Blair. Boris took a great liking to Marina, and would try to amuse her by rolling out of the car on to the ground when he was dropped off at school each day.

Marina would just think 'Oh God' when she saw this trick, which became a bit of a joke in her family. Nor was she any more impressed when, for her benefit, he rolled into a boat during a school trip to some caves. She was much less impressed by Boris than he was by her, and decided he was 'generally to be avoided'. But because their parents already knew each other from Washington, the two families continued to see a certain amount of each other.

To Marina and her sister, the Johnsons seemed 'incredibly rough – they were all so wild and out of control'. If you were playing a ball game with them, the ball would hit you hard on the nose, you would burst into tears and would feel you were being feeble. Marina's mother, Dip, one day relayed the exciting news that Boris had actually been shot with an air pistol by his brother Leo. To visit the Johnsons on Exmoor was also for Marina a shocking experience, 'so much harsher than I was used to'. It was freezing cold and everyone had holes in their socks. She thinks Stanley has 'mellowed' since.

Boris's intelligence was already apparent. He was an ardent reader: when his siblings wanted him to play with them, they would sometimes receive the unsatisfactory reply, 'Let's play reading.' At the European School, his mother was one day taken aside to be informed that he was '*un enfant doué*' – a gifted child.

In 1974, a year after moving to Brussels, when her and Stanley's youngest child, Jo, was still very small, Charlotte had a nervous breakdown. She was in the Maudsley Hospital, in London, for nine months, suffering from depression. As she herself says, 'It was terrible because I'd had before this all that time when I was so, so close to the children, and then I disappeared.'

It is painful even to think how harrowing this period must have been for Charlotte and her children: 'They used to come and see me. It was so mad. I would suddenly see my children running down the passage. And when they had gone I would feel completely destroyed.' Until she and Stanley were divorced, Charlotte was 'in and out of hospital quite often'.

Brussels was to become, in the early 1990s, the scene of Boris's first journalistic triumphs, and also of the collapse of his first marriage. In the 1970s, it was the place where Stanley and Charlotte's marriage fell apart. But before they parted, Boris had already been sent away to school in England.

5

Greek Before Breakfast

IN 1975 BORIS ARRIVED AT ASHDOWN HOUSE PREP-aratory school in East Sussex. Here the process started, as he later put it, of filling him 'up to the gills with the finest education England can provide'.

This period is so recent, yet in many ways it already seems impossibly remote. Boris caught the last years when Latin and Greek were at the heart of the curriculum. Ashdown's tradition of brilliant classical teaching had been set by Billy Williamson, headmaster from 1949, whose pupils won many awards to Eton and Winchester. Among them was Clive Williams, who got a scholarship to Eton and returned as a young man to Ashdown first as an assistant master and from 1974 as headmaster.

Some readers may assume from this account that the school, accommodated since 1886 in a fine country house at Forest Row in East Sussex, was simply a machine for getting scholar-ships, but this would be unfair. As Williams says of his predecessor: 'Billy was a past master at getting Eton awards – that was what he liked to do and he was very good at it – but he also took a great deal of trouble with those less able.'

Boris had a meteoric career at Ashdown. He went there as a boarder in the autumn term of 1975 when he was eleven years old, so the school had only two years to prepare him for Eton. It is normal for a boy destined for public school to spend five years, from the age of eight, at a preparatory school, so Boris had a vast amount of catching up to do, especially as he had never studied Latin or Greek.

We see Boris moving with almost unbelievable rapidity up the school. Williams showed me a notebook containing a record of all his pupils, including their form lists, aggregated marks, what prizes they won and which schools they went to. At the end of his first term Boris was placed fifteenth out of the fifteen pupils in Form II B, so he must have been struggling. At the end of his second term, the Lent term of 1976, he had already moved up to sixth place: as Williams remarks, 'he was getting the hang of things'. At the end of the summer term, he came top of II B and was awarded the form prize.

Half-way through that summer term someone brought Williams a piece of Boris's work: 'For the first time I thought there was something rather special about this boy. We had a discussion about this fantastically able boy in the common room.'

For his last year Boris was placed in Form I. Williams now taught him himself. Form I was divided into Division I and Division II, with Boris placed at first in the lower of these. Williams remembers: 'I don't think I've ever taught anyone who learned quicker. He was very good, very good, but I think it was the speed at which he learned which was so impressive. He just lapped it up, and the great thing was that he found it fun. Not all children enjoy Latin and Greek, but he did. He thought the paradigms of *luo* was rather fun – we used to do those before breakfast.'

Luo, the basic Greek verb, has an extraordinary number of different forms, and at Ashdown some of the pupils studied these at early school from 7.30 in the morning, while the rest did PT outside. As Williams remarked in a modest tone: 'We did seem to be a street ahead in basic grammar which in something like Greek makes quite a bit of difference.' The boys in Form I did fourteen periods of Classics a week, which in Williams's opinion 'you can't possibly justify'. Like all successful upholders of tradition, he saw the need for change: 'I think in those days we were rather too keen on our Latin and Greek.'

Ashdown was not one of those dangerous schools where all the pupils are unusually bright and tend to drive each other mad, but Boris was stretched by two other boys in Form I. As Williams said: 'Having two pretty competitive characters in Meyrick Cox and Tim Moon brought out the best in him. The rivalry in the top three was fairly intense, though never less than friendly. Meyrick Cox was much more a mathematician, so they were nicely balanced. Tim Moon was good at them all.'

Williams nevertheless doubted whether Boris would be ready for the Eton scholarship exam: 'The papers were quite difficult in those days.' But after only five terms of preparation – for the exams took place early in the summer term – Boris duly won a scholarship to Eton. Stanley still remembers how moved Williams was on ringing him in Brussels to give the good news. Meyrick Cox also won a scholarship to Eton, while Tim Moon was fourth on the scholarship roll at Winchester.

Boris's education was not confined to the Classics. Children at Ashdown were expected to take part in a wide variety of activities, whether they showed much aptitude or not. For example, as Williams says, 'Everybody was always in teams. He was certainly in the rugby side because of his size, and was quicker on his feet than you'd think. He enjoyed participating in all his games. He was not a great expert but he was by no means hopeless at any of them. But the things he did well he was astonishingly good at. He was a wonderful King Rhesus in the Greek play [performed in Greek]. He was particularly good as counsel for the prosecution in the mock trials we used to have. He was a good debater and he won the poem prize. He had a marvellously optimistic outlook – he would always go for anything – and he was also genuinely entertaining – he always was funny as a boy.'

Williams found Stanley an ideal parent: 'He was marvellous at encouraging us all to get on with it. He took lots of interest, but never interfered. He was always very jolly and extremely supportive. Running a school in those days was less complicated.' In the age before the mobile phone, anxious parents had much less scope to interfere in the running of boarding schools, which meant children enjoyed greater independence than is the case today.

Stanley had only one unusual demand, concerning Boris's sister: 'He told us we'd got to take Rachel. It was marvellous for us – we had already decided in 1974 to take girls. My predecessor was fairly old-fashioned, he ran the school on military lines. We wanted to be different, and the great different thing we wanted to do was have girls. Stanley's support was crucial. Stanley said, "I'll provide you with your first pupil," and sent us Rachel. She was not as brilliant as Boris, but she won a scholarship to Bryanston. Rachel was very good as a pioneer girl. She was tremendous.'

Boris and Rachel's younger brothers followed them to Ashdown: 'Leo and Jo – they were terrific too. Leo was a terrific chap. He only just missed a scholarship to Eton. Leo was a commanding figure in the school – an excellent games player and head boy too.'

This distinction eluded Boris. As Williams put it: 'He's always rather cross with me – in joking asides – not to have been made a dorm captain or a prefect.' But as Williams explained, it would have been 'rather unusual' to confer such posts on a boy who had only been in the school for one year.

Williams's wife, Rowena, who was involved in every aspect of the school, said: 'He wouldn't have been nearly such a good head boy as Leo.'

'He'd have given a very good speech,' Williams countered.

The Williamses remember Boris's mother with great affection: 'She gave us a lovely present – she gave us a portrait of us – a jolly nice thing to do.'

Stanley, Boris and Rachel have all been down to Ashdown to give away the prizes. As so often with Boris, he had a problem with his clothes. The zip on his trousers was broken. Rowena Williams said: 'I had to safety-pin his flies. If I was around a bit more often I might have saved him a lot of trouble.'

She added in a maternal tone: 'I always get nervous watching him on anything. Our feelings are nothing but affectionate towards him and his family.' When the news broke in November 2004 of Boris's affair with Petronella Wyatt, Rowena found herself having to explain it to her father 'as if Boris was one of my own children'.

Ashdown, like many independent schools at this time, was immersed in a headlong process of liberalisation, in which the admission of girls played a key part. Williams one night came upon a number of children, including Rachel, having a midnight feast of Coke and crisps. He offered Rachel the choice of losing two half-holidays or being beaten. She confounded him by opting to be beaten. Williams realised he could not beat a girl, nor could he have half the school eligible for a beating and half not, so corporal punishment ended at Ashdown.

Conrad Black, who was later to make Boris editor of the *Spectator*, said: 'His schooldays were one of the few subjects where he became quite serious and even quite believable – he is a passionate opponent of corporal punishment. He told me how when he was at school he would hear the younger boys crying, in terrible pain, and just how awful it was.'

Boris told me it made him deeply angry when he was chastised at Ashdown, not that he harbours any personal grudge.

Here was another English tradition of which he caught the final years, but not one which, like the study of Latin and Greek, he would spend the rest of his life celebrating. For while the Classics uplifted him, he was degraded by being beaten, and Boris is too proud to accept that.

– 6 –

An Etonian Performance

WHEN BORIS WAS FOURTEEN YEARS OLD HIS PARENTS got divorced. Stanley broke the news to the children, against Charlotte's wishes, when they were all at Nethercote. Boris lined himself and his three siblings up in the yard, stepped forward and said: 'Why did you have us?'

Charlotte and Stanley made it their policy to get on with each other. She says Stanley has been 'a very good father', while he is loud in her praises. But however well people behave – and the Johnsons behaved much better than many couples – divorce is still deeply miserable.

Charlotte returned to London and moved in to a maisonette at the top of a high, stuccoed building in Notting Hill with her four children. She was still a very attractive woman, only thirty-six years old, by vocation an artist and by birth a Fawcett, with grand Catholic friends, not one of those rackety Johnsons. For a time the roof leaked, but she loved filling the rooms with a rich profusion of things, and all the time she painted and drew. Her friends gathered that Stanley had been 'one amazing womaniser', and she was fed up with it. According to Charlotte, 'I couldn't stay with him. He was so inaccessible, not to say completely unfaithful. I couldn't live with him never allowing anything to be serious. That's the essential difference between Boris and his father. I can talk to Boris about anything.'

When Boris and his siblings were with their mother, he felt he was the man in the family, who must protect her. Charlotte's friends remember that he had a kind of seriousness about him, and a gentle reticence, and was conscientious and careful when given a responsible task, such as looking after a smaller child. He was tall for his age, and shy, and blushed when he spoke, gazing out through his hair like Lady Diana.

This is not the Boris the public have come to know and love. A friend of the family said: 'He had a dignity about him. You could see he was a very nice person. He understood what had happened to his mother, he knew it was dreadful and humiliating, and he was enduring it.'

Boris has continued to care for his mother. She lived in Notting Hill for ten years, supporting herself by selling portraits. In 1988 she married an American academic, Nick Wahl, with whom she went to live in an apartment in Washington Square, New York. He had no children of his own and was very fond of hers, but died in 1996, after which she moved back to Notting Hill.

As early as 1982, Charlotte noticed something wrong with her foot, which felt like a flipper when she went swimming, but it was not until 1989 that she was diagnosed with Parkinson's disease. It has progressed very slowly, but makes her hand tremble and is exhausting, and if she did not take her pills she could not swallow. She said Boris is very, very protective of her, often comes with her when she goes to see her consultant, and minds people talking about her illnesses.

The atrocious pain of the divorce encouraged Boris to create a mask which hid how he felt from the outside world. Many years later he confided to a woman with whom he was in love that after his parents split up, he decided to make himself invulnerable.

Any sensitive adolescent might hope to do this, but few have been able to model their escape bid on quite such a father. Stanley claims that apart from sending his children to good schools, 'My parental impact has been strictly zero. I'm quite ready to concede that a good school is probably going to do a better job of bringing up your kids than you're likely to do. In my view it took the pain out of parenting. It was a safer bet, particularly in the circumstances of Charlotte and I splitting up. Probably kids would prefer their parents to stay together. In many ways it was more difficult for Jo [the youngest of the four children]. Boris was already at Eton.'

The pretence that he has had no parental influence is Stanley at his most preposterous. Anyone who has met both father and son is struck by the extraordinary resemblance between them. They talk in an amazingly similar way, and Boris has learned a great part of his comic art from his father. They behave like stage Englishmen, often pretending to be impossibly baffled and stupid, while behind this screen they calculate what would be to their own advantage. This manner makes it hard for them to do seriousness, nor do they detect any great public demand for it.

Stanley said as he recounted his own political career, 'Nothing is more gloomy than making a speech that has no jokes in it. I don't think that on the whole people can take too much seriousness.'

In the late 1970s, as the first European elections in Britain approached, Stanley looked around for a seat where he could stand as a Conservative. He was interviewed in Leicester, where the Duke of Rutland, chairman of the selectors, asked if he had ever been there before. Stanley says he replied: 'Your Grace, I have never been to Leicester before but I have been to Leicester Square.' This joke went down badly.

After failing at three selection contests for European seats, Stanley put in for the Isle of Wight and East Hampshire. The other contenders were Bill Cash 'and his very scenic wife

Biddy', and Sir John Peel. Stanley said: 'I was in the process of separating very amicably from Charlotte. I was the only person of the three of us who didn't visibly have a wife there.'

The selection committee asked Stanley, 'Will Mrs Johnson be coming to live with you in the constituency?'

Stanley replied: 'Mrs Johnson will possibly be coming to live in the constituency, but certainly not with me.'

This joke went down well, and Stanley got the seat, which he held from 1979 to 1984.

But while Stanley joked about his divorce, it would be wrong to suggest he is completely incapable of seriousness. The stage Englishman usually has a hobby which he invests with the sanctity of a religion: his golf clubs mean everything to him.

Stanley cares deeply about the environment. As the lawyer Philippe Sands recalls: 'He used to instruct me a lot fifteen years ago in a lot of environmental cases. Stanley's terribly principled, even if it's totally unfashionable.'

Not that Stanley is unable to leaven even his environmentalism with humour. At the World Trade Organization meeting in Seattle, he dressed up as a turtle. Sands said: 'There are some great photographs of Stanley dressed up as a turtle haranguing Al Gore.'

When I put it to Stanley that Boris has followed him in many things, but not as an environmentalist, the father leapt to the son's defence: 'He's been jolly good on the Brazilian Macau question; but that was I think partly under my influence. And he has been particularly sound on the hunting question.'

Boris has entered the same competitions as his father. Like Stanley, he is a passionate rugby player who won a classical scholarship to Oxford, married young, had lots of children, and pursued careers as a writer and a Tory politician. But Stanley grew self-deprecating when I mentioned some of the similarities between him and his eldest son: 'Boris does almost all of those things better than I did. He gets very large advances [for his books] and I over the years have not had those. I think the talent comes from Charlotte – she's a wonderful lady.'

When an interviewer asked Boris about his parents' divorce, he replied: 'Yes, I was upset when they broke up.' But a minute later he added: 'Oh good Lord, they will read this,' after which he tried to retract it, before saying: 'No, it had some effect. They handled it brilliantly.'

Boris had to handle the divorce soon after he started at Eton, the most famous school in the world. It stands on the low ground on the other side of the Thames from Windsor Castle, whose towers can be seen in the distance. Eighteen British Prime Ministers have been educated there.

Eton is synonymous for many with idle privilege, but what people often overlook is how hard the school has worked to avoid becoming an irrelevant survival, and to stay at the top on its merits. Patrick Hennessy, who went to Eton slightly ahead of Boris, recalled, 'I disapprove of it fantastically and in many ways it's a disadvantage to have been there. But the education, and the way you were treated as an adult, and taught to become extremely independent, and have a very, very questing mind – there was nothing you couldn't do. McCrum [the headmaster] was very keen on the pursuit of excellence.'

As often happens, Boris spent his first half (as the school term is called at Eton), the autumn of 1977, in another house, D. J. S. Guilford's, before there was room for him in College, the house where the scholars live.

Boris's hair made him immediately recognisable, but there were about 1,200 boys in the school, and one should bear in mind that Boris would have been unknown, except by appearance, to many Etonians. Hennessy said: 'We didn't have much to do with Collegers. I do remember him though, very well, because he looked exactly as he does today. He was incredibly scruffy and had that sort of straw-coloured hair. Collegers had to wear gowns, which made him look all the more extraordinary.'

Boris's first housemaster, John Lewis, who in 1980 left to become headmaster of Geelong Grammar in Australia before returning to Eton as headmaster, remembers very little about Boris in his first three years at the school: 'He had a touch of the self-deprecating air which has become part of his political persona now, but he certainly wasn't a clown.' This period when Boris's parents were divorcing was no time for clowning. Boris, by Lewis's account, was a model schoolboy: 'He was a very good member of College: humorous, loyal and (in the politest possible way) irreverent.'

It is during his last two and a bit years at Eton that the familiar Boris emerges into the limelight. We see him develop into a public performer who is one of the great Eton characters of his generation, but who does this at the expense of the steady, unglamorous work needed to make the most of his intellectual gifts. Boris adores the Classics, but he cannot give them his exclusive devotion.

Boris has often said that for him 'the really inspirational teacher was Martin Hammond'. Hammond became Master in College in September 1980. A distinguished classical scholar, he has recently published a new translation of the *Meditations* of Marcus Aurelius and is now at work on a translation of Thucydides for the Penguin Classics. By great good fortune, or perhaps by sheer efficiency, Hammond has kept copies of the seven school reports he wrote on Boris. These take the form of a letter to Boris's father at the end of each term, and Hammond wrote to me: 'I would gladly release these reports to you, but that of course must depend on the agreement not only of Boris but also of Stanley Johnson, to whom they were addressed.'

When I rang Stanley to ask for his agreement, he laughed and said yes. When I rang Boris he said: 'Um, er, um, um, I don't see why not.'

These reports almost constitute a biography in miniature of

Boris, unclouded by hindsight and throwing brilliant shafts of illumination into the future. Nobody has ever been in a better position than Hammond to try to get the best out of Boris, and a fascinating duel develops between the master, who knows how things ought to be done, and his apprentice, who is intent on following a more risky but amusing path to success.

The first letter, which would have accompanied a sheaf of other reports by Boris's teachers, was written on 30 December 1980:

Dear Mr Johnson,

I had of course met Boris before this half, and had come to know something of his considerable intellectual ability . . . Closer acquaintance this half has enabled me to get to know him much better . . . I've found Boris a quite delightful person, a real life-enhancer. I like his open friendliness of manner, and his ready wit . . . I remember in particular a magnificent performance in Prayers, when he read with spectacular effect the hell-fire preacher's sermon from *Cold Comfort Farm*.

In his next report, dated 3 April 1981, Hammond says Boris has 'a finger in a wide variety of pies', is 'asserting his intellectual ascendancy powerfully but modestly' and presents 'the *disiecta membra* of a very considerable scholar'. But '*disiecta membra*' is the Latin for 'scattered limbs', and Hammond is growing worried that amid a diversity of other activities, Boris will fail to do justice to himself as a scholar.

This worry becomes even more pressing in Hammond's third report, written on 22 July 1981:

Boris' favoured pace is the amble (with the odd last-minute sprint), which has been good enough so far, and I suppose enables him to smell the flowers along the way. It's time, though, that with a greater commitment to the real business of scholarship (reading widely and deeply, unbidden; approaching each task with a craftsman's eye and a craftsman's deliberation; constantly probing for something deeper, or truer, or more accurate) Boris could turn himself into a classicist of real distinction, one of the best that we've had for years. To do that he must become a professional: and the first step, on which I think we must insist next year, is the production or preparation of work on time.

Similar criticisms – gross unpunctuality, failure to organise himself, refusal to submit to the discipline needed to become a professional – were to be levelled time and again against Boris in the decades to come. In his fourth report, written on 29 December 1981, Hammond is relatively content with Boris: 'His success in the Newcastle Classical Prize was deserved, narrow though the margin was.'

But the report after that contains one of the fiercest attacks on Boris which can ever have been written, the effect heightened by the friendly and fair-minded praise which is heaped on him at the start and finish.

Each boy at Eton has his own room, and every evening after house prayers, Hammond would walk the corridors of College from 8.45 until about 11.15, dropping in on one boy or another. There was, he says, 'virtually never any disciplinary aspect to these visits', though one can guess that the housemaster's presence helped to keep the peace.

'The Bill' which is mentioned refers not to the police, but to the form of punishment at Eton which entails being fetched from one's classroom before lunch by a praepostor, or prefect, and hauled before the headmaster. Boris's offence was to have done no work. The post of Captain of the School means the head boy of College. The letter was written on 10 April 1982 and is given in full:

Dear Stanley,

I was delighted that Boris achieved some success in the Newcastle [Divinity Scholarship], and he deserved it. He did in fact work quite hard towards the examination (which is not to say that he could not have worked harder): I was pleased to find him one evening reading St John's Gospel in Greek, and exclaiming, 'This is really exciting!' – as indeed it is.

Of course Boris did take on several large extra commitments this half, and one does not want to discourage diversity: but there is no doubt, as these reports make very plain, that his regular academic responsibilities were sadly neglected as a result. The tone of Andrew Hobson's letter is pretty damning, but its contents can hardly be gainsaid, and a very similar picture is painted by Ian McAuslan. Boris really has adopted a disgracefully cavalier attitude to his classical studies, and the scandal of the Bill would be followed by an even greater scandal if he did drop a grade at A level through sheer fecklessness. It is a question of priorities, which most of his colleagues have no difficulty in sorting out. Boris sometimes seems affronted when criticised for what amounts to a gross failure of responsibility (and surprised at the same time that he was not appointed Captain of the School for next half): I think he honestly believes that it is churlish of us not to regard him as an exception, one who should be free of the network of obligation which binds everyone else. I'm enormously fond of Boris, and saddened that he should have brought upon himself this sort of report. All is not lost, by any means: he can easily effect a full return to grace by showing obvious commitment next half.

I thought very well indeed of his contribution to the success of the College Play. He worked hard at it, and made Sir Politique Would-be a memorably comic figure (who

reappeared, with suitable adjustments, in the French Play):
he handled the dropped-stick episode superbly, and
throughout kept a marvellous rapport with the audience,
communicating his enjoyment to them.

Will the decision on Harvard have to be made at the
very beginning of the half?

Yours ever,

Martin

There was at this time some question of Boris going to Harvard,
the most famous university in the United States. According to
Stanley, 'Harvard came through with a terrifically generous
financial offer – who can tell what would have happened if he'd
made his life in America?'

Mr Hammond's next report, written on 25 July 1982,
brought little respite:

Although there has been no repetition of the disgrace of last
half's academic torpor, it's clear that Boris has still not been
working at anything like the limit of his capacity in any of
his three subjects – in fact, in comparison with what might
have been, this has been a pretty disappointing year. Boris
is pretty impressive when success can be achieved by pure
intelligence unaccompanied by hard work (he shines in
unseens, which are of course unprepared): but he doesn't
have the instincts of a real scholar, and tends to 'sell himself
short' when an exercise requires intellectual preparation.
He is, in fact, pretty idle about it all ... Boris has
something of a tendency to assume that success and
honours will drop into his lap: not so, he must work for
them.

Efficiency and organisation have been constant problems
(there was trouble this half with his running of the Political
Society, and an unprecedented rebuke from the Provost).

The Provost of Eton, Lord Charteris of Amisfield, had spent most of his life in royal service, latterly as Private Secretary to the Queen, and although he was a genial man, he liked things done properly. When the Queen Mother felt like visiting Eton, which she did at fairly regular intervals, Lord Charteris would make the arrangements. He also acted as host for the eminent speakers who came to address the Political Society, which Boris was then running.

Lord Charteris died in 1999, so it seemed unlikely that anyone but Boris would be able to say what the 'unprecedented rebuke' was for. Even Boris appeared, when I put the question to him, to have difficulty remembering what had gone wrong: 'Oh yes. I got into terrible trouble – he got terribly cross with me because I wanted to invite Ronald Reagan – I think that might have been it.'

It is amusing to find that even then, Boris had no hesitation in pursuing the famous. One of his strengths as a journalist is that he has always pushed for an interview with the most powerful person.

But Boris then corrected himself about his trouble with the Provost: 'No. I'm afraid I just turned up late to see him one day. I mean I wasn't very late. About forty-five minutes.'

Most schoolboys would not have dared to turn up late to see Lord Charteris, and even most of those with the self-confidence to do such a thing would have tried to avoid it, assuming they liked the Provost, because they would know it to be so rude. One suspects that Boris aggravated his offence by appearing not to understand how rude he had been.

Boris liked the Provost very much indeed: 'He was such a nice man. A wonderful man, Martin Charteris. I used to have to pour the wine [at Political Society events].' Boris did not mention to me that the Provost was also a friend of his mother's parents.

The next sentence of Martin Hammond's report, immediately after the reference to the 'unprecedented rebuke', marks an astonishing change of tack:

It was perhaps a bit of a risk to make Boris Captain of the School: but he clearly has the personality and the respect necessary for the job, and it's my hope that the imposition of a public responsibility will energise all else. It's a particularly important job in the Michaelmas, and involves a number of administrative tasks which simply must be done well. Certainly I look forward to working with him – he's excellent company, and has a mature understanding of people and things.

Boris has triumphed. Even though 'efficiency and organisation have been constant problems', he has been given a post which 'involves a number of administrative tasks which simply must be done well'. Hammond has been forced to recognise that Boris's claims to the top job are too strong to deny. The Captain of the School is the top boy in College, and not in the entire school, where the other two grandees were the Captain of the Oppidans, appointed from the rest of the boys by the headmaster, and the President of Pop, appointed by the boys.

Looking back on Boris, Hammond said: 'He was passionately loyal to his House, his school. In an odd way, he likes an ordered world, not a random world. Boris was not a rebel at all. He was a fully signed up member of the tribe. He was jolly nearly the custodian of the ark. Everything that went into the traditions of being at College Boris embraced whole-heartedly – Latin prayers, bellowed hymns.'

Another Eton tradition into which Boris threw himself wholeheartedly, and which still means a lot to him, is the Wall Game. The main match of the year takes place on or near St Andrew's Day, 30 November, between a team drawn from the 70 Collegers and one from the more than 1,100 Oppidans, and Boris played three years running in the College team.

Part of the charm of this game is that it is almost incomprehensible. But an article in the *Eton College Chronicle* – the

fortnightly school newspaper – of St Andrew's Day 1982 by
Oliver Van Oss, who taught at Eton and was Headmaster of
Charterhouse, allows one to get some flavour of the contest. The
Wall Game turns out to be the perfect preparation for life.
Substantial quotation is needed even to begin to convey its
strangeness:

> The ground is about 100 yards long, bounded on one side
> by a high brick wall and on the other by a furrow. At no
> point is it more than 15 yards wide. The object is to drive
> an under-sized football over a line, beyond which the
> aggressors may attempt to score. One end is called Good
> Calx, because the ball cannot go over the dead ball line; the
> other Bad Calx, because it can, which offers some slight
> advantage to a hard-pressed defence.
>
> Each team has 10 players . . . The centre of the battle is
> the Bully (scrum) and the leaders of it are the three Walls,
> men chosen for their huge size, physical strength and that
> exceptional length of arm which so seldom correlates with
> intellectual power . . . At first nothing happens . . . The lull
> seems permanently established when suddenly the Bully
> erupts . . . This pattern of alternating trance and frenzy
> continues until one side has forced its way into Calx and is
> in a position to score . . .
>
> It sounds bizarre, almost Boeotian [stupid, dull], yet all
> who have played it rate it one of the great games. It is
> enormous fun and utterly exhausting. It demands secret
> skills and an equable temperament. Though Rule XII
> forbids 'tripping, kicking, stamping, striking' and now alas
> 'knuckling' and goes on to disallow 'any methods of play
> whose sole purpose is to cause pain', it can be excru-
> ciatingly uncomfortable.
>
> The Wall Game is the supreme non-spectacle, the last
> sport totally to disregard the spectator . . . As a preparation

for life, the Wall Game has two special merits. It teaches one to push oneself to the limit of endurance and discomfort without losing one's temper. It provides the perfect training for later work on boards, committees, royal commissions and governing bodies. The unmovable and the irresistible are poised in perfect balance. Nothing is happening and it seems unlikely that anything ever will. Then, for two seconds or so, the situation becomes fluid. If one can take one's chance – and there may not be another – the day is won. If one miskicks or mistimes or is timid or was not attending, all may be irretrievably lost.

The *Chronicle* was in the custom of publishing short descriptions of the players. Boris first appears on St Andrew's Day 1980, when he is described as 'Completely non-directional, has to be pointed the right way or he may push the Wall over.' A year later we find: 'He plays the Wall Game like an echidna on heat, according to his homespun philosophy, "If it moves, grunt at it. If it moves again, kill it, then grunt at it." The only Colleger able to take on the Oppidans at their own level.' For his last St Andrew's Day we read: 'Hey, hey, A.B.J. How many Oppidans did you kill today? Watch the Blond Behemoth crud relentlessly through the steaming pile of purple-and-orange heavyweights, until he's knocking on the Lower Master's door.'

Johnnie Boden, who played the Wall Game against Boris, said: 'I was bitten by someone and it could well have been him.' Boden in later life launched a mail-order clothing company, of which Boris is a strong supporter, sometimes referring to Boden as his tailor. When I asked Boris if he had ever bitten Boden, he replied: 'I might have done. No, no, I wasn't a biter. My tactics in the Wall Game are sudden spasms of uncontrolled aggression.'

Boris adopted a similar style of play on the rugby field, where he played for the First XV. In Hammond's words, 'On the rugby field Boris was an absolute berserker. There was a lot of yelling and hurling of himself reckless of life and limb, both his own and other people's. He took it very seriously.'

I suggested to Hammond that Boris was not a typical Etonian, having in mind Boris's willingness to have a go at things he does not know how to do, and to risk making a fool of himself. But Hammond had detected another quality which distinguishes Boris: 'He's much more generous-hearted than most Etonians are. I didn't know him at school be unkind to anyone.'

Andrew Gilmour became friends with Boris at Eton. He remembers Boris performing at Speeches, an Eton tradition where Sixth Form Select – the top ten scholars and the top ten Oppidans – recite pieces of poetry or prose.

Boris recited the first page of *Decline and Fall* by Evelyn Waugh, which begins: 'Mr Sniggs, the Junior Dean, and Mr Postlethwaite, the Domestic Bursar . . .'

Gilmour recalls: 'The way he said "Sniggs" made people laugh, and then he turned to the prompter and said, "What's his name again?" That brought the house down. Even the Provost I remember roaring with laughter. I think from that time Boris realised that if you forget your lines and carry it off with aplomb, then you're made. He performed in a Molière play in French, *L'Ecole des Femmes*, with a very strong English accent and had to be prompted throughout.'

Unpreparedness had become one of Boris's hallmarks. Sir Eric Anderson, who was Tony Blair's housemaster at Fettes and Boris's headmaster at Eton, says: 'Boris had some similarity with Blair as a boy – both of them opted to live on their wits rather than preparation. They both enjoyed performing. In both cases people found them life-enhancing and fun to have around, but also maddening.'

But while the young Blair rebelled against the system at Fettes, 'Boris wasn't a rebel at all – a satirist and a humorist rather than a rebel,' in Anderson's words. He paid tribute to another of

Boris's qualities: 'Boris has terrific intellectual energy and terrific physical energy as well. The great Dr Arnold said there is more difference in the amount of energy of boys than in the amount of intellect, and that it was more important. Energy matters.'

Boris agrees with this and may well have heard it first from Anderson. As Boris put it in an interview in 2003: 'Intelligence is really all about energy. I mean you can have the brightest people in the world who simply can't be arsed. No good to man or beast.'

Eric Anderson taught Sixth Form Select once a week: 'I tossed them an intellectual bone and let them chew it. I wrote "Business, Industry, Commerce" up on the board and asked them to spend ten minutes writing down what these words suggested to them. Boris wrote: "These three words suggest to me that the headmaster dined in London last night."'

'Correct,' Anderson responded with a smile.

Boris went on: 'Some ignorant people attacked him for not sending enough Etonians into industry or commerce. What they do not realise is that industry is making things, commerce is selling them, while business is making all that happen, which being much more interesting is what Etonians head for.'

Sir Eric admired this answer for its intelligence and wit, but it also betrays the arrogant, or confident, or perhaps just the realistic belief that Etonians will end up running the show.

'I do remember,' Anderson said, 'that he was a member of the Headmaster's Essay Society – twenty-four bright boys on a Sunday evening three times a term – one of them read a paper and the others tore it to pieces. I do remember meeting him at Sunday lunchtime and he said he hadn't started working. But we still got a very stimulating paper.'

The word 'stimulating' is possibly a charitable way of concealing the annoyance Anderson felt at the time. As Boris himself was later to remark, Anderson 'was frightfully anti-me at school'.

Anderson offered his last anecdote of Boris: 'My third story is not particularly to his credit. At that time – it's now ceased, partly no doubt because of his performance – there used to be something called Shakespeare in the Cloisters, where members of College acted some scenes from Shakespeare out of doors. This had become less interesting as school drama became more developed. They were doing some scenes from *Richard III*, with Boris as the King. He hadn't had time to learn the lines, so had pasted them up behind various pillars. The whole performance consisted of him running from one side of the stage to the other and failing to read it properly.'

Boris wrote some of his first journalism at Eton. In the *Chronicle* of 10 October 1980, when Boris was sixteen, we find a short and unexciting report of a visit by Edward Heath to the Political Society. Boris ended with the words, 'Good sense like this must continue to provoke' – a sentence which could be ironical. One cannot pretend, in his articles for the *Chronicle*, that Boris stands out from his contemporaries. Nothing comes off all that well. In one piece, published on 4 June 1982, he is 'filled with a nameless horror' at the idea of becoming an Old Etonian banker.

But as a performer, Boris is already in a class of his own. On 2 November 1980 the Debating Society held a debate on the proposition 'This House would rather be tight than loose', proposed by Boris and by Hugo Dixon, a fellow scholar who had also been at Ashdown and became a lifelong friend. We are told that Boris 'spoke in such an authoritative manner that the audience almost believed him'.

In the autumn of 1981, Boris was elected to Pop, the self-perpetuating group of the grandest Etonians. We also find Dixon and Boris, 'whose speeches are always full of sound and fury, even if signifying nothing,' in the final of the House Debating Competition, which they lost. A quarter of a century later, Dixon recalled what happened. He was still cross about it, for a competitive Etonian is as competitive as anyone in the whole wide world: 'This was the high point of my debating career. Boris stood up and he hadn't prepared a speech. The judge said basically I'm afraid Dixon and Johnson have lost, although Dixon made the best speech of all four.'

One of the effects of glancing through these *Chronicles* is to start to get a sense of a whole generation.

On 15 May 1982 Hugh Fearnley-Whittingstall published a poem entitled 'Whither Apathy?' which was so bad that I did not bother, during an enjoyable day spent reading back numbers of the *Chronicle* in the library at Eton, to copy it. I did not then realise that many years later Boris would still be raging, as we shall see, against Fearnley-Whittingstall.

Near the end of Boris's time at Eton, a few articles by a boy called David Cameron appeared in the *Chronicle*. But it seemed clear to me – I carried out this research in July 2005 – that Cameron was unlikely to become so prominent as to make it worth asking the Eton archivist, Penny Hatfield, to go to the trouble of photocopying his juvenilia. Within six months, Cameron had become leader of the Conservative Party. In May 2006, when he went on *Desert Island Discs*, he attracted a certain amount of adverse criticism by choosing a cookery book by Fearnley-Whittingstall.

In the *Chronicle* for 5 June 1982, we read of a visit by a group of Etonians to debate with the girls at Wycombe Abbey. Boris received by far the most mentions in this short account: 'Boris Johnson was still asking if anyone wanted to speak instead of him, as we got into the minibus . . . Boris . . . unlikeliest cult-hero, won the debate on gestures . . . Boris was nearly left behind a tree.'

Almost everyone who remembers Boris at school remarks at some point on his acting. Jesse Norman remembers the College production of *Othello*. Boris played Brabantio, the father of Desdemona, and Norman said: 'I very much remember Boris looking out through a window and Iago telling him, "An old black ram / Is tupping your white ewe."'

Andrew Gilmour said: 'He had a great rivalry with Kabir Nath. There were two genius musicians in my year. Paul Richardson won the piano competition every year, except one year when Kabir Nath got it. Boris found this insufferable. He took up the piano, thinking he'd win it next year. He had no idea how difficult the piano was. He had such confidence in his own ability he just thought he'd come sailing in.'

Chris Bayston, who was a singer by profession, taught Boris the piano: 'He came to me for piano lessons as a beginner. It very soon became evident that he was incredibly bright, but he found the business of reading notes on two staves simultaneously, and also co-ordinating his hands, really remarkably difficult.'

Many people would either have decided the piano was not for them, or would have continued with the lessons but done virtually no practice. Eton has over 1,000 music lessons a week, given by 64 teachers, and as Bayston said, 'the tail of the dragon is very, very long – a large number of boys did very little practice'.

But Boris reacted quite differently: 'Whether it was the novelty of finding something he couldn't do easily, or a fascination with music, I've never taught a senior boy who struggled so manfully.'

Boris's housemaster, Hammond, could hear Boris struggling, and wrote in his report of 30 December 1980: 'As to his piano work, I can testify both to his determination and to the glacial progress: Boris plies his art on the instrument in Lower School, just across the passage from my study.'

A year later, on 29 December 1981, Hammond wrote: 'I could not fail to be aware of his flurry of preparation for the piano exam, sitting as I was just a few yards from the instrument that shared his agony.'

But Bayston has no bad memories of Boris: 'It was a joy to

teach him. He loved doing something very, very difficult. He never lost his temper – our lessons were such fun. What made the experience of teaching him the more memorable was that I plied him with very old-fashioned pieces by Walter Carroll, whom I learned from in my own childhood. Walter Carroll's first book was called *Scenes at a Farm* and had desperately out-moded pictures of peasants in smocks. I think he eventually graduated to a second book called *Sea Idylls* which had little poems. I taught him as if he was a young child, but he lapped it up, he derived enormous pleasure from it. I can't remember whether he took Grade One in his last year, but I do know he went on to the end, even when he was in Pop, and reached the standard of Grade One. I just felt that I actually achieved some-thing heroic in getting him that far.'

Grade One is the lowest of the eight grades which pianists can sit. As Bayston observed, Boris understands what it is like not to be successful.

One of Boris's closest friends at school and university said: 'Boris read the Classics and was very influenced by the Classics. He likes the heroism. And I think that secretly – but unfortu-nately you can't say this in politics – he likes the aristocratic value system of the ancients, meaning rule of the best – the heroic values. I would imagine he's always found it slightly frustrating to have to say what the newspapers want. I secretly think he would have preferred it in ancient times.'

Hammond's last report on Boris, written on 2 January 1983, contains forebodings about the future:

> Of course I was delighted by the news of Boris' Scholarship at Balliol, a real achievement in a year of extremely tough competition. His performance was described as 'very powerful' by Jasper Griffin: oddly, though, they could not get very much out of him at interview. The Scholarship is a happy ending to an academic career here which in its

latter stages was not always quite so happy: and this last half, as these reports show, was no significant improvement on those that went before. My fear is that Boris may take his easy-going ways with him to Balliol, and add to the damaging statistics of Etonians who do little work at Oxbridge. I very much hope that this does not happen, and that Boris sets himself with proper determination at the First which should be within his capability. I think it true to say that Boris has no real academic bent, and he'll be an easier prey than some to the temptations of Oxford life: but he has a penetrating mind and a very sharp intelligence (not to speak of a big helping of personal charm), which should ensure a response to the intellectual stimulus of Balliol.

Boris remains intensely proud of his achievements at school, and loved being a leader there. But his page in the College Leaving Book, which every member of College fills in, referred to a different form of competition. It contained a large photograph of himself, with two scarves and a machine gun, together with an inscription about his determination to achieve 'more notches on my phallocratic phallus'.

7

Genuine Bogusness

WHEN BORIS ARRIVED AT BALLIOL COLLEGE, OXFORD, IN THE autumn of 1983, he had several ambitions, not all of them quite normal for a nineteen-year-old. A close friend recalls: 'He came to Oxford wanting to find a wife.' Boris believed Oxford was the place where one would find the pick of the potential wives.

His Eton friend Charles Spencer (then known as Viscount, or Charlie, Althorp) pointed out to him: 'Your parents did that.'

Boris refused to be put off: 'Well, they did pretty well. Twelve years.'

There is a kind of ambitious man who wants to get married just in order to have his private life settled, so he can get on with the serious business of his career. Boris's urge to marry so young seems more likely to be a sign of his desire to emulate his father's achievements. He may also have wanted to create a new and intact family.

Boris was optimistic, and willing to throw himself into enterprises which others would have regarded as too dangerous. He was certainly precocious. Toby Young, who went up to Brasenose College, Oxford, in the same year, noticed that Boris was more grown-up, or more focused, than other undergraduates: 'Boris had a real head-start on the rest of us. He seemed so fully formed, even in those days.'

At a time when many of us are still in a state of utter confusion, Boris knew where he wanted to go. A close friend said of him: 'At the age of eighteen he set himself the target that he was going to be in the Cabinet by the age of thirty-five.'

Toby Young was not nearly as close as that friend to Boris, but offered a grander, though less reliable, version of our man's ambitions. Darius Guppy, an Etonian who was later to go to prison for fraud and drag Boris into his misfortunes, told Young that while at school, Boris had confided in Charles Spencer that his secret ambition was to be President of the United States. Boris had an American passport, so this was not beyond the bounds of legal possibility, but as a leap of imagination it is worthy of Ian Fleming, the Old Etonian author of the James Bond stories.

As a more immediately practical step, Boris set out to become President of the Oxford Union. He also yearned, with a passion barely conceivable to some of us, to take a first-class degree.

Boris aimed higher than most of his contemporaries, but was not alone in being ambitious. Born at the height of the post-war baby boom, this generation of students was alarmingly competitive. Some of them must have led quiet and meritorious lives, but the ones who chased the glittering prizes could be rude, nasty, spiteful, petty and arrogant. Boris was not like that, except for a hidden well of arrogance, but he noticed the obnoxious behaviour of many of his contemporaries, and when he returned to Oxford in 1999 to give a speech, he reported that the students seemed 'nicer' than they were in his day.

David Ekserdjian, who came to Balliol as a junior research fellow in October 1983, was struck by the careerist atmosphere: 'They were terribly keen on working out what they were going to do and how they were going to get there. In my recollection, the thing people in Cambridge in about 1976 thought was

incredibly cool was to get into the BBC. Boris's generation I
don't think gave a stuff for the BBC. They thought the *Spectator*
was frightfully gripping.'

Balliol has long been a nursery of statesmen. The last great
crop consisted of Edward Heath, Roy Jenkins and Denis Healey,
who all held high office. Before them came Asquith, Curzon,
Macmillan and a host of others. This history mattered to Boris.
Like other men who have aspired to greatness, he scorned to
measure himself merely against his contemporaries. When an
interviewer tried to console him, at the age of thirty-nine, by
telling him, 'You've come a long way very young,' Boris replied
in a gloomy tone: 'Not by historical standards.'

Balliol was founded in about 1263, but rose to pre-eminence
in the nineteenth century under Benjamin Jowett, who encouraged public service as well as intellectual brilliance. According to
Jowett, 'One man is as good as another until he has written a
book.' Jowett's pupils and their successors took so many leading
positions that Cyril Asquith, a son of Asquith the Prime
Minister, observed: 'At the "top of the tree" in every profession
we find a sort of congested arboreal slum of Balliol men.'

When Boris went up to Oxford, *Brideshead Revisited* had been
shown only two years before on television, and undergraduates
could be found who were attempting to imitate Evelyn Waugh's
version of undergraduate life in the 1920s. But Balliol was not
that kind of place. It was a friendly and informal college, archi-
tecturally one of the less distinguished parts of the university. In
the main quadrangle, Garden Quad, students were at liberty to
lounge about on the grass in the summer, dons and students
drank in the same bar, and like most of Oxford it was allergic to
the then Prime Minister, Margaret Thatcher, and clung to the
faded dogmas of the 1960s.

Jonathan Barnes, who was one of Boris's college tutors and is
now Professor of Ancient Philosophy at the Sorbonne, says it was
no advantage at this time to have been to Eton if you wanted to go

to Balliol: 'On the contrary, there was a pretty strong prejudice against public schools. I should say that it was the college's policy – powerfully urged by some tutors and implicitly accepted by most – that, other things being equal, a candidate from an "unfavoured background" should be preferred to one from a favoured background (anglice: prefer the rotten schools to the good).'

Boris had entered a college where Tory politics were virtually unknown. As the Master of Balliol in Boris's time, Anthony Kenny – now Sir Anthony – recalls: 'The Balliol JCR [Junior Common Room, representing the undergraduates] was in those days very, very left-wing. The Communist Party was the right wing of it. Boris avoided it. An SDP MP approached me, to ask if I could recommend a young man to work for him. I asked Boris if he would be interested. Boris burst out laughing and said: "No, I'm a true-blue Tory."'

Boris, it will be seen, did not wear his Conservative colours on his sleeve, and even such an astute and friendly observer as Kenny supposed he would support the SDP, the new party launched by Labour rebels in 1981 with the intention of breaking the mould in British politics.

Lloyd Evans, who went up to Balliol from a left-wing household and a state school in 1982, said of the JCR: 'They were all these stupid public-school idiots who were showboating – it was a lifestyle choice for them – pretending to have a bond of affection for the working man.' According to Lloyd, these lefties had 'posh accents, donkey jackets, working men's boots and Mummy and Daddy paying the battels [college bills]'.

Boris, like Lloyd, was repelled by this kind of politics. He has since said, in the kind of language that some might use to describe how they discovered they were homosexual, that he was 'conscious of right-wing feelings' and 'realised I had Tory tendencies' when he saw students at Oxford collecting money during the miners' strike, which lasted from March 1984 to early 1985. As Boris told *GQ* in May 2003: 'I was appalled by the way middle-class kids were going around supporting Arthur Scargill when it was quite obvious he was leading the poor miners to utter perdition and doing them no bloody good at all.'

Lloyd had heard Boris's name before meeting him: 'The first time I saw him he was standing in the quad. There were a group of people standing round him and he said: "I think I might pop up to my room and have a peek at Plato."

'So I said: "Why, have you got him in the cupboard?" I got this enormous laugh. The thing about him is how personally warm and charismatic he is. You always get this gale of laughter. He leaves you with a terribly good feeling about yourself.'

Jasper Griffin, who has spent most of his life at Balliol, was one of Boris's teachers and remembers him with much affection: 'He was a very entertaining figure about the place. He was generally liked. He was a conspicuous figure.' Griffin added that Boris 'doesn't have the stuffy and tiresome habits' which might be thought to go with his manner.

Barnes, brother of the novelist Julian, remembered Boris's charm, and described the impression Boris made:

The charm was part of the Old Buffer persona which he already had at Balliol. Not a Young Fogey – he wasn't in the least fogeyish. Rather, a young Old Buffer. It showed up in his clothes (suits, not jeans and T-shirt; occasionally a tie; shoes, not trainers; etc), and in his speech (the drawl; 'a tome' for 'at home', 'orften' etc; and especially the Gollys and the Goshes), and also in what for want of a better word I call his manners (he was polite, courteous, witty). He wasn't the only Buffer in the world; but at the time bufferdom was not at all widespread, and it certainly marked Boris out. It was, I think, generally supposed that the bufferdom was sedulously cultivated. I can't judge – but, cultivated or natural or a mixture of the two, he wore it very well.

As Hammond had feared, for most of the time Boris did virtually no academic work. Barnes said: 'My exiguous tutorial notes read "feeble", "hasn't read the text", "no essay", and so on. He wasn't lazy, and he wasn't uninterested in Plato (at least, I don't think he was). Rather, there were other things which engaged most of his interest.'

Ekserdjian claims that Barnes one week reproached Boris for copying a piece of work word for word out of Loeb, which gives a straight English translation next to the original Greek or Latin text.

Barnes said: 'Oh Boris, I'm incredibly offended that you should underestimate my intelligence to such a degree that you thought I wouldn't realise you'd just nicked this out of Loeb.'

Boris gave the amusing reply: 'I'm terribly, terribly sorry, I've been so busy I just didn't have time to put in the mistakes.'

Barnes does not remember this, but says of his attempts to teach Boris philosophy: 'If you're intelligent enough, you can rub along in philosophy on a couple of hours a week. Boris rubbed along on no hours a week, and it wasn't quite good enough.'

At the end of each term Balliol has a ceremony called 'handshaking', when each undergraduate appears before the Master and tutors in his subject. The tutors report on how well or badly the student has done, and Barnes recalls telling Kenny: 'This term, Master, Mr Johnson has been a pain in the arse.'

Yet all Boris's teachers remember him with affection. Barnes said:

On the whole, I find politicians perfectly odious (and I haven't the slightest interest in what they do). Balliol has produced more than its fair share of MPs: while I was a Fellow I met many of them, and taught three or four. Most of them strike me as frightful people – vainglorious and yet very stupid, moralistic and yet deeply dishonest. Boris

strikes me as one of the few exceptions. I might even be
tempted to vote for him . . . I confess that I have forgotten
the irritations, and am left with the conviction that, at
bottom, Boris is really a Good Egg.

Justin Rushbrooke, a Harrovian who was also reading Classics
at Balliol, became a lasting friend of Boris when they had rooms
next to each other, and defends him against the charge of idleness: 'Considering how thinly he spread himself, he was
disciplined, and he did *love* certain parts of the subject. He was
by no means a slacker. I was a complete slacker. Boris viewed me
with a degree of horror. We had different lifestyles: I would still
be in bed at eleven o'clock in the morning. We both had scholarships but I lost mine in my third year and took a gentleman's
third.'

Boris played rugby for Balliol for four years running, as a prop
forward, but his social life extended far beyond the college. In
Oxford terms, though not by any more demanding standard,
Boris was a toff, having been to Eton; but he tended to be seen
more as an exotic flower, or an English eccentric, than as a toff.
What Boris carefully hid from view, or at least took care not to
emphasise, was that many of his friends were toffish – a fact not
readily apparent among the workers, peasants and intellectuals of
the Balliol JCR.

Yet Boris was also one of the most conspicuous undergradu-
ates in Oxford, and had other conspicuous friends. Patrick
Hennessy, who had gone from Eton to Oxford ahead of Boris,
recalls: 'When he was at Oxford he associated with Darius
Guppy. Guppy was an obviously dodgy character. It was a flaw in
Boris in my view. I found Guppy very unpleasant.'

In a later chapter, we shall describe Guppy's downfall, and
how Boris became ensnared in it. But at this time Guppy was
enjoying social success and a relatively innocent notoriety. He
was at Magdalen College, as was his great friend Charles

Spencer. Boris was very fond of Guppy, and also on close terms with Spencer.

A large number of undergraduates were ready to take offence at the ostentatious behaviour of some members of this circle. A body calling itself the Magdalen Women's Group passed the following motion by an overwhelming majority: 'Henceforth, Magdalen women will not pander to the whim of Darius Guppy.'

Guppy revelled in such attention, which only made him more provocative. To insult the spirit of the age was part of the point. It was around this time that Peregrine Worsthorne, the then editor of the *Sunday Telegraph*, coined the expression 'bourgeois triumphalism' to describe the vulgar behaviour of some beneficiaries of Thatcherism, and such triumphalism could certainly be found among Oxford undergraduates.

Boris was elected to the Bullingdon, the most famously riotous dining-club in Oxford, which had only twenty-four members. The dress for the Bullingdon, including a navy-blue tailcoat with white silk facings and gold buttons, cost nearly £1,000 at 1984 prices, and the dinners, at which vast amounts of drink were consumed in the most expensive restaurants, about £400 a time. But according to Guppy the less wealthy members were subsidised at this period, and allowed to pay only £200 a dinner, by a rich benefactor who some believed had been elected to the club for this purpose.

Champagne breakfasts were held once a term at hotels such as The Bear in Woodstock and were attended, Guppy has recalled, by 'two or three top-class strippers from London' who 'would be heralded into the dining-room when the champagne had been flowing for some time' and 'would always be well-paid for their services and would never become annoyed, even when the more drunken undergraduates went too far'.

Elections to the Bullingdon took place in one or another member's rooms late at night at the end of each term, and

were often hotly contested. Boris had great difficulty persuad-
ing the other members to agree to admit Guppy, who in turn
faced a titanic battle to get Radek Sikorski in, at an election
held in the rooms of Toby Mansell-Pleydell in University
College.

By Guppy's account, some of the members did not want
Sikorski because he was a foreigner and, as they put it, 'not suitable material'. Sikorski was a fiercely anti-Communist Pole who
had managed to get out of Poland and into Oxford, where he
was elected President of the Union. In 2005 he became Poland's
Defence Minister.

Sikorski told me: 'I vividly remember the night of my election
to the Bullingdon, which happened as I was asleep in my room
in Walton Street. In the middle of the night a dozen screaming
figures burst in to my room and demolished it completely with
my hi-fi and books piled up in the middle of the floor and my
heavy desk chair put through the wall. I vividly remember Boris,
a very solid and friendly man, saying, "Congratulations, man.
You've been elected."

'The secretary or mistress of the landlord came down the stairs
and screamed: "What do you think you're doing?"

'And Darius Guppy ran up the stairs, put his face very close to
her and said: "Don't worry, baby, it's his birthday."'

The tradition was to smash up a new member's room, but
when Andrew Gilmour was elected, Boris warned the other
members not to break up his room, telling them that if this were
to happen, Gilmour would refuse to join.

Gilmour went to the first dinner after he was elected, at Le
Manoir aux Quat' Saisons, Raymond Blanc's restaurant outside
Oxford. In Gilmour's words, it was 'a pretty awful occasion –
someone vomited'.

After dinner the members asked each other, 'Who shall we go
and trash?' This prompted a protest from Gilmour: 'I got rather
pompous and said as the only member who was the son of an

old member, that didn't used to be done. I had the coat and all that – it was my father's.'

Gilmour's father is Sir Ian Gilmour, one of the patrician Tory wets who were appalled by Margaret Thatcher. He was ennobled as Lord Gilmour of Craigmillar. While still a young man he bought and for a time edited the *Spectator*.

Charles Spencer, who shared a house with Gilmour, was also elected to the Bullingdon, but declined to join. As with so many institutions which are popularly regarded as smart, it seems it may have been smarter not to belong to the Bullingdon.

Patrick Hennessy, himself an Old Etonian, said: 'It's often thought the Bullingdon was crammed full of Old Etonians. Quite a lot of Old Etonians wouldn't have gone within a mile of the Bullingdon and thought it was a load of tossers.'

The club still invited Gilmour to its farewell dinner, held at Cliveden, reached by boat down the Thames: 'I had an argument with Boris about Israel – Boris had read Conor Cruise O'Brien's book – don't give an inch of Gaza ground – Boris and I were arguing about it even as we went down to this ludicrous event in our Buller tails. I remember Guppy being anti-Semitic and Boris getting really very, very angry about that.'

In the photograph of the Bullingdon that can be found in the plate section, Boris is sitting on the steps, and although he appears to have the correct kit, he manages to subvert the effect by wearing odd socks. Most of the Buller men look very young and vulnerable, but determined to seem manly and self-assured. The pressure at that age to enjoy oneself, and to do supposedly glamorous things, can be pretty much intolerable.

Toby Young recalls that Roland Rudd, a Social Democrat ally of Boris who was President of the Union and later built up a financial PR company worth many millions of pounds, was debagged by the Bullingdon 'and took it very badly'.

According to Gilmour, Boris backed out when the Bullingdon went after Rudd. Boris seems to have kept a more level head than some Buller men. But if one moved in these circles, one was bound to find oneself witnessing the odd debagging. When Charles Spencer celebrated his twentieth birthday with a group of Oxford friends including Boris at the Notting Hill restaurant La Paesana, they tried to debag the disc jockey Tony Blackburn, who told the press: 'I got the message that Althorp and co. wanted to get my trousers off. I thought it was all very odd, but the waiters stepped in and asked them to return to their tables. There was a lot of shouting and suddenly a rubber plant hurtled across the room and landed in somebody's meal.'

In March 2003, by which time Boris was editor of the *Spectator*, he got Peter Oborne to include this incident in a cover piece for the magazine about the decline and fall of the Hooray Henry. But Boris exercised his editorial prerogative of removing all reference to himself from the piece.

Toby Young, who has himself achieved a degree of fame as a journalist in later life, is not sure where he first met Boris, but thinks 'it may have been at a Cheese and Wine Appreciation Society' meeting. Chapsoc, as it was usually known, just as the Lesbian and Gay Society was known as Gaysoc, was 'an opportunity for male undergraduates to meet secretaries'. Guppy and Spencer were both members.

According to Rachel Johnson, Boris's sister, who went to New College, Oxford, Chapsoc was 'easily the raunchiest society in Oxford, far surpassing the tame transvestitism of the Piers Gaveston . . . The bacchanalian quality of its meetings derives not so much from the amount of wine drunk as from the sexual excitement generated by the proximity of so many secretaries. Rendered incapable of small talk, difficult at the best of times in noisy rooms, the boys throw French sticks and packets of supermarket cheese at the girls they fancy.'

This account appeared in Rachel's essay on sex in *The Oxford Myth*, a collection she edited of ten pieces about the university, published by Weidenfeld in 1988. The book was denounced by reviewers, partly because of Toby Young's unpleasant and inaccurate account of the people he found in Brasenose: 'Small, vaguely deformed undergraduates would scuttle across the quad as if carrying mobile homes on their backs . . . In America, these people would be called "nerds". In Brasenose we referred to them as "stains".'

Rachel and her collaborators were recognised, as Young later conceded, as 'a bunch of insufferable jumped-up prats who deserved criticism'.

But even as Boris pursued earthly glory, he could see with perverse amusement how bogus it all was, and how the words of a poet might long outlive the power of a ruler.

One of the debates Boris had many times with his friends in his room at Balliol was whether 'bogusness' or 'bogusity' is the noun that goes with the word 'bogus'. Twenty years later, when telling *Esquire* magazine why the Rolling Stones are one of his favourites, he plumped for 'bogusness': 'What I like is the bogusness of them. I love the idea of these four middle-class white kids pretending to be rough around the edges.'

Oxford offered an inexhaustible supply of bogusness, and for Boris that was part of its attraction. He himself has a kind of genuine bogusness: a ludicrous manner which has nevertheless become part of him. And at Oxford he was about to demonstrate that he could conquer a far wider public than at school.

8

The Oxford Politician

BORIS THE WOULD-BE POLITICIAN REFINED HIS ORATORY, and the no less necessary crafts of intrigue and deceit, at the Oxford Union, where so many statesmen have taken their first steps. In the Union's Victorian debating chamber are found the images of Gladstone, Salisbury, Asquith, F. E. Smith, Curzon, Macmillan, Roy Jenkins and Michael Heseltine. But none of these great men has left so penetrating an account as Boris of how to get on in Oxford politics. His analysis of how to become President of the Union is worthy of Machiavelli.

Boris's twenty-page treatise, simply entitled 'Politics', appeared in *The Oxford Myth*, the collection edited by his sister Rachel. The triviality of the subject matter in no way invalidates the fascination of the work.

Boris understands the bogusness of democracy. He has an infallible eye for the distinction between the high-flown theory of how the Union is supposed to work, and the sordid reality. Rule 33 of its constitution expressly forbids the soliciting of votes, yet this is the 'distinctive activity' during the elections in which the President and other officers are chosen.

To succeed at Union elections, Boris explains, what you really need is 'a disciplined and deluded collection of stooges' who will get the vote out for you in their respective colleges. The key word here is 'deluded', for you attract stooges by implying that you are going to do as much for them, in their attempt to gain election to a junior committee, as they will do for you in your campaign to become supreme leader, or President.

Yet as Boris says, the 'brutal fact' of the candidate–stooge relationship is that the candidate can never do as much for his stooges as they can do for him. No candidate can give effective support to more than one stooge, while he must have support from several stooges if he is to become President. In short, 'The relationship . . . is founded on duplicity.'

Why then, he asks, do people consent to become stooges? There are several reasons: they can be flattered into doing so, they are vain enough to think that they themselves could have a shot at the top job, and their empty lives are given meaning by their humdrum activities within the organisation, or machine, which they have joined.

The essence of the stooge's role is a kind of wilful self-deception. In Boris's words, 'The tragedy of the stooge is that even if he thinks this through, he wants so much to believe that his relationship with the candidate is special that he shuts out the truth. The terrible art of the candidate is to coddle the self-deception of the stooge.'

One cannot pretend that Boris does justice to every motive which might inspire a man or woman to a political career. It does not seem to occur to him that some people might enter politics with disinterested motives, and he appears to think that everyone down to the humblest party worker secretly believes he can get to the top. On the other hand, the way in which many Tory MPs who were totally unknown to the outside world either entered the contest in 2005 to succeed Michael Howard as Tory leader, or seriously considered doing so, more than confirms Boris's view that politicians are amazingly vain.

So much for the theory. What of Boris's practice at the

Union? Michael Gove, who became a successful journalist at *The Times* and in 2005 followed Boris into the Commons as a Tory MP, cheerfully admitted: 'I was Boris's stooge. I became a votary of the Boris cult.'

Gove recalled how Boris hooked him: 'The first time I saw him was in the Union bar. He was a striking figure with sheep-dog hair and penny loafers, standing in a distinctive pose with his hands in his trouser pockets and his head bent forward. He seemed like a kindly, Oxford character, but he was really there like a great basking shark waiting for freshers to swim towards him.'

This vision of Boris as a shark does not, of course, do full justice to him. Gove, who had himself become an accomplished debater while still a schoolboy in Scotland and who appeared at the Union in a kilt, said of Boris: 'He was quite the most brilliant *extempore* speaker of his generation. I can still remember him mentioning "the Bell curve distribution", after which he went on: "I'm sure we all know what a Bell curve is. It is a curve which is shaped like a bell."'

As Gove said, 'Boris has the capacity apparently to lose his way in a sentence, like a child in a nativity play. You want him to succeed, and when he does you share in his triumph.' Gove also recalled that Boris was much more interesting to talk to than most of the Union hacks, and did not just take a 'close-the-deal' approach.

But a deal was closed: 'The real reason why I became a stooge in the Boris machine was that Oxford politics was essentially a matter of the college that you found yourself in. I was in Lady Margaret Hall [LMH], which was a small satrap of Balliol, like a colony in Sicily aping the manners of our betters. Slates need balance, and an LMH debater fitted into the balance.'

The recruitment of a team of stooges such as Gove was not the only means by which Boris became President. He also practised a series of bold deceptions about his own political opinions, in order to appeal to several different constituencies at the same time.

This behaviour was witnessed by Frank Luntz, an American at Oxford, whose outrage at Boris's conduct can be heard even down a transatlantic telephone line twenty years later. Luntz says: 'He renounced his Conservative affiliation and fully embraced the SDP and the principles and people who supported the SDP to help him get elected. At that time being a member of the Social Democrats was the best thing to be at Oxford. I said to him, "You don't do this, this is a very small country and it's not right and it will come back to haunt you." He abandoned them to get elected and after he was elected he said he was a Tory again.'

Radek Sikorski confirmed this: 'Boris made these SDP speeches at the Union which was how he got elected.'

But Luntz also remembered that Boris was capable of saying unpopular things: 'He was probably the most popular debater – when he spoke he was entertaining and emotional and effective. But he also stood up for Israel, which was not a popular thing to do. He stood up and said this thing about the bully in the school yard. The Jewish students at that moment just wanted to make him king.'

Luntz has since become a successful pollster in the United States, where he prides himself on having helped 'move the language' so that, for example, 'school vouchers' become 'opportunity scholarships'. His name cropped up in British politics in October 2005 when the Cameron campaign team distributed footage of a focus group organised by Luntz which showed that Cameron was 'exactly what swing voters are looking for in a Conservative leader' and represented 'the future of Britain and a new generation'. Some people thought this footage, which was shown on *Newsnight*, was unduly favourable to Cameron.

Whether or not that was so, Luntz still has close links with

Boris: 'I see him, I like him, I think he's a great guy.' At the Republican convention in 2004, Boris arrived without the right pass, but Luntz got him in and he ended up sitting in the seats reserved for the family of Vice-President Dick Cheney.

To pass himself off as a Social Democrat was not Boris's only deception. At Balliol, according to Lloyd Evans: 'He never stood in the Conservative interest. When he stood for the Union he told us he was an environmentalist.'

Jessica Pulay, of Christ Church, who was herself to become President of the Union, and is a great admirer of Boris, admits that he was 'extremely clever at not really revealing his political cards at any point'.

How did he veil his real opinions? Pulay said: 'His humour. And the fact that he's not an ideologue – or if he is, he keeps it very well-concealed. He's a life-enhancer. He had a lot of acolytes who maybe he didn't regard as friends. I was sure that he was going to be a success, absolutely. He just had an aura about him that made him instantly recognisable. Boris was a great showman – without doubt the best showman of his generation. He just made people laugh when he opened his mouth.'

Pulay recalled that Boris only succeeded in becoming President of the Union at the second attempt: 'The second time he was running against someone from Christ Church [her own college]. It was not the done thing not to support your own college, but I was a college renegade. The Balliol machine was very much the SDP machine. The Christ Church machine was the Tory Reform Group machine – the slightly wet Tory machine.'

Boris has since sought to diminish his great essay about how to succeed at the Union. In 2003 he said: 'I think my essay remains the *locus classicus* of the English genre of bogus self-deprecation.'

One can see what Boris means. In his essay, he undervalues his own talents as a debater, which were plainly a major factor in his success. He stood as a debater, the alternative being to commend himself as an administrator who would save the Union by means of tight financial control. For the administrative side of things, he relied on Brenda Goodall, who is now dead, one of the first in a line of strong-minded women, devoted to his interests, who have helped Boris.

But Boris's essay on politics is not bogus. His Union career was over when he wrote it, so he could afford to be amazingly, though not completely, candid about a political process in which he himself had played a leading role. Although we find no mention in his account of his SDP period, we still see a sophisticated and instinctive grasp of the role played by deceit in the electoral process, and a joyful, one might even say an honest, willingness to play this game.

And although the Union is easily mocked or despised, it is one way in which Oxford keeps in touch with the wider world of politics, and it is a very good way to meet people from London. Charles Moore, who was at that time editor of the *Spectator*, said: 'I first met Boris at the Oxford Union. It's the only time I've met a President of the Union who I thought was really, really interesting. We had a conversation about creationism.'

At Boris's final debate, the speakers included Melina Mercouri, the Greek actress and politician who was determined to retrieve the Elgin Marbles from the British Museum. Jonathan Barnes said: 'He was a splendid President of the Union – he looked and acted the part, and generally managed to juggle the thing along thanks to a mixture of authority and bonhomie. He asked me to speak once or twice – always at the shortest of notices, because one of the speakers he had booked jacked at the last minute. I only did funny speeches (and not very funny at that).'

If the Union politics of this period seem tawdry, Oxford journalism was truly atrocious. For callow nastiness, it is hard to beat some of these publications. As Alexander Connock observed in *The Oxford Myth*, 'Writing such magazines requires a ruthless willingness to sell one's friends down the river.'

Many of these student journalists made it to Fleet Street in one capacity or another. Toby Young passed on the editorship of *Tributary*, an Oxford imitation of *Private Eye*, to Boris, Guppy and Charles Spencer. According to Toby, 'When I did it, it was like the first half of *Private Eye*, with stories about real people. Boris didn't want to make any enemies, so he made it more like the second half of *Private Eye*. I think he's got an absolute anathema to being disliked. He clearly thrives on popularity and adores winning popularity contests of any description.'

Boris's most amusing cover, published in May 1985, had a picture of a nude woman on the cover who was saying, 'Why am I so lonely at Oxford . . .? But wait!' A small phial of liquid was sellotaped to her hand, and on page two it was explained that this was a 'LOVE-PHILTRE' which would make you 'positively sexy'.

Lloyd Evans and Aidan Hartley were the next editors of *Trib*, as it was usually known, and Evans recalled a decisive intervention by Boris:

> He could get really angry. There's a real toughness to him. When we were editing the magazine, and he was going for the presidency of the Union, he became fixated about what we were writing about him, and he came down to Aidan Hartley's house in the middle of the night – Aidan was living somewhere in Jericho and it was three o'clock in the morning – and picked up the thing we'd written and it contained a whole stream of abuse of Boris. We called him an exiled Armenian chicken farmer. The other thing we called him was the Aryan bull pig, victim of a hideous Nazi war experiment in Munich in 1936. We'd also called him incompetent. That was the thing he picked up on. He said,

'You can call me an Armenian chicken farmer or an Aryan bull pig, but don't call me incompetent.' He was absolutely incandescent. He really went mad. He grabbed the typewriter and said, 'Damn it, I'm a journalist,' and started writing his own version of the whole thing. We ended up not publishing any of it. I was surprised by how angry he was. He's a war leader. He is one of the two or three most extraordinary people I've ever met. You just feel he's going somewhere. People just love him. They go along with him and they enjoy being led.

To make people enjoy being led by him was an aspect of leadership which Boris mastered at a very young age. He made people helpless with laughter, and so great was their enjoyment that they scarcely cared what he did with their support, as long as he kept on amusing them. Only in retrospect did people start to ask whether this comedian could ever be serious. In Oxford, he looked to many of his contemporaries like a future Prime Minister.

9

Boris in Love

BORIS FELL IN LOVE WITH THE MOST BEAUTIFUL GIRL IN Oxford. He met Allegra Mostyn-Owen in early 1984, half-way through their first year. She was a radiant beauty, of such sweetness that it was virtually impossible not to fall in love with her. If you managed to amuse her, you were rewarded with an eager, loving smirk. If you annoyed her, she could get frosty.

Boris had many drawbacks – he was poor, scruffy, unreliable about practical matters and obsessed by student politics – but he amused her very much indeed. With unflagging single-mindedness he set out to win her. He decided to make her, first his girlfriend, then the wife whom he had always intended to find at Oxford.

They met because of an error on his part. He was invited to a party in her rooms at Trinity College, next to Balliol, which she had thrown jointly with another girl, and arrived on the wrong night with a bottle of wine.

Allegra was reading a book: 'The problem was I was reading this economics textbook. Quite a big textbook. I think it's by R. J. Lipsey. The fifth edition. Or the seventh edition. In fact I was falling asleep. I was lying on the carpet, reading it on the carpet in my lovely double set in Garden Quad. A lovely living-room with two huge windows looking on to the garden.

'There's this stranger at the door who goes, "Oh, oh, oh, oh, oh." I'd never met him but he said he'd seen me at a Union debate, and he was known to the girl I'd co-hosted the party with.

'So we drank the bottle and talked. I don't know what we talked about. I think we got on very well and he became my best friend, a much better friend than any of the girls I knew at the time. Because anyway he made me laugh. He introduced me to poetry, which I didn't know at all, and there were lots of good jokes, and lots of bad jokes. And in my own way I didn't really think he was making a play for me, despite the fact that there was lots of curry *à deux* at the Kismet Tandoori.'

Unlike many of the bolder male students, Boris did not spend his time at Oxford chasing women in general. He pursued Allegra in a manner that made him faithful, and continent, compared to some of his disreputable friends. His girlfriend before Oxford was called Alexa de Ferranti, who went to school at Bryanston with his sister Rachel.

Allegra was struck by her new friend's early intellectual development: 'When I got to know him I was very impressed that he'd started to read *Economist* editorials at the age of ten.' Some of Boris's uncles on his mother's side worked for *The Economist*. Boris used to ask Allegra: 'If I added up the IQ of my father and my mother don't you think they'd be more than the IQ of your father and mother?'

Allegra was too young to dismiss this ghastly question: 'I thought he must know what he was talking about, but of course he didn't. He was just talking from his own insecurity.'

Boris's scholarship-boy question, filled with cringing awe for the conventional measures of intelligence, does not begin to do justice to Allegra's parents. Her father, Willy, traces his ancestry to Owen Glendower. Woodhouse, the family seat in Shropshire, was remodelled in 1798, and he also had a castle at Aberuchill in Perthshire. While Willy was still at Eton, his father and both his brothers died, leaving him a man of independent means, free to go touring in his Rolls-Royce and to pursue his love of the arts.

Willy married Gaia Servadio, a high-spirited young Italian whom he met after returning to London from Florence, where he worked for five years for the great art critic Bernhard Berenson. Gaia as a tiny girl spent the Second World War on the run in Italy with her sister, their father, who was Jewish, and their mother, who was not. The father's mother and grand-mother were murdered at Auschwitz, after spending a dreadful time in an internment camp in Italy from which they were able to send only one message: 'I need money and a comb.' Allegra is a Jewish name.

Gaia's first book, *Melinda*, was a spectacular success, and was translated into many languages. Willy became Director of Old Masters at Christie's. They had three children, but their marriage did not survive Gaia's stardom.

When Allegra disapproves of something, she can be quite severe. Boris once told her: 'What I like about you is that you've got principles.'

They saw more and more of each other, and at Easter they went on holiday together in Turkey, visited some of Boris's rela-tions in Istanbul and saw Troy and Ephesus: 'In Seljuk, close to Ephesus, we rented a motorbike. We spent at least half a day in this place. I liked sketching – every child seemed to be called either Attila or Genghis – and a small number had yellow hair, just like Boris did.

'We had a lovely time, and at some point quite late in the summer term we were just saying goodbye at the gate of Trinity and he said, "I don't know if I'm coming or going. If you don't go out with me I'm not going to devote so much time to being your friend. I'm actually going to devote most of my time to the Oxford Union." Which he did anyway. No, it was fine.'

Boris had pushed Allegra into a commitment. His ultimatum, and the priority he went on giving to his own career, indicated a ruthless determination to run their relationship on his own terms. Whether he had found, in Allegra, a woman strong enough to tolerate his egotism, is not the kind of question Boris has ever allowed to hold him back. He had won the most desirable woman in Oxford, whom any number of undergraduates would have been happy to call their own, and together they made a glamorous sight. Boris and Allegra became the Posh and Becks, or Mick and Jerry, or Bogart and Bacall, of their generation.

Toby Young said: 'Allegra was by common consent the most attractive undergraduate of her year. Boris very quickly became a legendary figure, scaling the wall between Trinity and Balliol to bed Allegra.'

That was not how Boris got into Trinity, but Young expresses a common feeling of admiration. Radek Sikorski said: 'He and Allegra were the perfect couple. She was the girl from the cover of *Tatler* and he was the future Prime Minister.'

Allegra was photographed by Terence Donovan for *Vogue* and by David Bailey for *Tatler*. Bailey began by saying to her: 'You're a bit posh, aren't you?'

His next words were: 'Go on then, just fuck the camera.'

Allegra says of the resulting cover: 'That's my look of horror and shock when he's telling me to fuck the camera.'

The bad aspects of this picture did not end there: 'Having done the cover shot for *Tatler*, people decided I must be beautiful because *Tatler* says so. Then I got these declarations of love every day. I didn't want anything to do with them. Boris felt like a safe place, but not for very long. Like most human beings, he'll exploit weakness.'

One of her innumerable admirers was Hugh Fearnley-Whittingstall, who had been at school with Boris and has since achieved fame as a food writer. He sent her a note which said: 'Why have steak and chips when you can have *foie gras*?'

Allegra was amused by this: 'It really made me laugh. Of

course I responded to Hugh with a note saying I found *foie gras* ethically repugnant.'

Boris was less amused. In November 2005, in a brief contribution to the *Observer Food Monthly*, Boris said: 'As for Hugh Fearnley-bloody-Whittingstall, he's got a lot to answer for. That man has persuaded thousands of innocent people to pick nettles and boil them up in the delusion that they are making something fit for consumption.'

Many undergraduates were inhibited by a proper sense of shyness from approaching Allegra. Michael Gove remembered: 'Allegra, an Oxford goddess, and editor of *Isis*, seemed unimaginably distant.'

Not everyone liked Allegra: to some people she seemed cold. In the pages of *Cherwell* she became Ms Allergic Mostyn-Owen.

Boris and Allegra showed from the first some irreconcilable differences of taste. She could never understand what he could see in Darius Guppy, of whom she said: 'I got on with him OK. It seemed to me he didn't have much respect for women in general. We had arguments about that. I think he's the only person I've ever thrown a glass of beer over.'

Guppy would say to Allegra: 'Do you love me?'

Allegra would reply: 'Come on, Darry, you're too sweaty and feverish.'

But because Allegra was with his friend Boris, Guppy 'didn't step over the line with me'.

Boris and Allegra were in adjacent colleges, but wrote to each other continually: 'We really enjoyed the pigeon post. I respond very strongly to the written word and so does he. We would leave each other notes at least twice a day.'

Many of Boris's notes are jokes. He would tell her that she had been selected to play on board one for Atletico di Roma chess club against the USSR, against Boris Spassky, and should bring a packed lunch. Or he would ask her what is Plato's Theory of Recollection, to which the answer is 'I forget'.

In another note, Boris said Allegra reminded him more and more of his mother. He perhaps found some of the same moral seriousness, and sensitivity, and sweetness, in Allegra as in his mother.

But as if to make up for this confession, the note ran immediately into a joke about whether her bed was made, to which the answer was that it was made in Birmingham. He added that he had been making this joke since about the age of eight.

Trinity, Allegra's college, made Boris welcome, despite the fact that he was from Balliol: 'He would regularly borrow books from our library – Trinity was remarkably tolerant. The Trinity porters were always very courteous to him.'

Work occasionally intruded. Boris usually wanted to see her that very evening, and would suggest an amusing range of possible diversions, but once, when Jasper Griffin had told him he would get a delta in Greek lyric poetry, he asked if she could face not seeing him for a whole week.

During his first long vacation, or summer holiday from Oxford, Boris went with his sister Rachel to stay in Israel on a Kibbutz. Through their stepmother, Jenny, who was the stepdaughter of Teddy Sieff, the chairman of Marks & Spencer, they were connected to one of the most prominent Jewish families in Britain. Rachel recalled with pleasure that on the Kibbutz, Boris was forced for six weeks to do the washing-up. According to Allegra, 'He was in a subterranean room being punished for his blondness.'

In his second long vacation, he went with Rachel and his school friend Sebastian O'Meara to Spain and Portugal to investigate animal cruelty. During this expedition he wrote on 8 August 1985 from the Pension Amazonas in Lisbon to Allegra, asking her if she had broached the subject of marriage yet with her parents. Boris wondered on paper if she could bear the idea of getting married to him – a characteristic piece of self-deprecation – but also asked if she might emasculate him.

Allegra's parents were appalled by Boris. Her father, Willy, described him as 'rapacious', and would get into competitive conversations about Eton with him, in which it would invariably emerge that of the two of them, Boris had had the more glittering schoolboy career. Boris dressed in a wilfully scruffy manner, which might have been calculated to upset the Mostyn-Owens, who valued elegance and beauty. When he went on a skiing holiday with Allegra, her brothers and her mother, Gaia, he left his passport behind, which meant he had to catch a later flight, and when he opened his suitcase it turned out to contain only his dirty sheets from Balliol. Such behaviour added to Gaia's general sense of horror. Boris went skiing in his normal clothes, a tweed jacket and moleskin trousers, and liked going very fast straight downhill.

One way Boris saved time was by simply not doing some of the chores which fall to most students. Allegra said: 'He never had the time to wash laundry or buy shampoo and somehow he was terribly good at getting other people to do things. I ended up doing all his laundry at Trinity.' Boris pretends to be old-fashioned partly in order to hide the fact that he really is old-fashioned. He most likely believes laundry is for women, but would never be foolish enough to say it. Instead he has brought the art of masculine incompetence to such a pitch of perfection that women take pity on him. But it was still quite an achievement, albeit ungallant and not very good for his character, to get the most desirable girl at Oxford to wash his clothes.

Allegra liked the fact that Boris had to dress formally for the Union and the Bullingdon, as then he 'looked quite handsome'.

In the summer of 1986, Boris and Allegra engaged in a journalistic collaboration which caused her deep embarrassment. An article which Boris had helped to write appeared under Allegra's name in the *Sunday Telegraph*. It described the descent on Oxford of Tina Brown, a famous British journalist working in New York. Brown wanted to find out all about Olivia Channon, daughter of the Trade and Industry Secretary, Paul Channon, who had been discovered dead, choked on her vomit, in the rooms at Christ Church of Gottfried von Bismarck.

A delightfully hostile portrait was drawn of Brown on her hunt for 'tasteless details', but Allegra had made a disastrous error. She pretended she had been at a lunch which Brown threw for a group of fashionable undergraduates, when in fact only Boris had been there. It was the kind of mistake which would have counted for less than nothing in Oxford journalism, but it would not do in a national paper, for it enabled Brown to get one of her sidekicks to dismiss the whole article as 'untrue'. One of the distinctive products of Boris's journalism had already emerged: the powerful and amusing article, utterly convincing in its general drift, but weakened by cavalier treatment of mere facts.

Because Boris was reading Mods and Greats, as the undergraduate course in Greek and Roman literature, history and philosophy is known, he spent four years at Oxford, while Allegra left after the more normal three. After she had finished finals, they went on holiday in Perthshire, in Scotland. On the way back down, Boris insisted they have a picnic at Windscale, as the Sellafield nuclear reprocessing plant used to be known.

Allegra started work in London for the *Evening Standard*. She was on the paper's gossip column, 'Londoner's Diary', but did not enjoy it, and resigned the following April.

The separation during this year was difficult. Boris wrote many letters in which he tried to mend things after unsatisfactory telephone conversations. It is clear that he loves her deeply, and is determined to keep their relationship going. His passion and his fighting spirit are fully engaged. Where a faint heart might have decided things were not working out, Boris presses forward. He is worried whether he will get a first in his final exams, and the prospect of taking a job in the then fashionable field of management consultancy fills him with dread, but they are engaged to be married and that at least he regards as certain. But in a postscript to one letter he warns her to watch out for men and adds that they are all the same.

In March 1987 the great world came to Oxford, when two former Balliol men, Edward Heath and Roy Jenkins, contended for the chancellorship of the university, for which Lord Blake was also a candidate. Boris was entranced by the contest, and by the sight of Heath and Jenkins canvassing in Balliol with the quad full of bodyguards, and correctly predicted that Jenkins would win.

At the end of his Oxford days, Boris knocked on Anthony Kenny's door and asked for extra tuition in Aristotle's ethics before being viva-ed – interviewed – to see whether, despite written papers which were not on their own quite good enough, he could be given a first. 'But alas,' Kenny said, 'my efforts were in vain.'

Allegra remembered: 'He did really want a first. He had nightmares after it. He had one about his viva. The stumbling block in the viva was lyric poetry.'

Jasper Griffin said: 'He just cut it a bit too fine.' Griffin asked the don who had marked Boris's finals papers how he had done. The don replied: 'He got the top 2:1 in his year.' Griffin said of this don: 'I could have spat in his eyes, you can imagine.'

Boris in years to come was to make a speciality of cutting things too fine. A more humble – or humdrum – character would have said to himself, 'I really want a first and I'm quite clever enough to get one as long as I prepare carefully for the exam.' Boris instead said to himself, 'I really want a first and I'm so clever I can wing it.' It was with this enterprising attitude that he entered the world of work.

10

Troubled Times

ON 5 SEPTEMBER 1987 BORIS AND ALLEGRA WERE MARRIED AT St Michael and All Angels, West Felton. It was a grand and elegant occasion. Anna Steiger, the daughter of Rod Steiger and Claire Bloom, sang from *The Marriage of Figaro*. The congregation also heard the world premiere of a piece by Hans Werner Henze called 'Allegra e Boris – Duetto Concertante per Violino e Viola all'Occasione delle loro Faustissime Nozze il 5 Settembre, 1987'.

The reception was held on a perfect summer's day in the garden at Woodhouse. The guests were cosmopolitan, drawn from London, Italy and Oxford. A string quartet played in the drawing-room and the confetti were proper sweetmeats – sugared almonds – as in Italy, instead of the pieces of coloured paper which are flung about at weddings in England. To a guest like myself who was barely involved with the two families, it looked like a stylish and light-hearted Italian film shot on location in the green depths of Shropshire. The bride and groom were both only twenty-three years old.

Boris misquoted P. G. Wodehouse in his speech and was corrected by a man who had arrived in a helicopter, whereupon Boris recovered by saying: 'Good chap. Give the man a coconut.'

During the wedding, Boris did something which Allegra described as 'hilarious and totally exasperating', though many other brides would have used stronger language. As she described it, Boris was not taken by the idea of wearing a ring (after all, Stanley never did). 'Strangely, it fell to Darius to bring the rings up to Shropshire; I think Boris may have forgotten to fetch them from Hatton Garden. Rings were exchanged, but by the time we had lunch he no longer had his. He always insisted he knew where it was, i.e. somewhere in the garden, but he had somehow dropped it and lost it within an hour of receiving it.'

This is not the behaviour of a man who is going to be very solicitous of his wife's feelings. The normal course for an Englishman who disliked wearing a wedding ring would have been to accept it and gradually get used to it, while a few die-hard conservatives might have indicated before the wedding that they were not going to go along with the modern custom of men wearing rings. But Boris accepted his ring only to get rid of it immediately afterwards.

Nor did his bounderish behaviour end there. He also arrived for his own wedding without the right clothes. As Allegra said, after relating the story of the ring: 'What's more, he was wearing John Biffen's trousers at the time [Biffen then being MP for Oswestry] . . . Some weeks later I had to send the mortgagees our wedding certificate, but it was nowhere to be found. Naturally Bozzer showed not the slightest interest. Months later the Biffens were much amused to find the missing document in the pocket of the famous trousers.'

When Lady Biffen was reminded that Boris got married in her husband's trousers, she replied with indignation: 'And in his cufflinks, and the reason he didn't get married in my husband's shoes is that his feet were larger – he would have limped to the altar, which would have been worse than the holes in the soles of his own shoes.'

One reason why Boris delights audiences so much is his

willingness to burst the bounds of good behaviour. He offers a joyful liberation from all the petty inhibitions which weigh so heavily on respectable and conscientious people. As he crashes about like a bull in a china shop, the result is general hilarity. But the joke is often lost on whoever happens to be running the china shop.

All the Johnsons stayed with the Biffens for the wedding, where they made a very poor impression on Lady Biffen. According to her, Boris and his brothers had hired 'a job lot' of morning coats and other wedding clothes in Taunton without trying anything on, and found they had shirts which needed cufflinks to fasten, 'and things that didn't fit'. They therefore had to borrow clothes off their host, John Biffen.

Lord Biffen, who seems to have been less affronted than his wife by the chaotic behaviour of his guests, said in a mild tone: 'Something borrowed, something blue.'

Lady Biffen added that there had been a dinner at the Gowries' house the night before the wedding – Lord Gowrie had served as arts minister from 1983 to 1985 – at which Stanley Johnson 'behaved disgracefully, sticking a sort of cine camera up everyone's nose'. Charlotte Johnson, Boris's mother, was staying with the Gowries.

At the wedding itself, Stanley suddenly stood up and started making a speech, but Lady Biffen stopped him by saying, 'Shut up, Stanley.'

Looking back on her wedding, Allegra said, 'When we got married, that was actually the end of the relationship instead of the beginning.' Boris's hunt for her had been crowned with success, but he was already embarking on another hunt, for success in his career, which would prove almost impossible to combine with any kind of settled married life.

They went on honeymoon in Egypt with no money, bought a flat in Sinclair Road in west London, and Boris started work as a management consultant, at the then very high salary of

£18,000 a year. But he knew immediately that he had made a mistake: 'Try as I might, I could not look at an overhead projection of a growth-profit matrix, and stay conscious.'

Many of us would have struggled on, in a dispirited way, for months or years before conceding defeat, but Boris was decisive enough to cut his losses. In his *Who's Who* entry we read: 'LEK Partnership, one week, 1987.'

According to Stanley, Boris stayed at LEK 'long enough to get the joining fee'.

It was time for Boris to activate the contacts he had made in journalism. At the end of 1986 a select party had driven from London to Shropshire to see in the New Year at Woodhouse: the literary journalist Miriam Gross, her then boyfriend Frank Johnson, and the novelist Edna O'Brien.

O'Brien said they should take a present of some champagne: 'I don't think a bottle, darling. I think half a dozen at least.'

Frank had won a reputation while writing the *Times* sketch as one of the wittiest writers and talkers in England. He was grateful for Boris's company: 'He kept me laughing and engaged the whole weekend. He was a throwback to minor, marginal figures in history I'd read about before the First World War. He had a knowledge of all sorts of things young people by then didn't have to pay attention to. I thought he was too original and had too little command of detail to become a politician. I said to him: "If you want to try journalism, give me a ring after your finals." He did, and I got him in to see Charlie Douglas-Home [then the editor of *The Times*]. That was why he got the job. I then went abroad for *The Times*, first to Paris and then to Bonn, so I wasn't working with Boris.'

Miriam Gross recalled meeting Boris with Allegra when he was at Oxford: 'And I was completely bowled over by Boris. I thought he was exceptionally charming, sophisticated, witty, erudite at that age, and he didn't at all have that slightly bumbling thing which he has now, which is a defence mechanism.'

Perhaps Miriam put Boris at his ease, and made him feel appreciated, which was why with her he did not need his defence mechanism. Miriam immediately became a fan of his work, and thought she could detect traces of it even in pieces by Allegra: 'I was fond of Gaia Mostyn-Owen, so I read Allegra in the *Evening Standard* – it was absolutely brilliant – I just knew having met Boris he must have had a hand in it. I immediately started telling every editor I knew they should employ Boris, and was slightly influential in getting him appointed to *The Times* and the *Daily Telegraph*, where I was at that time Arts Editor. When I was at the *Sunday Telegraph* I used to say how attractive he was – all my male colleagues thought I was mad – but I've been proved right. Everyone I know including Barbara and Conrad Black is completely charmed by Boris.'

That winter *The Times* sent Boris to train for three months on the *Wolverhampton Express & Star*. He lodged with a woman called Brenda. She lived near Bilston and had two other lodgers: a man on the run from his wife and children, and a probation officer who introduced Boris to some of the grittier realities of Wolverhampton, and who reappeared many years later in Boris's novel, *Seventy-Two Virgins*.

Brenda loved doing a cooked breakfast, and quite heavy cooked dishes in the evening. According to Allegra, 'She was particularly delighted that Boris liked her special oven dish of meat, potatoes, cheese and butter. It was quite tasty. Boris could finish it off – Brenda was radiant with pride.'

Allegra and Brenda got on well: 'She liked this combination of ginger wine and whisky – I would drink it with her quite merrily. In the bathroom you would find her discarded mules and wig.'

It was quite a difficult time in the marriage and when Allegra was there, Brenda once turned to Boris and said to him: 'Boris, you've got to treat her like porcelain.' But that was not Boris's way. He was in too much of a hurry, and too full of energy and ambition, to treat his fine and delicate wife with the tenderness she needed.

In a letter to Allegra written from the *Wolverhampton Express & Star* in February 1988, Boris reported that his task for the day was to write the caption for a picture of a man drinking a pint of beer while having his hair cut. But the opening paragraph on his neighbour's screen was: 'When Mrs Jean Perry thought she'd clean out her budgie's cage, she did not reckon with the suction power of her new Hoover.' This, Boris thought, was bound to make the front page.

He also reported that he had been out for a drink the night before with a belligerent social worker called Bruce who drank seven pints of beer incredibly fast and at one point grabbed Boris's lapel and told him not to patronise the Black Country.

Boris added that without Allegra, life was a cold cup of urine. It was an unromantic image, and indicated that he was not enjoying himself. Some of the toughest jobs in journalism are at the very bottom, where you are given the feeble stories nobody else wants to do, and have no scope to write them in the way that might suit your talents.

After Wolverhampton came the task of proving himself on *The Times*. George Brock, who was then Foreign Editor, remembered Boris as 'an immediately striking figure with red braces and albino hair. Inevitably, he was found a bit woolly and shambolic: news editors expect you to be sharp. But he wasn't in the slightest bit difficult, just a bit messy. I think he always thought people at *The Times* took life a bit seriously.'

Boris has written, in the introduction to his volume of collected journalism, *Lend Me Your Ears*, that Brock 'had the misfortune to be my trainer'. Brock was not appreciative of Boris's efforts, many of which resulted from the inglorious activity of rewriting stories supplied by news agencies. According to

Boris: 'It seemed to be one of the rules that you could rewrite agency copy, and claim it as your own, if you made at least one phone call to show that you had "added value" to the story.'

Peter Stothard, who later became editor of *The Times* and was already an influential figure, said: 'I was responsible for the Graduate Trainee Programme. It was quite radical. The idea was to try to attract clever people into journalism instead of merchant banking, by making sure that they didn't have to start on the local paper in Hemel Hempstead.

'Boris was one of the early ones. He was a classicist, which obviously appealed to me, and he came with the strong backing of Peter Utley, whom I had rescued from the *Telegraph*.' T. E. Utley, known as Peter, was blind from childhood, a distinguished Tory thinker, and also very good company. For a long period he was an adornment of the *Daily Telegraph*, and of the King & Keys, the low pub next door to it in Fleet Street, where he drank whisky and held court amid clouds of tobacco smoke in the most democratic manner. That was one of Utley's paradoxes: he had a deep understanding of the need for authority and hierarchy, yet he himself was the least hierarchical of men. He was encouraged to leave the *Telegraph* by Max Hastings, and spent his last years at *The Times*. Utley would try to help any stuttering young man or woman who sought his advice about getting into journalism, and his recommendation of Boris would certainly have carried weight.

The story that led to Boris's sacking from *The Times* came, Allegra says, from their neighbour in Sinclair Road. Stothard remembers things slightly differently: 'The trainees worked in different bits. Boris was in the newsroom and had been given a "new discovery" story. These stories almost always turn out to be wrong, for the discovery is seldom, in fact, new. Boris was given the story because he was the person who might have the best idea of who Edward II was. The news desk could be quite rough and Boris felt under the gun to add to the agency copy. So he concocted a quote to add to the Press Association story, to boost it up a bit.'

The quote was by Colin Lucas, a history don at Balliol who also happened to be his godfather. Lucas would not have been most people's first choice to comment on London in the reign of Edward II, or even their second choice, since his speciality was the French Revolution, which took place in Paris nearly 500 years later. But Boris has never allowed himself to be discouraged by a technicality of that kind, and duly concocted a racy comment for Lucas to make. Boris was unfortunately unable to contact Lucas, to check he was happy for his name to be used in this way.

The story 'by Boris Johnson' duly appeared in *The Times* on 20 May 1988, under the headline 'Edward II's "Rosary" Palace found in London'. One can see the kind of not particularly inspiring material Boris had to work with, as well as the manner in which he used Lucas to perk it up:

Archaeologists working on an urban development site on the South Bank of the Thames have discovered the long-lost palace of King Edward II. They have also found the remains of the large house of Sir John Fastog, thought to be the model for the Shakespearean character Sir John Falstaff.

A large stone corner of the royal palace, built in about 1325, first came to light at the Hay's Wharf site last week, but excavators have tried to keep the discovery quiet because of the danger of attracting treasure hunters . . . The palace was a large moated building, about 80 yards square. Known to historians as the 'Rosary', it was a retreat on the far side of the river where the king could escape the cares of office.

According to Dr Colin Lucas, of Balliol College, Oxford, this is where the king enjoyed a reign of dissolution with his catamite, Piers Gaveston, before he was gruesomely murdered at Berkeley Castle by barons who felt he was too prone to foreign influence.

The story continued for several more paragraphs, ending with a dubious speculation about the 'new light' cast on Sir John Fastog: 'The discovery near the house of riverfront installations suggests that Sir John was quite unlike the rumbustious devil-may-care Shakespearean character.'

The note of parody struck by Boris in this last sentence is worthy of Kingsley Amis. But that was not what caught the eye of readers. At high tables the length and breadth of the kingdom, a roar of laughter went up at Colin Lucas's expense.

Boris had scored a hit, but it was not the hit he had intended. He had managed to sex the story up – a catamite, after all, is a boy kept for homosexual purposes – but had also committed a grotesque historical error. Gaveston was beheaded in 1312, so could hardly have cavorted with Edward II in a palace built in 1325.

As Andrew Gilmour, who had been at Eton and Balliol with Boris, put it: 'Lucas was a laughing stock. Every sub-lecturer from Sheffield wrote in to point out his error.'

Lucas himself failed to see the joke, and wrote a letter of bitter complaint to *The Times*. He naturally took his own reputation and career prospects more seriously than anyone else did. For although he was at this point a relatively obscure history don, who had risen from an assistant lectureship at Sheffield to a fellowship at Balliol and lectureship at Oxford, he soon afterwards became a professor at Chicago University. From there he returned to become Master of Balliol and Vice-Chancellor of Oxford, and a knight as well as a member of the Légion d'Honneur.

Boris said that Lucas's behaviour 'lent a new meaning to the word godfather'. Lucas has declined to talk about this painful episode, but the estimable Brock has not failed us, and it has proved possible to reconstruct a rough outline of what took place. Boris was sunk not by the original story, but by his foolish attempts to deny or make light of it.

According to Brock: 'Colin Lucas complained and someone wrote back to him saying that our reporter stands by the story. Lucas then wrote back to *The Times* and said there was no way on earth Boris could have spoken to him. What got Boris into most trouble was lying about it. He had got the first *Times* person who wrote to Lucas to lie to Lucas.'

Brock's recollection that Lucas was at first rebuffed is supported by the following bizarre story which appeared in *The Times* of 24 May 1988, four days after the first piece, under Boris's name and bearing the sober headline, 'Timber may show date of Edward II's palace':

The discovery of timber supports near the 'Rosary' palace of King Edward II may help to determine the exact date of the building, archaeologists said yesterday. Two walls of a stone building, which is believed to have been the royal residence, were found on an urban development site at Hay's Wharf, south London.

The timber includes stakes and planks, which served as wharfing at two inlets, as well as wooden revetments supporting the palace moat.

The find shows how the Thames has shifted since the Middle Ages. Trading and wharf facilities at the time were much greater than had been suspected. The age of the timbers will be accurately determined using the dating technique of dendrochronology.

The only documentary evidence of the Rosary dates it to 1325, two years before Edward II was killed at Berkeley Castle. He would have had little time to use it as a retreat, as has been described.

Dr Colin Lucas, of Balliol College, Oxford, said:

'Edward II is reputed to have led a life of wine and song with his catamite Piers Gaveston. But if 1325 is correct, that could hardly have taken place in this building since Gaveston was executed in 1312.'

One can well see why Lucas might have regarded this contorted quote as inadequate recompense for making him a laughing stock.

Boris was summoned to appear before Charlie Wilson, the editor of *The Times*. Even at this late stage, he could almost certainly have saved himself if he had shown a fitting sense of how badly he had behaved. But according to Frank Johnson the following dialogue took place:

Wilson: 'All the quotes are made up.'

Boris: 'But so are most of the quotes in your paper.'

As Frank later remarked, 'This was perfectly true, but it was the wrong reply.'

John Bryant, who was then number three on *The Times*, remembers an 'inquest' on Boris in which Wilson said, 'You can't make up quotes on *The Times*,' to which Bryant replied, 'You can't make up quotes on any paper.'

Wilson himself cannot remember exactly what was said to him – Boris was, after all, an insignificant figure at this time. But Wilson does remember the general drift of his errant trainee's remarks: 'At the time Boris didn't seem to take making up quotes as a very serious matter. I thought it was a heinous crime. However, during my time as editor we had to dispose of only two trainee graduates and the other one was Toby Young, so you could argue that being fired by Charles Wilson was a guarantee of career success.'

The plain fact was that these Oxford men had no idea how to behave. This could have been the end of Boris as a journalist. The editor of *The Times* had found him wanting. Part of the trouble was that Boris also found the editor of *The Times* wanting: he was later to describe Wilson as 'a man straight from a Britflick gangster movie'. But Wilson was not the first or the last person who decided that Boris simply would not do. The general verdict of journalists at *The Times* on Boris was summed up by Brock: 'It was not clear he was going to be a success.'

11

Our Man in Brussels

BORIS THREW HIMSELF INTO THE SEARCH FOR A NEW job. Frank Johnson remembered: 'Boris phoned me up one day and said he was in a bit of a spot – it could be a P45 job. I said don't be so ridiculous, Boris.' But when Frank realised how grave the situation was, he promised to see if there was an opening for Boris at the *Daily Telegraph*.

Frank summed up his contribution: 'I have both given this man his start in life, and saved him, but history will not remember it.'

The greatest credit for giving Boris his second chance in journalism should actually go to Max Hastings, the then editor of the *Daily Telegraph*. Hastings was unimpressed by Boris's brilliant career at Eton and Oxford, which he knew was 'often the precursor of a lifetime of obscurity', but agreed to take him on as a leader-writer. There was a cavalier dash to Hastings, seen when he scooped every other correspondent in the Falklands war by being the first man into Port Stanley. He saw the point of Boris, a man as energetic and competitive as himself, and less than a year later he made him the *Telegraph*'s man in Brussels.

Allegra had meanwhile abandoned journalism and enrolled at law college. In the spring of 1989 Boris started the job where he

was to make his name. His stories about the idiocies of the
European Union were received with rapture by an ever-growing
circle of fans, and he became the only Brussels correspondent of
whom ordinary mortals have heard. His work was so marvellously enjoyable because he debunked an institution which
almost everyone else reporting from Brussels was still treating
with reverence.

Boris infuriated many of his colleagues. According to Rory
Watson, an experienced and scrupulous correspondent who was
at that time working for the *European*: 'He made stories up. The
classic one was the Berlaymont. It was when the Commission
decided to leave the Berlaymont building because it was leaking
asbestos. Boris's story was that the Berlaymont was going to be
blown up.'

Charles Garside, the editor of the *European*, was so excited by
this news that he rang Watson and told him: 'It's a pity you
missed that great story about the Berlaymont. Find out which
company is going to get the contract to blow it up.'

The *European* wanted to arrange for one of its readers to push
the plunger on the detonator. The problem for Watson was that
there was actually no plan to blow up the Berlaymont. An
explosion seems to have appealed to Boris as being the cheapest,
quickest and most dramatic way to get rid of a building, or at
least to get his story into the *Daily Telegraph*. But dynamite is not
an approved method for dealing with asbestos and the structure
of the Berlaymont is standing to this day, with the asbestos-
ridden cladding replaced by what looks like a completely new
building.

David Usborne, the *Independent*'s Brussels correspondent, said
of Boris: 'He was fundamentally intellectually dishonest, in my
view. He was serving his masters in a very skilful way but I never
felt he believed a word.'

Sarah Helm, who observed Boris while working as the
Independent's diplomatic correspondent, agreed with this: 'I

remember developing an instinctive feel that Boris was a complete charlatan. He was a highly intelligent man, much cleverer
than I was, he could see all these nuances and subtleties, but he
wasn't conveying them in his writing. It was a cheap thrill – a
stunt, and quite a dangerous stunt really.'

But Usborne, who had been in Brussels since 1984, recognised that the press corps was ripe for shaking: 'Boris came in to
a Brussels that was populated by correspondents who had either
been there a very long time – probably too long – or by people –
I would include myself in this – who were probably a little bit
guilty of becoming part of the institution they were reporting
on, and were inclined to defend it.'

Boris and Usborne became 'intense and friendly competitors'
for stories: 'Boris was always very flattering, telling me I was
number one, and like an idiot I probably believed him. To begin
with we were playing the same game, to see who could get the
best scoops and the best secret documents. But I began to realise
over time he was ploughing his own furrow, and a very different
furrow from me. Boris understood immediately what the
Telegraph wanted to hear and he delivered in spades. Once he got
his confidence up he started firing every torpedo he could at the
Commission. He was writing things without really believing in
his heart what he was writing. He would take something that
might make a few paragraphs and turn it into an atomic bomb.
He really began to eclipse all of us. He was having fun. He didn't
have to worry about all that serious stuff. He could just cherry
pick. I don't really think he was pursuing a political agenda about
Europe – I think he was pursuing his own future. I don't think
he was half as antagonistic to Delors as you would think.'

Jacques Delors, the President of the European Commission,
was driving forward the process of European integration and tri-
umphing over the British. A bitter power struggle was in
progress and Boris admired the ruthlessness with which Delors
and his henchman, Pascal Lamy, were waging it: 'With his

virtually shaven head and parade-ground manner, Lamy runs the upper echelons of the Commission like a Saharan camp of the French Foreign Legion.' British officials were, Boris lamented, 'limp-wristed' and 'impotent' by comparison: 'With their shy grins and corrugated-soled shoes, they are no match for the intellectual brutality of Lamy and his stooges.'

Like a brilliant caricaturist, who knows exactly what parts of his subject to exaggerate, Boris knew how to ridicule the European Union because he saw so clearly what was going on. He may have been a wrecker, but he was a highly intelligent wrecker. He revelled in the chaos he caused.

When asked if Boris often 'went the extra mile' in pursuit of a good story, Usborne replied: 'He often went the extra five hundred miles I think just for the pleasure of watching the rest of his colleagues scurry the next morning to catch up.'

Boris has confirmed that this could be a pleasure. He has related, in the introduction to his book of collected journalism, how 'the great George Brock', who had been so unimpressed by Boris's work at *The Times*, arrived in Brussels as the correspondent for that paper: 'One of my keenest pleasures was to hunt for scoops, exclusive stories that might cause *The Times* to ring Brock up, long after he was tucked up in bed. "Stand by your phone, George," I would say, tapping my nose. I like to think that Mr and Mrs Brock had several interrupted nights on my account; and at least once, annoyingly, I was rung by the *Telegraph* and asked to chase up one of his.' The playful tone and the concession in the last line save this from being nasty, but Boris has never been averse to getting even with those who disparage him.

Michael Binyon, Brock's predecessor as the *Times* man in Brussels, said: 'What he realised was that there was a cartel of Brussels correspondents, and if you broke the cartel you would stand out. He wrote some grotesquely exaggerated stories. He would get a story and then he would speculate on it. This drove everyone berserk, because they all had to follow it and it all turned out to be a load of tosh, but it didn't matter. He was never malicious. There was one about how Brussels was going to build the highest tower on earth.'

Boris had a highly personal style, symbolic of his determination to plough his own furrow. Binyon remembered Boris always arriving late for the daily press conference at noon, a fixed point around which the journalists' day revolved. Boris would shamble in at about 12.10 looking as if he had been pulled though a haystack, and a French journalist once asked Binyon: '*Qui est ce monstre?*'

Some of Boris's competitors were crippled by an excessive scrupulousness, which prevented them from cutting through the monstrous quantities of mostly very dull material with which they were confronted. Meanwhile Boris fell with joy on stories about changes in the rules governing crisps and sausages, which could so easily symbolise the threat posed by Brussels to the British way of life. Allegra said, 'He knew he could get a front page with a sausage.'

Boris could not have shone in Brussels without a big story to cover, and this he got. Charles Grant, *The Economist*'s correspondent, arrived in Brussels at the same time as Boris, in April 1989, 'just when the subject was getting interesting'. Jacques Delors, the President of the Commission, that month published his report on economic and monetary union, and in June, at the Madrid summit, Margaret Thatcher tried and failed to stop progress towards the single currency. The fight had begun which would lead to Thatcher's downfall. Brussels had become a British news story.

For a man with an anarchist streak, it was a marvellous opportunity to do some vandalism in a good cause. Boris has often fallen back on a favoured image, of throwing rocks over a garden wall, to describe his activities in Brussels. As he put it on *Desert Island Discs* in October 2005:

I saw the whole thing change. It was a wonderful time to
be there. The Berlin Wall fell and the French and Germans
had to decide how they were going to respond to this
event, and what was Europe going to become, and there
was this fantastic pressure to create a single polity, to create
an answer to the historic German problem, and this
produced the most fantastic strains in the Conservative
Party, so everything I wrote from Brussels, I found was sort
of chucking these rocks over the garden wall and I listened
to this amazing crash from the greenhouse next door over
in England as everything I wrote from Brussels was having
this amazing, explosive effect on the Tory party, and it really
gave me this I suppose rather weird sense of power.

Thatcher fell as a direct result of the Rome summit in
October 1990, at which she was ambushed by the Italians, who
sprang the date of 1999 on her for the launch of the euro.

Her message on 30 October 1990, when she reported to the
House of Commons on the Rome summit, was: 'No, no, no.'
On 1 November, Sir Geoffrey Howe resigned the post of
Deputy Prime Minister, in protest at Thatcher's European policy,
and on 22 November she herself was forced to resign. Like many
Tories, Boris felt this as a deep personal blow. He has written
that his future wife, Marina Wheeler, says 'she came upon me,
stumbling down a street in Brussels, tears in my eyes, and claiming that it was as if someone had shot Nanny'.

Boris did not invent euroscepticism, but he became one of its
most famous exponents. According to Grant, who was strongly
pro-European, 'For his first year or two, Boris wasn't very sceptical at all – he was a reporter. He does work incredibly hard. He
hasn't got a swottish image, but the truth is that he's always put
his career first. It's probably true that very successful journalists
have to do that. His supreme point is to entertain so he doesn't
worry too much if his facts are wrong. He'd always put a good

joke above the facts. I do remember as Boris became more sceptical, thinking it was an act, because he did it to make his name in the *Telegraph*. He wasn't particularly happy when I said that.'

But Boris remained on friendly terms with many people who found his growing euroscepticism abhorrent. This puzzles Grant: 'The interesting thing is why pro-Europeans like Boris. Why? I don't know, except he doesn't take himself seriously. I suppose he's not an extreme eurosceptic. Some of the more visceral eurosceptics are quitters.'

There is something about euroscepticism which can turn sensible men into cranks. They decide, quite reasonably, that the European Union is a mortal threat to our ancient liberties, including our form of government, and adopt a tone of intense hostility towards Brussels which starts to make them seem narrow and paranoid. On finding themselves ignored or dismissed by the pro-Europeans, the anti-Europeans become ever more vehement and ever more suspicious, until in the end they can only preach to the converted.

Boris never started on that downward path. He delighted in showing up the absurdities of Brussels, but he did it in a humorous rather than a bitter tone. And he began to make a European reputation. When European Foreign Ministers held an informal meeting at Guimaraes, in Portugal, on the first Saturday in May 1992, the Maastricht Treaty had recently been signed, but had yet to be ratified. Grant said: 'I remember Boris running around very excited at Guimaraes.'

Boris has written: 'I remember going to a payphone at teatime that Saturday, standing in the dusty square and watching the dogs lying in the sun, and ringing Frank Taylor, the Foreign Editor of the *Sunday Telegraph*, to find out what had happened to my story . . . "We've made it the splash," he said with his beardy chuckle, "and I've called it 'Delors Plan to Rule Europe'."'

And as Grant has written in his biography of Delors: 'The next day Britain's *Sunday Telegraph* carried an article which may

have changed the course of European history . . . Boris
Johnson . . . reported that Delors wanted to scrap the rotation of
the EU presidency and to centralise power in Brussels. The
member states would lose their remaining veto rights . . .
Meanwhile Denmark was in the thick of a keenly fought refer-
endum campaign on the Maastricht treaty. The *Sunday Telegraph*
article, widely reprinted in Denmark's newspapers, had a huge
impact. The "Nej" campaign, which had argued that the new
treaty would centralise power in Brussels and deprive small states
of their rights, claimed vindication. Before the article opinion
polls had suggested a narrow vote in favour of the Maastricht
treaty on 2 June; afterward they pointed to a narrow vote
against.'

Boris is naturally happy to accept Grant's verdict that his article helped sway the Danes: 'My boast, and I make it in the
confidence that no one gives a monkey's, is that I probably did
contribute to the Danish rejection of Maastricht.'

Thatcher formed a very high opinion of Boris, telling his old
headmaster, Sir Eric Anderson: 'He's my favourite journalist.'
But Douglas Hurd was greatly irritated as Foreign Secretary by
Boris's coverage. According to Charles Moore, who was then the
Deputy Editor of the *Telegraph*, 'Douglas Hurd made a serious
attempt to get Boris sacked while in Brussels. Max was very def-
erential to Hurd, who kept on at Max about how awful Boris
was. Max was in the end OK, but he did listen to Hurd a bit.
Boris was always a bit vulnerable because his stories weren't
always wholly accurate. I went to see Boris in Brussels when I
was Max's deputy. I told him about the Douglas Hurd risk, and
that I was completely on his, Boris's, side, but I noticed how
exceptionally worried Boris was at that point.'

Hurd denied to me that he ever tried to get Boris sacked: 'I
wouldn't have dreamed of it.' Nor does it sound quite like Hurd's
style. He said he and Boris 'were on cosy terms given the basically mischievous nature of his activities'.

John Kerr, then the UK Permanent Representative in Brussels and, later, as Lord Kerr, the head of the Foreign Office, respected Boris: 'I found him challenging in briefings. Disconcertingly, he made few notes. Even my usual ploy, when on thin ice, of attempting to distract with a battery of facts and numbers, some of doubtful relevance, rarely worked with Boris. He had the knack of spotting what I wasn't saying, and his subsequent product often drew heavily on intuition. Some of his flyers were way off-beam, sometimes irritatingly so, but some were spot-on, even more annoyingly.'

Boris's competitive instinct was not sated, as some people's might have been, by the ceaseless struggle to get stories into the *Telegraph*, and better stories than his rivals were getting into their papers. He was also becoming increasingly determined to go into politics himself: he and Charles Grant would discuss their ambition to become MEPs, Boris as a Tory and Grant for Labour. Meanwhile Boris took on a challenge of a quite different sort against Binyon of *The Times*. As Binyon recalled: 'We used to enjoy going down to Strasbourg – a weekend away from Brussels – we all had cubby-hole desks next to each other, and would be trying to hear what the other fellow was saying.'

Boris asked where 'the true, the blushful Hippocrene' comes from, to which Binyon replied: 'That's Keats. "Ode to a Nightingale".'

Boris said: 'No, it's not. It's "Ode on a Grecian Urn".' He went away, looked it up and having discovered that Binyon was right, came back and said: 'OK, but I bet you can't recite it.'

A general challenge then arose between Binyon and Boris to see who could recite all the great poems ever written in English. Binyon made an alarming discovery about his opponent: 'Boris to my horror had a considerable knowledge of long poems. He could recite reams of Milton. I said: "That's absolutely impossible. We have to have short poems."' So they drew up a list of about 130 poems which they would learn. The challenge was to be held at the Dublin summit. A week before the summit, Binyon said to Boris: 'I say, Boris old chap, how are you getting on?'

It emerged that neither of them was prepared, so they postponed the contest until the Rome summit. They decided that a public challenge would be humiliating if it went wrong, so they started with a private challenge, held in a restaurant with vaulted ceilings and marble floors.

Binyon said: 'All right, Boris. Sonnet 18.'

Boris responded: 'Shall I compare thee to a summer's day?'

When the sweet trolley came, Binyon waved it away with the words: 'Not now, he's in the middle of Gray's "Elegy".'

Binyon remembers that Boris did not care for many of the modern poems and would say, 'Awful tosh, that stuff.' But the private challenge had gone well enough for them to decide to hold a public challenge once they were back in Brussels.

And so one night they went to Kitty O'Shea's, the Irish pub near the Commission, with eight or nine other correspondents, and began the challenge. Binyon was getting 'awfully tied up' in the middle of 'The Love Song of J. Alfred Prufrock' when another correspondent burst in and announced: 'Shevardnadze's resigned and we've all got to go and write reaction stories.'

And that, for some reason, was the end of the great poetry challenge. But when Boris met Binyon he would greet him in verse: 'Ah, Binyon. They told me, Heraclitus, they told me you were dead / They brought me bitter news to hear and bitter tears to shed.'

– 12 –

Twelve Days a Bachelor

AS BORIS'S CAREER TOOK OFF, HIS MARRIAGE COLLAPSED.
Allegra joined Boris in Brussels in the summer of 1989, after her
law exams. She disliked the district in which he had found a
place for them to live: 'I never understood what had drawn him
to the flat in Woluwe St Pierre except that the ground floor was
taken by a dentist called Goris. It was quite a Flemish suburb,
and on the whole it wasn't very friendly. The newspaper shop
was unfriendly after two years, and if you left the rubbish out on
the wrong day you got anonymous notes.'

Nor could she detect any enthusiasm in her husband for the
glories of Flemish culture, including the paintings and the food:
'It didn't work with him. His favourite food was sausages. It's
true! I'm sure he'd still say so now.'

Boris recently declared, in a short interview about food: 'My
favourite thing is bangers, mash and mustard, with red wine.'

When they went on a skiing holiday, and Allegra was feeling
low, Boris said to her: 'What you need is a bit of buckismus.' She
found that comment 'absurd and funny and totally alienating'.
Things were past the stage when a bit of bucking-up would
mend them.

Allegra witnessed the beginnings of Boris's fame: 'He was

included in some more obscure version of *Who's Who*, and
under hobbies he put scuba diving, which was my hobby, which
he was rather bad at – I did laugh. He uses up his oxygen too
fast. I don't think he ever repeated it [scuba diving], so it was just
a bit of a fib, but kind of vaguely revealing.' On another occasion, Boris returned from an EU summit and said with
satisfaction: 'I was recognised by John Major.'

She remembers feeling 'a bit alienated' from the British journalists in Brussels: 'They were an interesting lot, the British press
corps, but all they could do was this competitive stuff.' Boris
himself specialised in the competitive stuff, which was not how
Allegra, with her gift of sympathetic appreciation, could bear to
live.

To Charles Grant, Boris and Allegra at first seemed fine: 'I
used to go to their rather nice flat by a church. They gave nice
parties and I rather liked Allegra. She was gorgeous to look at.'

In a letter written from the Holiday Inn, Strasbourg, Boris
told Allegra that he had spent all day in the bowels of the
Parliament building, waiting for any one of the MEPs to say or
do something remotely unexpected. He said the place felt like a
huge new airport, built by a third world government in the
middle of a jungle, and totally pointless.

Boris went on to say how vital it was to him that Allegra had
come and joined him in Brussels, though he feared she did not
really respond to that sort of rhetoric, which was why he had not
used it much.

She might have responded better if she had not come second
to his work. Boris is a humane man, in the sense that he feels
things deeply, and this emotional warmth has always drawn
people to him, and has saved his jokes from ringing hollow.
People sense that there is a suffering man behind the comic act.

But he could also be quite staggeringly inconsiderate. Intent
on doing exactly what he wanted to do, or what he must do to
maximise his chances of getting a piece in the next day's

1. Boris's great-grandfather, Ali Kemal, journalist and politician – a caricature drawn shortly before his death at the hands of a lynch mob in 1922.

2. Boris, aged one, comes to celebrate with his heavily pregnant mother Charlotte at the end of her Oxford exams in 1965, and is determined to have some of her champagne. Charlotte's family nanny, Miss Reid, looks on.

3. Boris with his father Stanley, whose motorcycle helmet he is wearing.

4. Boris at the age of about seven, sketched by his mother, Charlotte.

5. Boris with his mother, Charlotte, and sister Rachel.

6. Sibling rivalry in Brussels: Boris runs faster than Rachel, Leo and Jo.

7. The Johnson family (from left): Charlotte, Jo, Stanley, Rachel, Leo and a not very happy Boris.

8. Father's Day at Ashdown House: Boris takes tea with his father, who has longer hair.

9. Ashdown House: the three successful scholarship candidates (from left): Meyrick Cox (Eton), Boris (Eton) and Tim Moon (Winchester).

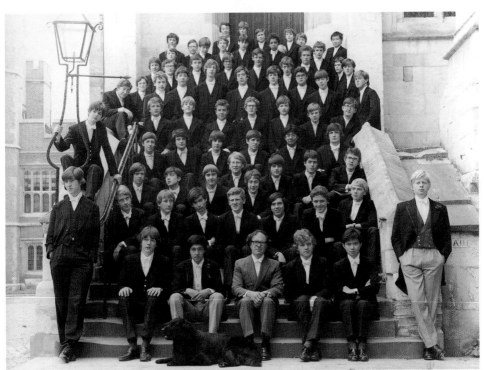

10. A commanding figure: Boris, wearing his Pop waistcoat, dominates this photograph of College at Eton in 1982. His housemaster, Martin Hammond, composer of penetrating reports of Boris's progress, sits in the middle of the front row.

11. Balliol rugby XV: Boris standing at the extreme left.

12. Boris (in odd socks) as a member of the Oxford dining club, the Bullingdon, in 1986. Darius Guppy is standing fourth from right; to the left of Guppy is Andrew Gilmour.

13. Boris as President of the Oxford Union, flanked by the Greek actress Melina Mercouri and by Gavin Stamp, with Jonathan Barnes next to Stamp and Allegra Mostyn-Owen behind them.

14. Allegra as cover girl, just after David Bailey has told her to 'fuck the camera'.

15. Boris and Allegra celebrate in 1987 after his final Oxford exams: but he perhaps already suspects that he has not done quite enough to get a first.

16. Boris and Allegra on their wedding day, 5 September 1987.

Telegraph, he accepted no obligation even to tell his wife where he had gone. One of his many gifts as a journalist is a willingness to board an aeroplane at the drop of a hat: he is excellent at rushing towards the sound of the gunfire, which in those days came with increasing frequency from the Balkans. As Yugoslavia disintegrated, Boris would fly in with whichever Brussels panjandrum was trying in vain to sort things out. Allegra often didn't know where he was: 'The really bad times were when he didn't tell me he was going to be away. There were two times when I had to ring the foreign desk to find out where he was. He got ribbed really badly. Then he was cross with me for having put him in that position. I used to get the paper – yesterday's news – and there's his by-line in fucking Zagreb. You get past caring and you start drinking malt whisky. But you know, I think he rather regrets all that stuff now. Though he finds it very difficult to play the part of a sensitive husband – it just doesn't come easily. He hasn't got a blueprint for that one.'

Allegra also said: 'I used to get a short haircut at the Flemish barber's because I wasn't very happy. I was very apprehensive that the Johnson family history would repeat itself. I adored his mother Charlotte but I was anxious to avoid the kind of experiences she had when she was married to Stanley.' When life in Brussels with Stanley had got too much, Charlotte checked herself into a clinic. Allegra felt she too was heading for a breakdown if she stayed with Boris. No note of recrimination entered her voice: that was just how things were. She could not take this kind of life: 'Boris didn't do much for my peace of mind. Bearing in mind that my own family was completely disintegrating at the time, and I was cut off in Brussels, I think I must have been vulnerable. But what the hell – it's all in the past.'

In February 1990 she left. This was a disaster which Boris could not conceal. As Charles Grant said: 'When Allegra left Boris, Boris was distraught. I do remember having a heart-to-heart with him at the Dublin summit in April 1990. Edmund

Fawcett [one of his mother's brothers who worked at *The Economist*] and I and Boris had dinner together and Boris let it all hang out. He desperately wanted Allegra. That was probably the only time when the comic mask dropped. He was very, very unhappy.'

Allegra was very, very unhappy too. A male acquaintance got a lift back to London with her at about this time: 'She was driving and she poured out her heart to me. She was obviously fantastically affected by the break-up. She was in a terrible state. She said she'd been shocked by some of his behaviour. You thought you knew someone so well and then you found out things about them.'

Boris wanted to make Allegra happy, and to this day he says he feels 'guilty' about her, but he could not make the sacrifices of his own inclinations which would have been required. Allegra complained to people at the time that he never did the shopping or the washing-up, but really he did not attend enough to her at all. There was a kind of selfish impatience about him. He was twenty-five years old and it was natural for him to please himself.

Some people in Brussels thought Allegra was histrionic and over the top, but she found most of them pretty frightful too. She would not enter into the rivalries of his career, nor was she careerist when it came to her own work, nor could she sit quietly at home waiting for him to return at some unknown hour from his latest triumphs. At the end, he asked her something about politics, and she said, 'I can't believe it. I'm not going to talk about that. I'm leaving you.'

Boris and Allegra started divorce proceedings which reached the *decree nisi* stage, but then they had a reconciliation. In September 1990, Allegra began her Law Society finals course in London and commuted to Brussels every weekend. In September 1991, she enrolled at the Université Libre de Bruxelles for a Masters in

EU law, as recommended to her by Boris's old childhood friend Marina Wheeler, who had taken the same course the previous year. According to Allegra, 'Marina lived in crappy digs and I'd have her round to dinner.'

Boris had never entirely lost touch with Marina, and on one occasion he invited her to some festivities at Eton. There was a bit of tittering from his friends, who asked him if she was his girlfriend: a question that made Marina indignant.

Marina is insistent that although Boris had been keen on her between the ages of nine and eleven when they were at school together in Brussels, she was not keen on him and did not become romantically involved with him until it was all over between him and Allegra. According to Marina, Boris was a bit frightened of not having anyone around and would quickly get lonely. Allegra had taken the furniture with her and Marina was there as a friend, helping him to pick up the pieces. They would go and do things together, and slowly their friendship became more romantic.

By the time Allegra made her last attempt to save the marriage, Boris was having none of it. He had reverted to the style of life, the chase, which came most easily to him. Marina resisted, but that only intensified his pursuit. She remembers crying with frustration that he would not go away. One of her friends said: 'Boris chased her mercilessly in Brussels. I do remember seeing her in Brussels and her saying this guy had absolutely targeted her and was going for her.'

Marina is the daughter of Charles Wheeler and his wife, Dip Singh, who is of Sikh descent. Boris's Tory politics were abhorrent to Marina, a left-wing lawyer. She went to Bedales, a rather bohemian private school, read law at Cambridge, and had already been called to the Bar in London. She was tough, intelligent, level-headed and nice, and whatever else she did she was going to pursue her own career in the law.

But she fell madly in love with Boris. Friends who went to

see her in Brussels found she cancelled meetings with them so she could see Boris.

When she introduced Boris to her friends in London, they were appalled. The first meeting took place at the birthday party of a lawyer who had known her since Cambridge, Philippe Sands, who has since become a Professor of International Law and a well-known critic of the legality of the Iraq war.

Sands said: 'The first time we met Boris was at my thirtieth birthday party in London. Marina turned up with Boris – the first time in front of her friends – and at the moment he made his grand entry there was no one who wished she was Marina. We were all totally appalled a) by the physical appearance – large and white. He was fucking ugly. I think he's become more attractive since – and b) when he actually opened his mouth. In October 1990, a month before Thatcher went, in comes our dearest, darlingest, teeniest Marina with a Tory – it was a ghastly moment. The idea of Marina turning up with a Tory was painful, hilarious and devastating all at the same time. This guy turned up and defended Margaret Thatcher. We were revelling in her misery. But I have to say that 98 per cent of people were won over.' Boris has always been brilliant at winning the support of lefties, including the lefty who became his second wife.

Yet Boris and Allegra continued to attend the odd event together. I happened to see them on the weekend of 9/10 November 1991, for the wedding of their Oxford friends, Andrew Gilmour and Emma Williams, at Lichfield Cathedral. Before the wedding, Boris had to go from Brussels to Rome for the *Telegraph*. The idea was that Allegra would go too, as her grandmother was dying in Rome, and she went with her suitcase to meet Boris at his office. Boris – who was finishing an article before he set off – told her it would cost £1,000 for her to fly to Rome and then to England for the Gilmour wedding, and then back to Brussels. Allegra took her suitcase home, went to watch a football match on the television with some British students and decided, as she put it, 'to change friends'. The end was now near, but she still appeared with her husband at the Gilmour party, which included a dance on the Saturday night.

A group of us, including Boris and Allegra, stayed the weekend with Nick and Madeleine Budgen on their farm at Rugeley. On the Sunday, Nick Budgen, who had succeeded Enoch Powell as the MP for Wolverhampton South-West, took Boris and myself to the Remembrance Day parade in Wolverhampton. A huge variety of people joined in the parade, including a Sikh mayor and a contingent of firemen in silver helmets: middle England did not seem to be disintegrating. Afterwards we went to a reception where Boris asked Budgen what he thought of John Major, who was at that time Prime Minister and the leader of Budgen's party. Budgen said Major would make a highly competent head of the social security office in Wolverhampton.

In about January 1992, however, Boris and Allegra's marriage finally collapsed. In October that year, I spent a couple of weeks in Brussels with Sally Malcolm-Smith, my future wife, who was working for the *European*. We stayed in the flat above the *European* offices, and one night had dinner with Boris and Marina. They picked us up in a car which had something badly wrong with the door on the passenger side – a chronic problem, it seemed, which Boris had not got round to fixing – and we went to a restaurant in one of the arcades in the middle of Brussels, where we ate Belgian delicacies with names such as Waterzooi.

There was a certain symmetry about the evening, for while Boris and I are Tories of some description, Marina and Sally are natural Labour Party supporters. Marina asked Sally how she could possibly marry such a right-wing man as myself. Sally explained that I wasn't homophobic or racist, so the gap was not as huge as it might seem. Marina was worried that the political gap between her and Boris *was* huge, but she was also crazy about him.

It was at about this time, October 1992, that Marina got pregnant by Boris. Allegra agreed to an accelerated divorce, but time was short. Paul Hill, foreign desk manager at the *Daily Telegraph*, said Boris 'got in a bit of a tizz' when getting married to Marina as he 'hadn't quite divorced his old wife yet'. Boris needed a copy of his birth certificate and Hill 'had to run over and get one'. Almost at the last moment a DHL delivery van came up a drive in Umbria to deliver a document for Allegra to sign. The divorce was straightforward and Allegra was a litigant-in-person. One of the questions she had to answer was: 'On what date do you think the adultery began?' Allegra answered: '1 April.' As she afterwards said, 'It was a grim business with one feeble joke.'

Boris and Allegra still get on well, on the rare occasions when their paths cross, but it is clear that they were not cut out to be man and wife. For him, the role of husband was fulfilled by going out and working immensely hard at getting on in the world, which happened to be what he wanted to do anyhow. But for her, his self-preoccupation was disappointing. Boris can get quite wistful about their break-up, but it was not just the timing that was wrong: they now come across as essentially incompatible. She has chosen a different path and currently works as a ceramicist and art teacher, with a very wide range of friends and interests. She finished her legal studies but did not qualify and did not remarry.

Boris was a bachelor for twelve days. His divorce came through on 26 April 1993 and on 8 May he married Marina at Horsham town hall in Sussex, near her parents' home. Marina was by now extremely pregnant and there was some doubt whether the Belgians would allow her to travel, but she told her gynaecologist: 'There's a wedding I want to go to in England.' The wedding was small, consisting of close family, including Marina's aunt from India, and five or six friends each.

Marina had never envisaged her father walking her down the aisle. They had a splendid honeymoon in East Grinstead, where they stayed for one night at an absurdly over-decorated hotel.

Their first child, Lara Lettice, was born a month later, on 12 June, and at the end of that month Boris wrote a piece in the *Spectator* headed 'Congratulations! It's a Belgian'. The difficulty was that although Marina and Boris were both British citizens, they were also both born abroad, and this meant, under the terms of Willie Whitelaw's 1981 British Nationality Act, that they could not transmit their nationality to any of their own children who were also born abroad.

The purpose of the Act was to prevent British citizens living in the Caribbean or the Indian sub-continent from transmitting their nationality to their descendants, who might then arrive in 'tidal waves' in the United Kingdom.

Boris addressed a humorous yet heartfelt plea to the then Home Secretary, Michael Howard, not to let Lara become a Belgian by default: 'Do you wish to see her claimed by a nation which refused to sell us ammunition in the Gulf war? Shall she scamper, her face gleaming with chips and mayonnaise, as thousands of Bruxellois did the other day, to watch the National Day firework display, her heart beating at the sight of the black-red-yellow flags?' Five years later they managed to have Lara registered as a British citizen.

Sally and I met Boris and Marina quite soon after at a dinner in London and a memorable argument broke out, during which it emerged that Boris thought North Korea was South Korea, and vice versa.

When Boris left Brussels in 1994, James Landale, who was working for *The Times* but has since joined BBC television, composed some verses in his honour. They were closely modelled on 'Matilda', by Hilaire Belloc, with the *Telegraph*'s foreign desk taking the place of Matilda's aunt, and they began:

Boris told such dreadful lies
It made one gasp and stretch one's eyes.
His desk, which from its earliest youth
Had kept a strict regard for truth,
Attempted to believe each scoop
Until they landed in the soup.

In Belloc's story, Matilda tells a lie – that her house is burning
down – with the result that nobody believes her when her house
really is on fire, and she is burned to death. In Landale's version,
Boris tells a lie – that Britain is to leave the European
Community – and all the other correspondents have to follow it
without any time to check the facts, and are forced to retract
when John Major and Douglas Hurd deny the story. Boris then
tells a second, even more implausible story, which the correspondents refuse to believe:

For every time he said 'Delors' the Messiah',
We only answered: 'Nah, it's a flyer.'

In journalism, a 'flyer' is an eye-catching story based on guess-
work rather than fact. To round off his verses, Landale wrote:

The moral is, it is indeed,
It might be wrong but it's a damn fine read.

The details of what Boris wrote might often be wrong, but his
general understanding of what was happening was right. He saw
that Brussels was intent on gaining much greater power over the
member states, and he dramatised this process more entertain-
ingly than any of his rivals. Boris had begun to show his
extraordinary ability to reach the widest possible audience.

– 13 –

The Fall of Darius Guppy

WHILE BORIS'S CAREER WAS STILL IN ITS INFANCY, IT was nearly ruined by the sympathy he showed for one of his friends. No scandal, or alleged scandal, has pursued Boris for longer than the bizarre case of his tape-recorded conversation with his Eton and Oxford chum Darius Guppy. After leaving university and spending a brief period as a bond dealer, Guppy had embarked on a criminal career. In March 1990 he arranged to have himself and his business partner tied up in a hotel room in New York, and to make it look as if they had been robbed of precious stones worth £1.8 million, a sum they successfully claimed from Lloyd's of London.

In the summer of 1990 Guppy became annoyed by the inquiries of Stuart Collier, a journalist on the *News of the World*, and decided to arrange for him to be beaten up and frightened off. Guppy rang Boris in Brussels and asked him to supply Collier's private address and telephone number. This twenty-one-minute conversation was bugged by Peter Risdon, who had been paid £10,000 to tie Guppy up in New York, but had now decided to betray him.

As on a number of other occasions, Boris would have got into fewer difficulties if he had managed to give a straight answer. If

he had kept his wits about him, he would have said something
like: 'For heaven's sake, Darry, you know I can't do that. Just
forget about this wretched journalist.'

But which of us can claim never to have had a telephone conversation which would look bad in print? Boris allowed his
friend to talk, and can be heard prevaricating. He is plainly
reluctant to provide the number, but also to say that he will not
provide the number. Guppy has rung him before, and Boris has
undertaken to get Collier's details from one or another of his
contacts at News International, publishers of *The Times* as well as
the *News of the World*. But Boris has not yet done so and is worried about the danger of discovery.

Guppy tries, by expounding the campaigns of Napoleon, to
show there is no risk of being found out. Boris breaks in to ask
how badly Collier is to be hurt, after which the following
exchanges occur:

GUPPY: 'Not badly at all.'
BORIS: 'I really, I want to know . . .'
GUPPY: 'I guarantee you he will not be seriously hurt.'
BORIS: 'How badly will he be . . .'
GUPPY: 'He will not have a broken limb or broken arm. He
        will not be put into intensive care or anything like
        that. He will probably get a couple of black eyes and
        a . . . a cracked rib or something like that.'
BORIS: 'Cracked rib?'
GUPPY: 'Nothing which you didn't suffer at rugby, OK?'

The conversation continued with Boris saying, in the manner of
one trying to wind up the proceedings, 'OK, Darry, I said I'll do
it and I'll do it.'

The two friends then turn to discussing the relative merits of
Second World War generals, with Boris reckoning Guderian was
the best, while his friend's top three are Rommel, Patten and

Alexander, after which Guppy makes some concluding observations about Napoleon.

In 1993 Guppy was convicted of fraud and sentenced to five years' imprisonment. Immediately after he was convicted, Boris wrote a short piece about him in the *Daily Telegraph*: 'He lives by an Homeric code of honour, loyalty and revenge.' Boris did not entirely spare his old friend. He told the horrible story of how Guppy pursued a vendetta against his landlord in Oxford: 'On one occasion, after the landlord had hung up weeping from a midnight call, he picked up the phone the following morning to discover Darius still on the line.' But he also said that 'the joy of knowing Darius is the humorous self-deprecation beneath the idiotic flamboyance', and he praised his friend's 'ascetic, contemplative intelligence'.

Only when Guppy was already in jail did the tape get sent to Boris's editor at the *Telegraph*, Max Hastings, with a letter from a media enquirer asking him what he was going to do about it.

The tape could have done Boris very serious harm. Hastings consulted Jeremy Deedes, the paper's Editorial Director, and relates in his memoir, *Editor*, what happened next: 'Jeremy and I thought that it was impossible for the *Telegraph* simply to ignore an issue touching on the personal integrity of one of the staff. We flew our correspondent to London for a serious discussion. Boris easily persuaded us that he had never taken any action in pursuit of Guppy's proposal, nor had he intended to. We sent him back to Brussels bearing only a strongly worded note from me, suggesting that he would be rash to make such an error of judgment again, or even to indulge such a man as Guppy down the telephone. As a virtue, loyalty to friends has its limits.'

Boris drew those limits more widely, and less prudently, than Hastings would have done. So did Charles Spencer, who when Guppy came out of prison provided a house for him on the Althorp estate.

Ever since extracts from the tape were published in the *Daily*

Mail, on 16 July 1995, Boris has faced questions about his friendship with Guppy. Again and again, he has pointed out that he never supplied the address and that Collier was never beaten up. Sometimes he adds that his unfortunate friend was being 'hounded', while at others he says that Guppy 'was always a bit of a fruitcake'.

Some will say Boris should not have been Guppy's friend in the first place, but I cannot go along with this. I could see why Boris and Guppy were friends. Guppy had great charm. It is true that some people, including some of Boris's friends at Oxford, hated him, but when I met him for the first time in 1987 I liked him at once. He described himself as a poet and showed me some of his verses, and I liked those too. He had a quality of impertinence which was very attractive.

When I spoke to Guppy on the telephone – he now lives abroad – his tone of voice was exactly as I remembered it: high-spirited, affectionate, witty, and crazy in a way which before his downfall there seemed no need to take seriously. He was no longer in touch with Boris, but spoke with great fondness of him: 'I loved Boris. I was very attracted to him. I felt an affinity – I appreciated not simply his humour, but the warmth within his humour.'

Guppy said if he were Boris and being questioned about the tape, 'I would play it slightly differently. I would say the journalist concerned needed a knee-capping. I'm only sorry I couldn't provide him with the address. The guy was a prick, he needed a knee-capping, and the people I know would think I was a pussy for not chopping his head off and putting it on the Internet.' (Let me interject, lest anyone misunderstand this, that I am not in favour of knee-capping, or of chopping the heads off annoying journalists.)

Guppy went on: 'To be fair to Boris, a) he did not provide me with the address; b) he should have. The world would be a better place if he had, and you can quote me on this. Because I don't like journalists.' He added that he liked me, but he didn't like journalists: 'In fifteen years I have not spoken to one journalist.'

According to Guppy, 'people are so concerned about appearances' that they worry about justice being seen to be done, but are less concerned that justice actually *is* done. He prefers the customs of earlier ages: 'The Duke of Wellington fought twenty-five duels. Now if that had been under today's conditions he would have faced twenty-five counts of attempted murder.'

It has since occurred to me that the Duke would not have condescended to fight a duel with a journalist, and would more likely have said: 'Publish and be damned.' He did fight a duel when he was Prime Minister, but against a peer, the Earl of Winchilsea, and was severely criticised in the press for doing so.

Guppy refused to acknowledge that Collier's inquiries were entirely justified. He insisted that even today, many people, including 'Spaniards, Turks, Mexicans and South Americans', would have done the same as himself and gone after Collier. But in Britain, he thinks, 'a dreadful moral sanctimoniousness' has replaced any sense of natural justice: 'The English have this *Daily Mail* mentality and it is absolutely sickening.'

Guppy published a wooden account of his insurance fraud, *Roll the Dice*, in which he tried and failed to justify what he had done. As one who had once admired his literary gifts, I asked whether there was any chance of his writing something now, but he said: 'What I have to say is too controversial, I can assure you. I just can't be bothered with it – publishing stuff – the inevitable snide comment from the *Daily Mail*. I would not be allowed by law to seek redress. If someone says something bad about me my instinct is to go and beat them up. I never had a problem in prison because the prisoners could see this in me. If I came back to England I know I would do time for grievous bodily harm.'

He made the point that in a conversation between friends, one does not interrupt and say, 'Oh Darius, for the sake of any tape recording . . .' and then place on record one's complete condemnation of what one's friend is saying.

'Now talking of addresses, Andrew,' he said in a joking tone, 'there's something you can do for me . . .'

Boris could see Guppy's defects. In June 1997, when commenting on the downfall of the Tory MP Jonathan Aitken, Boris wrote: 'There is a touch of Darius Guppy about him, to take an example from my own generation, a Walter Mittyish refusal to face up to reality, and an inability to sort out right from wrong.'

Boris went on: 'Like all tragic figures, Aitken was the author of his own downfall, and like most tragic figures, there was at least an initial dash of greatness, if not quite of heroism.'

Should we just pass by on the other side when our friends get into trouble? Part of Boris's trouble was his generosity. A nastier man would have cut Guppy without a backward glance.

One of the journalists who wrote most about this affair was Marcus Scriven, at the *Evening Standard*, the paper Max Hastings went from the *Telegraph* to edit in 1995. In 1997 Hastings invited both Scriven, who went with a girl friend, and Boris, who went with Marina, to a lunch party in the *Evening Standard*'s box at Newbury race course.

On the way to Newbury, Scriven played the tape to the girl, wishing to have a witness in case the subject of Guppy came up. After a pleasant lunch, for which Boris and Marina arrived late, Scriven wandered round the course and placed a couple of bets, before returning with his friend to the *Evening Standard* box.

Boris and Marina also returned to the box, and by Scriven's account, the following conversation took place.

BORIS: 'Why do you keep writing about me and Guppy?'
SCRIVEN: 'Well, I don't really. I've only written about Guppy a couple of times. If you would go into print and write an apologia for him [a reference to the

article, quoted earlier in this chapter, which Boris wrote after Guppy's conviction in 1993]. You know him better than I do and you shouldn't indulge him by asking if this bloke is going to get badly hurt.'

BORIS: 'I don't think I said that.'

MARINA: 'I'm sure Boris wouldn't say that.'

SCRIVEN [withdrawing the tape from his pocket]: 'Yes, you did. Would you like to listen?'

Boris, according to Scriven, 'did a Bateman. The hairs stood up on the end of his neck, the white mop took off. And he left, he walked out. He came back later and said, "Let's just call it pax, shall we?"'

A time would come when Boris proved able to devise, at a decisive moment, a way of turning the Guppy episode to his advantage. But at Newbury races it was still a rather dreadful embarrassment.

– 14 –

A Telly Star is Born

BORIS RETURNED FROM BRUSSELS TO THE OFFICES AT Canary Wharf of the *Daily Telegraph*, where he was given the grand titles of Assistant Editor and Chief Political Columnist. A dialogue along the following lines took place between Boris and one of the leader-writers.

> LEADER-WRITER: 'Welcome back. It's terrific you're going to do a political column.'
> BORIS: 'I'm a bit worried I haven't got any political opinions.'
> LEADER-WRITER: 'You must have some.'
> BORIS: 'Well, I'm against Europe and against capital punishment.'
> LEADER-WRITER: 'I'm sure you'll make something out of that.'

He did make something out of that. Boris was being self-deprecating when he said he had no political opinions, but he certainly had no carefully worked-out system, or none that he was going to preach in a tedious way in his column. He could be eclectic and light-hearted and shove in whatever floated into his head, or whatever he thought *Telegraph* readers would enjoy. In 1997, he was made Commentator of the Year at the 'What the Papers Say' awards.

Some journalists would have rested on their laurels, composed a column a week and enjoyed feeling self-important. Boris was also the father of a rapidly growing family. Lara Lettice, born in June 1993, was followed by three more children all born in London at University College Hospital: Milo Arthur on 3 February 1995, Cassia Peaches on 8 September 1997 and Theodore Apollo on 4 July 1999. Theo only narrowly escaped being given an extra name, Washington, in honour of American Independence Day, after a certain amount of pink champagne had been drunk.

But while Boris revelled in being a father, that did not stop him being the most driven and ambitious man at the *Telegraph*. He was an astonishingly prolific writer, who more than made up in energy and rate of fire for those pieces which did not come off as well as they might have done. For a short period after he came back he wrote the political column in the *Spectator*, and one could often see that he had not devoted nearly as much time to it as he should have done, though Dominic Lawson, the then editor, said, 'I thought it was always very good.'

Boris also purued his political ambitions. For the eighteen months up to the General Election of 1 May 1997, when the Conservative Party went down to its worst defeat, in terms of parliamentary seats, since 1906, Boris was the Tory candidate in the hopeless seat of Clwyd South, just over the border from Shropshire. He learned how to sing the Welsh national anthem and to order fish and chips in Welsh. But as he himself has written: 'I fought Clwyd South – and Clwyd South fought back.'

Losing Clwyd South was an excellent way of showing keenness to the party hierarchy, and Boris had done it in order to get a safe seat next time. Meanwhile he devoted himself mainly to journalism. One of the best things Boris did was a back-page

interview in Monday's *Daily Telegraph*. As Charles Moore, who
had succeeded Max Hastings as editor, says: 'He did it very well.
He didn't just suck up [to his interviewees], but nor did he tear
them apart.'

In September 2004, when Andrew Duncan came to interview
him for the *Radio Times*, Boris told him: 'Bad luck you having
to interview me. I used to interview people. Terribly difficult.
You have a wonderful time with this chap, or girl, end up with
a dumper truck of gravel from which you pick shiny pebbles to
make your mosaic. It's seduction and betrayal.'

It is typical of Boris to voice the reservations others may feel
about his work. He is a master of pre-emptive self-criticism.
Before it has even occurred to us to accuse him of seducing and
betraying his victims, he has accused himself. He enlists our sympathy by leaping to a harsher verdict on his conduct than we
would have reached ourselves.

Not that this stops him from conducting a robust defence of
his behaviour, in which he further implicates the rest of us. For
as he explains in the volume of his collected journalism *Lend Me
Your Ears*, while reverential interviews may still be acceptable in
France or America, 'British readers, with their jaded palates,
want something stronger. They want the revelations, the confessions. They want the sudden grabbing for the hankie. That is
why the British hack approaches his interviewee with what is
sometimes a frankly treacherous smile.'

This treacherousness, he says, has led PR men to become 'ever
more ruthless' in their treatment of journalists, which in turn is
why journalists 'have become ever more ratlike in their cunning'.
Boris declares that he is 'in principle' on the side of the hacks,
before saying a few more words in his own defence: 'For my own
part, I have always tried to be faithful to the drift and mood of the
conversation, even if there is a lot one must necessarily cut. I also
tend to like my subjects, though Chris Evans and I were probably quite relieved when our game of golf was over.'

His piece about Evans, a disc jockey who had also become the proprietor of Virgin Radio, describes how Evans agrees, not just to do an interview, but to 'give the *Daily Telegraph* a game of golf! . . . Just when he is needed most, Bill Deedes, the paper's answer to Arnold Palmer, is in Sudan. Someone, anyone, is needed to play golf with Evans. Have you ever swung a club in anger?' the features impresarios ask, and, like a fool, I say yes.'

Boris turns his incompetence into a running joke: 'The last time I played golf was at school when one Major Morkill expelled me from the course for using only one club.' But he only has to play a few holes with Evans, whose own golf turns out to be mediocre – 'unless – ghastly thought – he was only being polite'.

For a while, Boris was comment editor, a role Charles Moore remembers him performing with 'maximum idleness'.

It was at this time that Boris started to acquire a vast new public through his appearances on television. He became the nearest thing most of us have seen to a real-life Bertie Wooster, and people loved him for it. While everyone else was trying to sound more classless, Boris went in the opposite direction, which was a much more enjoyable thing to do. Like his hero P. G. Wodehouse, but in another medium, he took us into a world of upper-class lunacy from which all nastiness had been removed. He acted like a public-school twit from the 1930s, yet by going on programmes on which most politicians would have been unable to cope, and on which most Cabinet ministers would consider it beneath their dignity to appear, he bolstered his democratic credentials.

The programme with which Boris has become most closely associated, and which did most to make him a television star, is *Have I Got News For You*. His first appearance on the show, in April 1998, proved painful, as he had not realised that it was the custom to spring a nasty surprise on one of the guests. Ian Hislop, the editor of *Private Eye* and one of the regular panellists, said: 'He was absolutely livid because I brought up the Darius Guppy tape, which I found immensely funny. He was in a terrific strop and blustered about an elephant trap.'

Boris was so angry he took his revenge by writing an article for the *Spectator* under the headline 'I Was Stitched Up' in which he said the programme was 'a fraud on the viewing public' because 'all that lightning repartee' was actually the result of careful preparation, scripting of even the bits where people are supposed to be ad-libbing, and an entire day of tedious editing before the programme went out.

Paul Merton, the other regular panellist, was infuriated by this article, for as Hislop said, 'Paul Merton gets very cross with suggestions that he's done anything to prepare in any way.'

Boris's career as a contributor to *HIGNFY* might have ended there. But it is not Boris's way to allow a feud to fester, and he cannot have wished to be on terms of permanent enmity with the *Private Eye* set. Quite soon peace broke out and Boris was invited back. After all, his disaster had been a thousand times more entertaining than a safe performance by someone else, and when Hislop said to him of the offending article, 'What a load of bollocks, Boris – you must have knocked that out in about twenty minutes,' Boris replied, 'No, it was shorter than that,' after which Hislop said, 'I expect you were pissed as well,' to which Boris responded, 'I might have been.'

Hislop felt disarmed by Boris's willingness to admit to virtually any charge made against him, and said: 'He apologised on air the next time he came on. It was quite endearing.'

On one edition of *HIGNFY* Boris faced a quiz about his party leader, Iain Duncan Smith, in which he was unable to answer any of the questions. Audiences loved such towering ineptitude. With many contestants, such behaviour might have become embarrassing, but Boris knew how to carry it off. He was tough enough to take the knocks, and the worse things went for him, the more he could make people laugh. The boy who had made Etonians roar with laughter by forgetting his lines was now playing to a nationwide audience. And although he was sending himself up, he was also sending up the very genre, the television quiz, on which he was appearing, by refusing to allow his every word to be controlled by the programme-makers, or to give the kind of glib performance which professional television people cannot help trying to create.

Once, while waiting in the wings, Boris said to Hislop: 'Do you know what the Tory policy is on immigration?' Hislop said 'No,' to which Boris replied, 'Nor do I.'

Boris was soon being asked to present the show, a role in which he maintained his unprofessionalism at a level nobody else could match. According to Hislop, most presenters 'spend two days rehearsing it, but Boris turned up at six p.m. on the day and had never read the script, which he proceeded to read in that dazed way of his. His insouciance was extremely funny.'

Charles Kennedy, the then leader of the Liberal Democrats, was the only politician before Boris who had done well on the show, but 'Chat-show Charlie' was attacked by his own party for being so good.

Boris has appeared only a handful of times on *HIGNFY*, which makes the reputation he has won there all the more remarkable. On a recent occasion when he presented the show, Merton paid him the compliment of saying he had actually got worse.

Some people thought it beneath the dignity of a Member of Parliament to go on such a programme. Boris replied that he would be a coward not to, and it was a way of reaching a much wider public, and he got paid £1,000 a time, which was enough to take two children skiing. He also said the real shocker was 'not that people are so foolish as to appear on TV, but that people are so idle as to watch it'.

Part of Boris's childhood on Exmoor was spent without television at all. His first love was books and one reason why his performances come off so brilliantly on telly is their throwaway character. Boris had become one of the very few politicians who could succeed on the television programmes people actually wanted to watch, and he hoped this would prove a decisive advantage. As he put it in an interview with *GQ* in May 2003: 'If you don't go out and mix it up a bit on the stuff that everybody watches, if you don't get involved in things that everybody thinks are amusing and if you're not prepared to get involved in vernacular, real TV and you just stick on Andrew Neil's late-night yawn-a-thon, then you're never going to get anywhere.'

Television fell in love with Boris. He has been on *Parkinson*, *Question Time*, *Breakfast With Frost* and *Top Gear*, among other programmes. If he had wanted, he could have given up politics and become one of the dominant television personalities of our age. But to Boris's credit, he did not want to sell his soul to television. His fiercest ambition was still political, and he was also heading for the top as a print journalist. His well-hidden seriousness of purpose has preserved him from becoming a television star with an income and an audience of millions.

15

Ape Gets Ming Vase

BORIS WAS MADE EDITOR OF THE *SPECTATOR* IN JULY 1999, when he was thirty-five years old. This was a great chance for a youngish man, for although the magazine's circulation was only 57,000, everyone who was anyone in London read it. The *Spectator* was the oldest weekly in Britain and stood for a kind of irreverent conservatism, though much of it was not very political at all. It was part of Conrad Black's newspaper empire, which also included the *Daily* and *Sunday Telegraphs*. The post could be a springboard either to grander editorships within the group or to high political office. Having edited the *Spectator*, though in some cases after a considerable interval, Ian Gilmour became Defence Secretary; Iain Macleod Chancellor of the Exchequer; Nigel Lawson Chancellor of the Exchequer; Charles Moore editor of the *Daily Telegraph*; and Nigel Lawson's son Dominic editor of the *Sunday Telegraph*. There was no reason why Boris should not equal or exceed these predecessors.

Yet his appointment was not greeted with universal enthusiasm. When Sandra Barwick rang me up for a quote for the piece she was writing about Boris for the *Daily Telegraph*, I told her: 'It's like entrusting a Ming vase to an ape.'

How could I have said this? Partly because I thought Boris

would be slapdash, but mainly because I placed such a high value on the *Spectator*. I started reading it when I was a student, in about 1978, during the editorship of Alexander Chancellor. He not only persuaded interesting people to write for him, he also got them to do their best work, by giving them the intelligent appreciation that writers most desire. As a reader, you could relax in their company, and felt that they knew what was going on, but were not obsessed by politics or by success, and would laugh at people who deserved to be laughed at.

Richard Ingrams did a television column in which he treated telly people as the self-regarding idiots they so often are. One week he watched no television at all, but heard some through the wall of a hotel room in Hay-on-Wye. Jeff Bernard began 'Low Life', Taki reported on 'High Life', Ferdinand Mount was the political columnist, Xan Smiley went to Africa, Murray Sayle was in Japan, Christopher Hitchens in Washington, Sam White in Paris and Andrew Brown in Sweden, Roy Kerridge was at a gypsy encampment somewhere outside London, Patrick Marnham, Geoffrey Wheatcroft, Richard West, Peter Paterson and Peter Ackroyd were all in full flow, and the great Shiva Naipaul spent several years having lunch with Chancellor before going on a journey and writing something which could not have appeared in any other magazine.

Boris could not edit in this style. He was far too busy, and also too restless. *Spectator* lunches, held in the small dining-room at the top of the house, used to be enjoyable because they were so leisurely, as well as because of the mixture of guests, who often included a famous politician or writer, but also took in some of the most amusing, though not necessarily most productive, people from Fleet Street. Boris could not pay host to that kind of long-drawn-out affair. Charles Moore said: 'There was a long-meditated lunch he gave for Debo [Duchess of] Devonshire at the *Spectator* – a weird mixture of people – random – someone from marketing, a friend of Ann Sindall's [Boris's secretary].

Almost as soon as lunch began, he left for the House of Commons – very typical. He enchanted Debo for twenty minutes, then departed.'

Like most editors, Boris was more excited by stories than by writers. 'Scoops are us,' he would say. When one considers that he shot from the hip, his aim was surprisingly good. He was in many ways a very fine editor, who did not expect other people to be as go-getting as he was. I was at this time returning to London from a stint in Berlin. He kindly invited me to be his unpaid Foreign Editor, and found it amusing that I did no editing and almost never went abroad. On one occasion he suggested I go to Papua New Guinea to write about penis gourds. Boris would have been there and back in a week, and would have written an account of the gourds which was just within the fairly elastic bounds of modern taste, but although I spoke to a man at the Pitt-Rivers Museum in Oxford, who knew all about Papua New Guinea and warned me it was quite a dangerous place, I never got round to going there. The articles I did contribute to the Boris *Spectator*, about places as far afield as Hackney, Surbiton and even Burnley, were paid at the generous rate of £500 a time, and usually appeared with the note: 'Andrew Gimson is Foreign Editor of the *Spectator*.'

Some editors treat their staff like galley slaves and expect them to produce a constant flow of 'ideas' for pieces (which is one reason why so much journalism is such nonsense, for many ideas which will pass muster as a phrase at an editorial conference are exposed as vacuous when some poor journalist is sent off to write about them). Boris was a humane editor who did not seem to mind if nobody but himself had any ideas, though Peter Oborne, who wrote the politics column, was usually rather good at coming up with something.

Never have I been to editorial conferences where such freedom of speech reigned. Leaning back on one of the sofas in Boris's office, you could tell any joke that came into your head.

There was a slightly brutish desire to 'get' Blair, but brutishness is one of the traditions of our free press, and Blair would have been an amazing scalp.

Oborne reported one week that Blair had been pheasant-shooting in the West Country, and recalled: 'Boris was electrified. He wouldn't stop ringing me up about it. He became quite obsessive about it. The resources of the *Spectator* were never engaged quite so fully and with such personal attention from the editor himself as on the Blair pheasant-shooting story. Jeremy Clarke [author of the 'Low Life' column] was sent down to Devon and found someone in a pub who claimed to have been out beating when Blair was shooting. Then the trail went cold, until a Tory MP said he'd sat next at dinner to a backwoods peer from Devon who could authenticate the story. Boris was in a state of frenzy. Then the peer started to withdraw a bit. Finally Boris rang up Fursdon, the friend Blair stayed with in Devon, who said: "No. Never. No. Absolutely not."'

Boris's right-hand man at the *Spectator* was Stuart Reid, a man a generation older than him. Dan Colson – Conrad Black's man of business – wanted an older and wiser person at Boris's side. The idea was that Reid would supply the sober judgement and attention to detail which Boris was unable to provide.

Reid is unquestionably a brilliant sub-editor, who can improve almost any piece of copy by making tactful changes to it. He is also devoid of the slightest trace of self-importance. But Reid said that people like Dan Colson misunderstood him: 'They got me completely wrong. I'm just as irresponsible as Boris but I lack his courage. I have actually urged caution and been utterly delighted when he went ahead anyhow. I've always voted Conservative but I'm not a capitalistic, Wall Street right-winger – I'm more of the Perry Worsthorne/Michael Wharton school. I agree with much of what George Galloway says about the war in Iraq.'

As a young man, Reid went to Australia, where he worked

for various publications, including the *Australian*, in which he had a column called 'On the Contrary', signed 'Matilda', and *Poultry News*. He drank enthusiastically, but at the age of thirty-eight thought it prudent to become a total abstainer. In 1975 he served for three months as editor of the *Catholic Herald*, where the headline on the leader in the week after he left was 'Return to Sanity'. He said of this period: 'My heart was in the right place. I was right to support Catholicism at the *Catholic Herald.*'

Reid barely knew Boris: 'I first got to know him when I was comment editor of the *Sunday Telegraph*. I always found him tremendously charming but a bloody nightmare. There'd never be any question of his copy arriving on Friday, nor first thing on Saturday. I'd ring him and he'd say: "Any second."

'At the *Daily Telegraph* I got to know him a bit. The first time I can remember speaking to him was on 3 September 1997 when he did that great piece about Lady Di – "A Latin American carnival of grief" – I sought him out in his office and praised him at length. He looked confused, bewildered and modest, as he does when you praise him.

'Not long after, I found him wandering round and round in circles. He had to write a column and he was saying, "Christ, what can I write?" He was in the shopping mall area of Canary Wharf. His shirt was hanging out and he was running his hand through his hair. My mind went blank. I couldn't help him at all.

'But from 1999, at the *Spectator*, we worked together as if we'd been colleagues – fairly close colleagues – for a long time, a fiction that helped us both.' Reid, whom I interviewed in June 2004, looked back on his life with Boris: 'We've been together now five years, and in that time I've only lost my temper once, and I don't know that he's ever lost his temper. He really is the nicest person I've worked for other than Kim Fletcher, and he's easy-peasy at a personal level.

'He's basically unreliable in terms of delivering copy or being around, and he doesn't seem to bear grudges – it's impossible not to forgive him. You see, he has to be a really nice guy, because if he weren't a nice guy he'd be dead. The anger doesn't have to do with personal nastiness. It's to do with him not being there, decisions not being made – and yet they always are made in the end.

'He's got this wonderful streak of creative irresponsibility. He's the sort of chap who can't see a red button marked "do not press" without pressing it. He's seen as anarchic. This is his appeal. And he is anarchic. He's a liberal libertarian. Legalise drugs. Let's not be pious about sex. Life is for living. Keep government off your back.

'I don't know whether he has any passionately held views. There must be more to him than a pastiche of an Englishman. I remember when the Americans went into Afghanistan and Boris said, "Wouldn't it be funny if – yeah – the Americans took a hiding." He's not anti-American, but he's mercurial. It would have been a better story.

'He is naturally a nice man. The mother of a kid he'd been at prep school with wrote to him and said her son had died, and did Boris remember him? Boris sent her a hand-written letter of about three pages, in which he not just remembered him, but remembered him with affection and told affectionate stories about him.'

Boris brought Ann Sindall with him from the *Telegraph* as his secretary. She was a very important person in his life and it was vastly to his (and her) credit that he wanted her to help run things. Sindall is a blunt, warm-hearted socialist from Batley, in Yorkshire, who dresses as if she is about to set off on a nineteen-mile hike across the moors and is capable of ferocious rudeness, both to her employer and to anyone else who has offended against her sense of right and wrong. She brings her dog, a terrier called Harry, to the office, but is the antithesis of the demure and elegant home counties girl whom ignorant people might have expected to find at the *Spectator*.

Sindall started at the *Telegraph* as a temporary secretary on the leader-writers' desk, when the payments system for the comment writers had collapsed. She sorted things out and they asked her to stay on.

Sindall was sceptical: 'Don't you want posh here?'

Richard Ehrman, one of the leader-writers, replied, 'We've had posh here and nothing works.'

Even when she started, in 1996, 'most of the calls I took were from people asking "Where's Boris?" Even then he was a rising star.'

The more famous Boris became, the greater the number of people who rang up wanting some of his time. Sindall defended him from these supplicants. Susan Clarke, a freelance journalist, rang offering a piece on the royal family and mentioned that next Thursday she was coming to lunch at the *Spectator*.

Sindall replied: 'Just because you're coming to lunch doesn't mean I know who you are.'

Television people had an insatiable craving to get Boris on their programmes. One day I went into Sindall's office and she was telling a TV company: 'He hasn't got time to spend two days going off pretending to be a boy scout.' As Sindall said after this call, 'However you deflect it, they just come back in a different way. It drives you mad.'

She described with affectionate scorn how Boris at a party would spinelessly agree to do things for people who came up and pestered him: 'Nodding dog stands there and agrees to everything they say.'

Boris was more than capable of annoying Sindall, and everyone else with whom he worked closely at the *Spectator*, but he knew how to mend fences. Sindall said: 'We can all hate his guts, we want to kill him, but then he can get us laughing again.'

Sindall's manner of taking important people down a peg or two gave enormous enjoyment to anyone sitting within earshot of her. When she was still at the *Telegraph*, 'Peter Mandelson ran

up wanting to speak to Boris. He said, "He'll know who I am."
I said, "That's fine, but I'm taking the message." He said: "Peter
Mandelson." I said: "Can you spell that please?"'

Sindall's spelling was not actually very good. As she herself
says, she got to the age of eighteen 'not even knowing I could-
n't read and write properly'. After Paul Goodman, a *Telegraph*
leader-writer who is now a Tory MP, criticised Sindall's written
work, Boris reassured her: 'There's nothing wrong with your
spelling. It's just different to everyone else's.'

Boris and Sindall were once at a function attended by
Margaret Thatcher: 'He was like this schoolboy. He went running over to Margaret Thatcher saying "come on Ann, come on
Ann". I had to go over and meet Margaret Thatcher. I couldn't
think what to say to her. She was like a monster when I was
growing up. Where I grew up there was absolutely no work. I
said to her: "You changed the course of my life." I meant it sar-
castically. She really did. I moved from the north because of her
and ended up down south. She actually looked quite small and
defenceless. Boris says I just treated her like a queen.'

There were strict limits to what Sindall would do for Boris:
'One day he came in wearing these trousers with a big rip in
them. He was going on telly or something. He brought them in,
he said, "Ann, you don't think you could . . .?" I said, "No way
I could." The next thing, I walked in to reception and Alex
Whitaker was sewing his trousers. He was sitting at his desk in
his boxer shorts. Some girls will and some girls won't, but I
won't do dry cleaning or sewing up trousers.'

Yet Sindall did help Boris in many other ways. When she
started with him, his financial affairs were in total confusion.
Unpaid parking tickets would increase in cost to £800 and the
bailiffs would be about to break in.

She organised his speaking engagements and negotiated the
fees. I caught a glimpse of this lucrative trade when Boris was
asked by a German bank to speak at the tenth anniversary of the

opening of its Guernsey branch. Boris did not have time and the bank needed another speaker at short notice. Sindall suggested me, billed as the Foreign Editor of the *Spectator*. I asked her how much I should charge and she said that as soon as the word 'bank' appeared in the name of an organisation, she charged a lot. How much was a lot? She urged me to ask for £3,000.

My freelance career was going through one of its worst patches, so I plucked up my courage and followed Ann's advice. The sophisticated gentleman who ran the bank paused for a moment during our telephone conversation when I mentioned this outrageous sum, and then agreed.

Sindall had the onerous task of making Boris's travel arrangements. He has an extraordinary, one might almost say a self-defeating, capacity to go to the wrong station, or to the right station but get on the wrong train. When Boris goes to an airport, there is a good chance his passport has not gone with him. Sindall said: 'I think that's just because his mind's so full of everything else.'

Boris craves action, including the action that flows from things going wrong. As Sindall said, 'If he hasn't got a crisis, he'll sit and say he's bored. He edited the *Spectator* on a knife-edge. He couldn't do it otherwise.'

Trevor Kavanagh, the Political Editor of the *Sun*, recalled a characteristic Sindall intervention: 'I rang Boris up about the identity of some people who might be involved in a story. He was going to give me some information he just couldn't resist giving to me when I heard Ann shout: "You're talking to Trevor Kavanagh. You can't do that!" And Boris said, "I'm sorry." He'd been caught red-handed.'

On one occasion I asked Sindall for the telephone numbers of some people to whom I wanted to speak about Boris, and added: 'Please don't feed his paranoia.'

Ann replied: 'It doesn't need feeding.' Boris is in many ways so robust, and so good at taking jokes at his own expense, that we

16

Member for Henley

BORIS HAD REACHED, WITH THE EDITORSHIP OF THE *Spectator*, a very exposed place in journalism, but he also pursued with ardour his hunt for a parliamentary seat.

Going into politics was no mere afterthought, but the deepest goal of his existence. He had set himself the goal of being in the Cabinet by the age of thirty-five, yet he had reached that age without even getting into the House of Commons.

He was determined to put that right. Michael Heseltine, the former Deputy Prime Minister, was standing down as MP for Henley after more than thirty years in the Commons. In the summer of 2000, Boris competed against 201 other applicants for this safe Tory seat. In the final round, which included a question-and-answer session for which Boris's television experience gave him an advantage, he defeated two lawyers, both of whom were closer to Heseltine on the question of Europe. In Henley as elsewhere, Tory activists were obsessed by Europe. They asked many more questions about it than about anything else, and were inclined to choose someone less pro-Brussels than Heseltine, whom many Conservatives had not yet forgiven for his decisive role in Margaret Thatcher's downfall. Boris could cope convincingly with Europe: here his journalistic experience remained extremely helpful to his political aspirations.

But there was one other matter which threatened to derail him. A Henley Conservative stood up at the selection meeting and accused Boris of having a skeleton in his cupboard. It was the Guppy question, posed with such venom, according to Boris, that it offended the audience's sense of fair play.

The candidate was able to reply: 'In so far as you accuse me of keeping this Guppy business a secret, well, that seems a bit thin, since I have actually been questioned about it on a TV game show watched by I don't know how many millions.'

There was no need for Boris to add that he had not chosen to be stitched up by the resident wags on *Have I Got News For You*. The point was (as he says in his book about Henley, *Friends, Voters, Countrymen*) that he had shown the ability to recover under fire. This, he argued, 'was a bit of bad luck on the other two [candidates], since they lacked the advantage of an embarrassing past to brush aside'.

It is a wonderful argument for taking foolish risks. How better can a man show his resilience than by getting into trouble? Boris was not one of those percentage players, who never does anything daring, and whose life furnishes no materials for history.

Henley may sound small, but the constituency which takes its name from the pretty town on the Thames covers a vast tract of country between Reading and Oxford, and the *Oxford Journal* ran a whole page about Boris on the day after his victory, ending with the prediction: 'After the virtual disappearance of Michael Heseltine following the last election, politics in South Oxfordshire are about to get very interesting once more.'

Even in 1997, a disastrous year for the Tories, Heseltine had a majority of 11,167 over the Liberal Democrats, but the Lib Dems boasted that they could take Boris on: 'We believe the anti-Boris vote will be bigger than the pro-Boris vote.'

Boris himself used cautious language in victory. When something matters to him, he is perfectly capable of keeping quiet, and he had no desire to ruin everything in Henley by shooting off his mouth. There was a lot of stuff about being 'greatly honoured', and he insisted that his election to Parliament 'is absolutely not a foregone conclusion'.

But Boris also made clear that he hoped to pursue the risky course of remaining editor of the *Spectator*. 'I don't see a conflict of interest and it is not an unprecedented career path. I could mention Winston Churchill and Disraeli. It will probably be hard, but my plan is not to leave my job, not least because I would be broke.'

Disraeli and Churchill certainly showed that periods of intense literary activity were compatible with being an MP, though neither of them edited a weekly magazine. But from another point of view, these grand comparisons, offered with such skilful modesty ('I could mention'), were and are highly encouraging for Boris. Both men were written off as marginal figures, yet came to dominate politics.

Disraeli was an outsider who was at first regarded as ridiculous, and whose private life was scandalous, but who at the age of sixty-three 'climbed to the top of the greasy pole' and became one of the greatest of all Tory Prime Ministers. Churchill in the 1930s was likewise an outsider, who in 1940, at the age of sixty-six, reached the top. Boris still had another thirty years to achieve his ambition of becoming Prime Minister.

But it was nevertheless rather wilful of him to say that he saw no 'conflict of interest' between editing a magazine and being a Tory MP. The world of journalism looked askance at his move into politics, and predicted that he would fail. Richard Ingrams wrote in the *Observer*, 'What is rather sad about Johnson is that he has this desire to go into politics. For it is hard to think of a single successful journalist who has made any kind of mark as a politician. Most, including such illustrious names as William

Cobbett and Hilaire Belloc, failed utterly to shine when they were elected to Parliament.'

The assumption in Fleet Street was that Boris would be forced to give up the editorship once he actually became an MP, and Boris amused himself by inviting four of the candidates to succeed him – Michael Gove, Stephen Glover, Alice Thomson and Matthew d'Ancona – to lunch at the *Spectator*. In Gove's words, this was Boris's way of saying: 'I know what you buggers are up to – I can have a laugh at your expense.'

Less than a year later, when the election was called, journalists descended on Henley to write about Boris, confident that whatever else he did he would provide good copy. A. A. Gill wrote a notorious piece in the *Sunday Times*. He began by insulting the 'faux rural' area: 'Henley is a supermodel constituency – and like all supermodels it looks lovely on postcards but when you get up close and personal it's smug, selfish, demanding and vain.'

Gill moved on to Boris, whom he described as 'Quisling Boris' for abandoning journalism. The piece included a lengthy description of Boris struggling to find anyone to canvass on a summer morning in a commuter village, and ended: 'Boris Johnson is without doubt the very worst putative politician I've ever seen in action. He is utterly, chronically useless – and I can't think of a higher compliment.'

This verdict said more about Gill, and his desire to regard journalism as a higher calling than politics, than about Boris. The Liberal Democrats distributed Gill's verdict to the voters, but it made no difference.

At the General Election on 7 June 2001, Boris held Henley with a majority of 8,458 over the Liberal Democrats. The picture of him yawning which adorns the front cover of this book was taken not long before dawn, when he was sitting waiting with his wife, Marina, for the result to be declared. Boris was wearing a blue rosette which the art department at Simon &

Schuster has skilfully removed. In his victory speech, Boris urged people to 'go back home and prepare for breakfast'.

Henley was starting to take Boris to its heart, as a piece about him in July 2001 in the *Oxford Mail* made clear: 'It was the biggest ever attendance at the Macmillan Cancer Relief Lunch . . . The 37-year-old is juggling enough plates to dazzle a magician.'

Boris as usual arrived late, but nobody minded. 'I can't talk about politics because everyone thinks it's boring so I'm going to give a speech on the crisis of masculinity,' he confided to Katherine MacAlister from the *Oxford Mail*, while 'shovelling mouthfuls of duck noodle salad into his mouth'.

And the speech itself was a triumph: 'He had the Ladies Who Lunch eating out of the palm of his rather large hand . . . When his mobile phone went off in the middle he was terribly embarrassed and managed to utter, "Could you phone back, I'm in the middle of a speech," which had everyone splitting their Gucci sundresses with laughter . . . But don't be deceived. Beneath his famously dishevelled fair mop and innocent schoolboy face, lies a fantastic intellect and burning ambition that is making him more successful by the day.'

Boris told Katherine MacAlister: 'I don't go to parties. I'd much rather be at home with my kids and spend as much time as possible with them in the evenings and at weekends. My wife is being marvellous about everything.'

The last sentence of this reads a bit awkwardly. What exactly was the 'everything' to which Boris referred?

Boris's book about the campaign, *Friends, Voters, Countrymen*, came out in October. Simon Walters, who had written a book called *Tory Wars*, did a joint book signing with Boris at the 2001 Conservative conference: 'I'd written a serious book, while Boris had polished up a few sketches. One person came up to my desk. This person said, "You've libelled me – I'm going to sue." Boris was meanwhile being mobbed by hundreds of

women. It was like Mick Jagger. They were going crazy over
him. I thought, "This guy's got some special appeal, because the
book's nothing."'

It is unkind to describe the book as nothing. As a light-
hearted description of the trials and tribulations of life on the
stump, it is good fun. It was serialised in *The Times* because
Charles Moore, the editor of the *Telegraph*, would offer only a
small sum for it, and it was quite favourably reviewed by Roy
Hattersley, Jeremy Paxman and Christopher Silvester among
others.

Not everyone warmed to Boris, however. Early in 2002, he
was hit in the face with a bread roll as he addressed the Mayor of
Henley's annual dinner. The roll was thrown by Eleanor Hards,
a Labour councillor and the chairman of South Oxfordshire
District Council, who was sitting three places away from Boris
on the top table.

Councillor Hards said: 'He deserved it. He was making an
overtly party political speech, worthy of the Tory conference. He
mentioned at least three times that people threw bread rolls at
him when they got bored. So I took him at his word.'

According to Tom Boyle, who reported the attack in the
Henley Standard, 'The mayor's annual dinner is the social high
point of the civic year. Over 100 guests packed the upper hall at
Henley Town Hall on Friday evening, including dignitaries from
Thame, Marlow and Maidenhead.'

In his speech, Boris said: 'Many people ask me "what policies
the Conservatives have to offer?" At the risk of being hit by a
bread roll I shall tell you some of my ideas.'

Boyle reported that Boris had lamented the state of public
services, road conditions in Henley and rising crime, 'and was
explaining his theory on nurses' pay when he was struck by the
mini French baguette. Good-humoured heckling from the floor
turned to gasps of horror when the roll found its target.'

The Mayor of Henley, Councillor Tony Lane, said: 'In all my

thirty-seven years in local government I have never seen anything as disgraceful. It was not the time or the place and it's left a rather unpleasant taste in my mouth.'

At Westminster, Boris faced a harder opponent than Councillor Hards in the form of Alastair Campbell, Tony Blair's director of communications.

Matthew Pencharz, who worked for Boris at the Commons, said that only once did he see his boss 'shell-shocked', and that was after Campbell had made 'terrible threats' against him at a meeting outside the Commons in New Palace Yard. This confrontation took place because Peter Oborne had revealed in the *Spectator* that Downing Street had pushed for the Prime Minister to be given a more prominent role in the Queen Mother's lying-in-state in Westminster Hall in April 2002.

Campbell was infuriated by this report, and the *Spectator* lacked the hard evidence needed to prove it. Oborne described the weakness of the magazine's position: 'I told Boris, "I can't stand this up. I can't provide documentary evidence that this is the case." So when Campbell first came on to Boris, Boris was a bit windy. He gave Campbell the impression we were on very weak ground. It was a bit like Hannibal at Cannae: we lured Downing Street on. I had a sleepless night because I couldn't stand the story up. I thought Downing Street had got us by the balls.'

Campbell, confident of victory, overplayed his hand, and was forced to back down when Black Rod, the parliamentary official in charge of the lying-in-state, declined to back No. 10's version of events. Boris's luck had held and he found himself on the winning side. It is easy to say that at many points in his career Boris should have been more cautious, but in journalism as in politics, victory sometimes goes to those who take risks.

While other new boys at the Commons kept their heads down and learned their trade in an obscurity from which some of them will never emerge, Boris operated in the full glare of publicity. It was not just in Henley that he was becoming popular. Up and down the land, he was the darling of the Tory rank and file.

Anne Jenkin, who knows the Tory party as well as anyone, and is married to Bernard Jenkin, the MP for North Essex, said of Boris: 'When he came to speak at our constituency dinner, it was the only dinner that was not only sold out but had a waiting list. The kids all wanted their photo taken with him. He's absolutely my tip for the top. He's the only person who reaches beyond the political arena. Everyone else is so dull and political. Political life squeezes the character out of you.'

But Boris made a poor impression on many of his colleagues on the Tory benches. One senior backbencher described him as 'a blithering idiot. You never see him. I don't think I've ever seen him in the tea room.'

Another backbencher said: 'I was staggered at his economic ignorance. When he got in [in 2001], he was put by the Whips, to test his ability to do big, gritty subjects, on a committee giving detailed scrutiny to a Bill. He didn't make the reputation there he could have done for being able to do the nitty-gritty. There was a laziness.'

The 23-year-old Matthew Pencharz applied to become Boris's first researcher at the Commons, and went for an interview at which his future employer disconcerted him by scarcely giving him a chance to get a word in edgeways: 'Great for you to come in. Fantastic. Brilliant. So, err, well, um, not really given interviews before. How do you do it? Nightmare. Ah, you went to Haberdashers' School I see. Went there for a talk recently. Bright young thrusters. Fantastic. And you're a Cambridge man. Great!'

Pencharz began to grow desperate to say something. He blurted out that he was a 'genuine liberal', which caused Boris to bellow back: 'Not a Liberal Democrat!'

To Pencharz's astonishment, he got the job ahead of thirty or forty other applicants, apparently for the simple reason that he had the best degree. He loved working for Boris: 'He bounds into the office radiating bonhomie and energy, congratulating the team, asking for cups of tea and diet Cokes and barking orders.'

But according to Pencharz, his employer sometimes got 'very, very tired – the man overworked himself'. Boris was taking on too many commitments to be able to fulfil the demands of the Tories at Westminster. Pencharz witnessed how he could infuriate the whips, whose job is to get MPs to turn out and vote: 'After the fall of Baghdad in April 2003 Boris went to visit the city. Unfortunately he hadn't bothered to tell any of the whips. On Monday morning I received a very poor-quality call on a satellite phone from the "beleaguered Palestine Hotel" in Baghdad. "Hello old bean, Boris here!" the line crackled. "Yeah, I made it. Very interesting. Fascinating. What's going on? Any votes?" Yes, I answered, there's a three-line whip tomorrow. "Oh dear. Call up the whips and tell them I'm in Baghdad will you. Back Wednesday. Got a thing in Thame [a town in his constituency] to go to.'''

The line went dead. Pencharz informed the whips that Boris could not make Tuesday night's vote, and went to lunch. On his return, there was a message waiting from Boris's whip: 'Boris, I do not appreciate being told, quite nonchalantly, by one of your staff on Monday morning that you're in Baghdad. Frankly that's not acceptable. I expect you to be in the House on Tuesday night for the three-line whip.'

Boris was not there. Nor, sometimes, did he get to other events. Pencharz sometimes had to stand in for him, to the disappointment of the packed audiences who had come to see and hear Boris. Pencharz also had to pick up Boris's people-carrier from a pound somewhere in an industrial estate beyond Woolwich, and cope when it broke down on the way back to Islington.

One of Boris's trickiest relationships was with the Tory party leader, Iain Duncan Smith. William Hague resigned as Tory leader after losing the 2001 election. Boris backed Ken Clarke to succeed him, and Michael Portillo also stood, but Duncan Smith came through and won. Interviewers made a point of asking Boris how he could remain loyal to such a dimwit, but Boris, with barely veiled satire, would say things like 'Superb man. Fantastic.'

When an interviewer for *Varsity*, an undergraduate newspaper at Cambridge, asked him in June 2002 'if he seriously believes that IDS is the man to lead the glorious Blue revolution', Boris accused the interviewer, Luke Layfield, of 'defeatism', then pretended to be 'paralysed by incredulity' by 'this most unexpected and unusual of questions', and ended by saying: 'Jeepers creepers. I just can't stand this negativity. He's going to do fine, absolutely fine.'

Negativity was breaking out all over the place. In September 2002, Boris published a piece by Peter Oborne which said the Tories were in chaos under IDS and predicted that within months he would be replaced by the sacked party chairman, David Davis.

The *Daily Mirror* quoted 'a Central Office insider' who said: 'This is a clear declaration of war and even amounts to mutiny. Iain will not take this lying down and those behind it will be dealt with. For a sitting Tory MP to publish an article in a magazine that he edits portraying the leader as a failure is unforgivable.'

But another Tory source said: 'Iain will have to play this one very carefully. Boris is one of the party's only stars and as a future leadership contender himself is unlikely to be intimidated.'

One can see why IDS's people might have regarded Boris as a traitor. IDS needed all the help he could get as a public speaker, and tried to make use of Boris's gifts as a debater by getting him, along with David Cameron and George Osborne, to come and brief him at the crack of dawn on Wednesday mornings, in preparation for Prime Minister's Questions. *Newsnight* filmed Boris arriving one morning on his bike, dripping wet and wearing a baseball cap and promising that they were going to kick Blair's butt.

The Tory leader felt he was not receiving quite the support he might have expected from Boris. At a party held by the historian Andrew Roberts for Henry Kissinger, IDS said to Conrad Black: 'I'd like to have a talk with you about Boris. I suspect neither of us is getting full value.'

But in Black's view, 'By laying most of the work [at the *Spectator*] on Stuart Reid we got the best out of Boris – IDS was losing out more than we were.'

By November 2002, in an interview with the *Scotsman*, Boris was lamenting 'the breakdown of authority' in every area of life: 'Adults are treated disrespectfully by children. In the Conservative Party we have total failure to respect the hierarchy.'

But Boris immediately corrected this verdict: 'No, it's total bollocks, isn't it? It's balls. No, forget it. It's a paragraph in a crap column. I tell you what the real problem is: there's no *esprit de corps* or will to win.'

Nobody could accuse Boris of lacking the will to win. In May 2003 he told readers of the laddish magazine *GQ* why they should vote Tory: 'Your car will go faster, your girlfriend will have a bigger bra size. It's an attested fact that under Conservative governments the quality of living of the British people has immeasurably improved, leading to better denticians, higher calcium consumption, leading inexorably to superior mammary development.'

We do not know of another politician who has promised the men of this country that if they vote for his party, their women will have bigger breasts. People reacted with incredulous joy to a Tory who would say such things. Boris was becoming the exponent of a new and vulgar Merry England conservatism,

17

Conrad Black's Indulgence

HOW DID BORIS GET AWAY WITH IT? HOW DID HE manage at one and the same time to be an editor and an MP? There are precedents for this dual role, not least at the *Spectator*, but none which quite fitted Boris, who had in any case promised his proprietor, Conrad Black, that he would stick to journalism.

This Canadian magnate, who was ennobled as Lord Black of Crossharbour in 2001, rose and fell as a British press baron within two decades. Black bought the *Telegraph* cheap off the Berrys in 1985–86, acquired the *Spectator* in 1988, but suddenly started to lose control of his newspaper empire in the autumn of 2003, when his accounting practices came under intense scrutiny in the United States from disgruntled shareholders and from the Securities and Exchange Commission. In June 2004 the Barclay brothers bought the *Daily* and *Sunday Telegraph*s and the *Spectator*.

In the summer of 2005, Black and his second wife, the journalist Barbara Amiel, visited London, where they attracted a certain amount of adverse publicity. It was said that the American authorities were about to decide whether Black would face criminal fraud charges. Unkind souls also said that before arriving in town they had rung old friends encouraging

those friends to have them to lunch or dinner. Boris had Black
to lunch at the *Spectator*.

Black agreed to meet me for a drink one evening at the
Berkeley Hotel, the luxurious establishment close to Hyde Park
where he and his wife were staying. I have never had more than
a passing acquaintance with him, but have always enjoyed his
expansive manner, his love of the grand sweep of history and his
fondness for orotund jokes, while also feeling slightly frightened
of the power-mad bully who might at any time emerge. He is a
very large man, who generally looks as if he is fighting a losing
battle against his own greed.

His pugnacity seemed if anything to be intensified by his difficult circumstances. 'Envy is never far from the surface in this
city,' he announced in an angry tone. He later added that journalists have 'a sort of grunting herd instinct when they use their
position to destroy people with no sense of fair play'.

Black, who has himself written a considerable biography of
Franklin Delano Roosevelt, asked whether Boris approved of
having his life written. I said that at first he did, to which
Conrad replied: 'He's so ineffably duplicitous you never know.
FDR is one of the few people I know more devious than Boris.
If FDR hadn't been devious God knows what would have hap-
pened to the world.'

It will be seen that Black admires duplicity – in this case the
'self-confident and Machiavellian' duplicity shown by FDR in
the period before the United States entered the Second World
War, when he was declaring his determination to preserve the
peace while at the same time extending American territorial
waters from 3 miles to 1,000 miles and letting Britain have 50
destroyers.

I asked Black how he first got to know Boris. 'I read his articles, I guess when he was in Brussels. He was a name much
bandied about by Max [Hastings] in his last couple of years as
editor [of the *Daily Telegraph*]. I may first have met Boris at the

leader conference. I occasionally attended the leader conference when I thought Max's soggy tendencies were getting out of control.'

Black was intrigued by Boris: 'He's sort of like Hugh Grant in that he has rather predictable gestures. Boris tousles and retousles his hair and produces a number of imaginative adjectives – stonking – and he speaks in that syncopated upper-class way. He produces what purports to be a metaphor that's preposterous. I rang Boris up once and he said: "I'm hard at it transforming the *Spectator* into a McVitie biscuit. What I mean is an opening of solid meal followed suddenly and dramatically by a chocolate taste explosion." It's all rubbish, but it's imaginative.'

Black gave the impression that he was slightly over-awed by Boris, or at least felt powerless to control him. The powerlessness of the proprietor is one of the paradoxes of newspapers. In theory the proprietor is all-powerful, but in practice the only moment when he can exercise absolute power is when he hires or fires an editor.

The problem with sacking is that it cannot be done all that often without shaking confidence in the very publication you own. A disobedient editor therefore has much more freedom than may appear, at least as long as the publication in question is thought to be doing well.

Boris understood this. Black grew heated as he recalled how Boris had behaved: 'Jesus Christ, it all comes back to me, what a duplicitous scoundrel he is. When Max retired [as editor of the *Daily Telegraph*] we were in discussions with Dacre [Paul Dacre, editor of the *Daily Mail*]. Once Dacre just took our prospective pay packet back to David English [in charge at Associated Newspapers, owners of the *Daily Mail*], we re-interviewed Charles Moore and it became clear he was the man [to edit the *Telegraph*].

'Frank Johnson had a number of people call me to champion his cause – none of them was a grand elector – I didn't consider a call from a somewhat bibulous Woodrow Wyatt at midnight a clincher – but I told Frank he could have a try as editor of the *Spectator*. And then Frank didn't do anything.'

I said Frank was a good editor, who deserved to be backed rather than sacked, but Conrad swept on with his explanation: 'I again and again urged Frank to do the job. I said to him, look, you hired Anne McElvoy, if you want to change deputies it's up to you. Finally Dan Colson couldn't take it. The *Spectator* was rather lacklustre. There was no doubt the star in waiting, the man to make the *Spectator* a household name, was Boris.

'I saw Boris: he gave us his solemn word of honour that he would not seek selection for any party including the Conservatives. About two weeks later we found he'd thrown his hat in the ring in two constituencies. I was overseas so Colson interrogated him on the thing. Boris went through this tousling, oh God, I shouldn't have done this, you should fire me.'

Boris quite often told his employers he deserved to be sacked, but Black let him get away with it: 'We kind of endured it because the paper was doing well. Our view is that Boris's performance was outrageous, but the chief criterion is what's good for the *Spectator*, and Boris was a good thing for the *Spectator*. Still is.' This was how Black justified being so indulgent to Boris, under whose editorship the circulation of the *Spectator* rose from 57,500 to nearly 70,000.

When Boris became candidate for Henley, he rang up Charles Moore to ask his advice about how to handle Black, given that he, Boris, had faithfully promised that he would not become an MP. Moore at length wearied of Boris's apparent indecision and said: 'Look, Boris, what do you want?'

Boris replied: 'I want to have my cake and eat it.'

In only nine syllables, Boris had defined his programme, and on this occasion he actually managed, for several years, to carry it through. It is a popular programme, in the sense that it is what most people dream of doing, but by our mid-thirties most of us

17. A thoughtful Boris on honeymoon in Egypt.

18. Boris and Max Hastings, who gave him his second start in journalism.

19. Conrad Black, former proprietor of the *Spectator*, with his wife Barbara Amiel. Black would not only give Boris editorship of the magazine, but also fail to sack him when Boris sought election to Parliament.

20. Boris at the *Spectator*: his secretary, Ann Sindall, tells him to concentrate on something that bores him.

21. *Spectator* supremo. Boris with colleagues at Doughty Street: Mary Wakefield at his feet; Ann Sindall sitting with her terrier Harry on her lap; Stuart Reid with clasped hands; Michael Heath in black; Clare Asquith over Heath's shoulder, Mark Amory on the right; and production editor Clarke Hayes leaning on a bust of Pericles.

22. Boris and his second wife Marina, after winning selection as the new Conservative candidate for Henley.

23. Journalist, author, MP and now TV star: Boris as guest host on *Have I Got News For You*.

24. Boris, Kimberly Fortier and David Blunkett at a *Spectator* party.

25. Boris goes hunting with Charles Moore, former editor of the *Daily Telegraph*.

26. Operation Scouse-grovel: Boris narrowly avoids deep water by apologising to the people of Liverpool at Albert Dock in October 2004, having been ordered there by Michael Howard after a *Spectator* editorial described the city as being 'hooked on grief'.

27. Petronella Wyatt, whose affair with Boris he famously and disastrously denied as an 'inverted pyramid of piffle'.

28. Boris makes the cover of *Private Eye* – one of the most famous shots of him during the Petronella affair.

29. A slightly dishevelled Boris, taking refuge at the home of his old Oxford friend Justin Rushbrooke, notices the long lenses of the *News of the World* while Rushbrooke points out that his car is about to be clamped.

30. Johnson *père et fils*, competing as ever while on the campaign trail during the 2005 General Election. Contrary to appearances Boris won the match easily.

31. Expect the unexpected: Boris was a handy rugby player in his day, and applied his skills against Maurizio Gaudino in a charity match before the 2006 World Cup. Unfortunately he was supposed to be playing football.

32. Boris found himself overtaken by his fellow Etonian David Cameron in the party leadership stakes. Time will tell if Boris's unique style will one day find wider favour among his fellow MPs.

tend, in our unimaginative way, to have settled for something less.

Boris worked very hard to realise his dream. He lobbied everyone who might help him fulfil his ambition to be both an editor and an MP. At the *Spectator*, he spoke to his deputy, Stuart Reid, who recalled: 'When Boris decided to become an MP – to go for Henley – and I think he'd told the *Telegraph* there was no question of remaining editor if he got Henley – and vice versa – he asked me about it. Would I keep on working for him if he became an MP? I said yes. He was shoring up his position. But I did say to him I thought it was wrong in principle for someone to be both an MP and editor of a political magazine. And I still think it's wrong. But having said that, I think he's incredibly independent. He's run pieces about the Tory leader that I, as someone not committed to the Tory party, would have been terrified to run.'

When Boris appeared on *Desert Island Discs*, he was pressed by Sue Lawley to explain his conduct, and was unable to do so.

LAWLEY: 'You did as I understand it undertake to your proprietor Conrad Black that you wouldn't go into politics, you would just do the journalism, but you know, within a year you were running for Henley. I mean that was . . . dishonest?'

BORIS: 'Well, aaargh, it's probably fair to say I didn't tell them I was going to do it, that'd be a, you know.'

In April 2002 the *New York Times* did a profile of Boris, and it too asked him about his promise to Black. Boris claimed: 'The blessed sponge of amnesia has wiped the chalkboard of history.' Since Boris has an excellent memory, he must be referring to other people's amnesia.

The *New York Times* wanted a picture of Boris. I happened to be with him in his office at the *Spectator* when their photographer arrived downstairs, and Boris suddenly said: 'You pretend to be me!'

There was, we thought, a good chance that nobody in New York would realise, in the short time between getting the pictures and printing one of them, that they had got the wrong man. Boris went out and I posed for the photographer, who was completely taken in. Even when members of the *Spectator* staff put their head round the door and said, 'Where's Boris?' the poor man just said, 'Oh, are there two Borises who work here?'

But Kimberly Fortier, the American-born publisher of the *Spectator*, got wind of this childish joke, was not amused by it and put a stop to it.

One reason why Boris managed to remain editor was his ability to charm and amuse the many people apart from the Blacks and Dan Colson who thought they deserved to be amused. His predecessor, Frank Johnson, had found this an intolerable chore: 'There was this idiotic set-up where you had to suck up not just to Conrad and Dan Colson, but to the *Spectator* board.' This contained people like Norman Tebbit, the Tory politician who was most memorably described as a semi-house-trained polecat, and Algy Cluff, the former *Spectator* proprietor. Frank Johnson could not stand them, and would behave in a very surly fashion at board meetings. The consequence was that they could not stand him. Worst of all, he incurred the enmity of Kimberly Fortier. It is impossible to imagine that Boris would ever have made enemies in this way.

It was indicative of Black's continuing indulgence that, six months after Boris was elected MP for Henley, Conrad and Barbara threw a party in honour of 'the Boris Phenomenon'. Stuart Reid recalled the cardboard cut-outs of Boris which greeted guests as they arrived: 'I remember when Conrad and Barbara gave that party for him. Daniel Bernard, the French ambassador, was going up the steps. There were pictures of Boris everywhere and Bernard said: "It's a little bit like the cult of Pol Pot."'

Sarah Sands, then the deputy editor of the *Daily Telegraph*, and also the sister of the singer Kit Hesketh-Harvey, who performed at the party, said: 'The whole party was completely extraordinary – a celebration of Boris's treachery. My brother was asked to sing a song about Boris and his incredible unreliability. Everyone was laughing at things which were very, very close to the bone. At the end Kit went back to the piano to pick up the lyrics and they had gone – Boris had taken them, which was naughty.'

According to Kit, Black gave a speech in which he said that if Boris chose to run for No. 10, he, Black, was right behind him.

Charles Moore said: 'Kit and the Widow gave the cabaret and Conrad got quite angry because Kit was off-message. We left at midnight and my last sight was of Stanley Johnson in tartan trousers making a speech no one had invited him to make. The only words I can remember from it are, "One of my ex-wives . . ."'

But the Boris Phenomenon party was mainly famous for the indiscretions of the French ambassador. These would not have come to wider attention had Black's wife, Barbara Amiel, not publicised her guest's remarks in a piece for the *Daily Telegraph* in December 2001. Amiel said that during a reception at her house, the ambassador of 'a major EU country' had told guests the world's current troubles were all the fault of 'that shitty little country Israel', and had asked: 'Why should the world be in danger of World War Three because of those people?'

Other newspapers immediately identified Daniel Bernard, the French ambassador, as the author of these remarks. Bernard was outraged that a private conversation had been publicised. He at first said he could not remember saying what he was supposed to have said, and later insisted that his words had been distorted. But in July 2002 the French government transferred him from London to become ambassador to Algeria, and he died in April 2004 while still serving in that post.

I asked Black if he was intending to make Boris the editor of the *Daily Telegraph* when Charles Moore stepped down in the autumn of 2003, but he replied: 'More likely the *Sunday* [*Telegraph*] – and move Dominic [Lawson] to the *Daily*.'

Moore said Boris very much wanted the editorship of the *Daily Telegraph*: 'Boris tried pretty hard to get the job but they were determined not to give it to him. Colson was probably more adamant than Conrad.'

In Moore's account, this determination to deny Boris sprang from what Black and Colson saw as his deceitful behaviour as editor of the *Spectator*, when he had promised not to stand for Parliament only to go ahead and do so. Boris was no longer being allowed to have his cake and eat it. Some sort of high water mark had been reached.

According to Sarah Sands, Boris was offered the editorship, and said he would like to do it, but asked if the transition could be made to fit in with the next election, for he could not let down his constituents in Henley by causing a by-election.

Sands thinks Charles Moore, intent on arranging a smooth succession from himself to Boris, tipped off Boris about his departure several months in advance, while keeping her in the dark: 'I felt very hurt. I'd been Miss Goody-Goody, very loyal to Charles,' yet he did not tell her he was going until he actually did, which gave her no chance to campaign for the editorship herself. Charles had been in College at Eton, and she saw an 'Etonian understanding' between him and Boris. In the event, the relatively unknown Martin Newland was made editor, and lasted for about two years.

The embattled tycoon ended our conversation by declaring his innocence: 'It is more likely that I would get from here to John O'Groats by flapping my arms than I would ever violate the criminal statutes of the United States or any other serious country.'

One may note Black's assumption that it would be in order for him to break the law in those countries which he does not regard as serious. Conventions that might restrain lesser men were not for him. He had grand ambitions, and respected the grandeur of Boris's ambition to become Prime Minister.

On 17 November 2005 Black was charged by Patrick Fitzgerald, the attorney for the northern district of Illinois, with eight counts of fraud. Fitzgerald said: 'The indictment charges that the insiders at Hollinger [Black's company], all the way to the top of the corporate ladder, whose job it was to safeguard the shareholders, made it their job to steal and conceal.' Black denies the charges; his trial is currently scheduled for March 2007.

The day after Black was charged, I happened to see Boris at the *Spectator*. I asked him what he thought about Black. Boris was slow to answer: 'Let me think. He was terribly kind. He always treated me very, very well. No question of that.'

18

The Start of an Affair

A YEAR OR TWO AFTER BORIS BECAME EDITOR OF THE *Spectator*, he began a love affair which was to have very painful consequences.

Petronella Wyatt was already working at the magazine. She was the only daughter of Woodrow Wyatt, a raffish figure who as a young man had been a Labour MP, but was later raised to the House of Lords on the recommendation of his friend Margaret Thatcher. Woodrow moved in grand circles which encompassed the worlds of racing, politics and café society. He was in close touch with Rupert Murdoch, was chairman of the Horserace Totalisator Board and had innumerable famous people to dinner, about whom he wrote in his posthumously published diaries, which showed how rackety but also amusing he could be. Up to his death in 1997 he wrote a column in the *News of the World*, under the title 'The Voice of Reason'.

Petronella's mother, Verushka, was from Hungary and was the widow of Baron Dr Lazlo Banszky von Ambroz. Petronella had an exotic, hot-house air, and enjoyed behaving in a stylish and outlandish way. Michael Portillo, himself quite an exotic figure, has given an amusing description of her refusal to conform when as Defence Secretary he took a party of journalists to visit British forces in Bosnia:

It was winter and the troops' accommodation in the field was basic, so we issued a note to the press corps urging them to wear clothing that was warm and robust. We were billeted with the forces in a metal factory. At breakfast we joined the queue of soldiers in their fatigues and boots, rifles over their shoulders, with their mess tins ready to receive the man-sized dollops of scrambled egg, sausage and black pudding.

One figure stood out. She wore a tall Cossack hat, whose soft fur swayed like ripe wheat as she moved her lovely head. Her cashmere sweater plunged devastatingly at the neckline. Her legs were swathed in skin-tight moleskin jodhpurs and pirate boots. Petronella Wyatt looked wonderful, better for military morale than a whole concert performance by Gracie Fields. I asked one open-mouthed witness what he thought of her interpretation of the dress code. 'Very satisfactory,' he gasped.

Boris did not know Petronella before he went to the *Spectator*, but its offices are small and as assistant editor she would have seen him all the time. She was fascinated by political history, knew the Conservative Party well, including people like the former Chancellor of the Exchequer, Norman Lamont, and looked with favour on Boris's political ambitions. To be desperate to get to the top, but to make jokes about it, was for her a perfect mixture. His anarchic side chimed with something anarchic in her. Like her father, he delighted in causing consternation, or at least surprise, on social occasions where others were on their best behaviour.

A friend of the Wyatts said of Boris's attraction for Petronella: 'The key thing is that he's terribly like her father. He's identical to her father. They're both flamboyant, self-centred characters, very clever mountebanks, but what they've left behind is quite sparse.'

This is unfair to Boris, who is made to sound cruel and shallow. Petronella is also a very warm-hearted person. She may appear wilful and flighty, but she is capable of deep devotion, and she became deeply devoted to Boris. Friendship and the enjoyment of each other's company developed into love. They began a passionate affair.

From the first, there was one serious, and probably insuperable, obstacle to any kind of future together. Boris was married with four small children. A close woman friend of Petronella, whom for the sake of brevity we shall call Fop, defended her against the charge that she set out to break up Boris's marriage: 'She'd never before got involved with a married man. She didn't believe in it. I don't think women set out to take men away from other women unless they are complete bitches, and Petronella is not like that. She thinks divorce must be a terrible thing. She knows her father was terribly upset by his divorces, especially his third one.'

The affair was like any number of other office romances. It should not have happened, but once Boris and Petronella were attracted to each other, at least one of them would have to have shown a degree of self-restraint, if they were to avoid taking advantage of the opportunities open to them.

Boris and Petronella's warmest admirers would not say that either of them is notable for self-restraint. They incline towards boldness and impetuosity, rather than to the careful weighing-up of risks. They went out for long lunches and had assignations at the house Petronella shared with her mother in Cavendish Avenue, St John's Wood, which was within easy reach of the *Spectator* (by coincidence, the same road on which Boris's mother Charlotte had lived).

There was no reason why Boris's political or editorial colleagues should know he had broken his journey by bike from Westminster to Doughty Street at Petronella's house. Nor, if he went out to lunch, need anyone be certain where he had been.

If he wanted to see Petronella, he could postpone whatever lunch he had that day, tell the postponed character not to tell his secretary, Ann Sindall, what he had done, and pedal off to Cavendish Avenue.

Things were going very well for Boris. He saw no need to make the choices – politics or journalism, wife or mistress – which other men had to make. Boris got carried away and thought he could have it all. He said as much in an interview in the *Daily Mirror* in May 2002: 'I hate it when people say I'm a part-time MP. I work jolly hard. I am always at the 10 p.m. vote. I am a feminist icon. That's it! I am a juggler. I can have it all!'

Yet although the lovers were, as Fop puts it, 'basically very happy', Boris was also troubled: 'I know Boris felt guilty. He's family-minded. He adores his children – I think that was the big problem. And of course the children were very young. I mean, they still are quite young. But I don't blame him for not leaving Marina because I think it's impossible to leave four young children.'

Soon after the affair began, a woman of the world, a generation older than Petronella, asked her: 'How's your love life?'

Petronella: 'I'm having an affair.'

Woman: 'Oh good.'

Petronella: 'It's bad. He's married.'

Woman: 'Anyone I know?'

This sympathetic and intelligent woman takes up the story: 'I suddenly had a flash of intuition. I said, "Is it Boris?" I've always thought of Boris as a very faithful man. Petronella was very much in two minds about the whole thing – but obviously also rather smitten and very flattered. I think she was very thrilled by it all. And of course she hoped he'd leave his wife. And Boris quite rightly didn't. But I think she felt very betrayed by him. But this was a classic case of a man perhaps hinting he'd leave his wife. It's a classic story. It happens all the time. In this age of equality between the sexes, you would think it would work both ways. But single women are still very vulnerable to this. Someone like Boris has got so much energy, and is so political – one can see how it would happen in an office. Boris behaved as well as one can under these very unfortunate circumstances, where one is bound to hurt people – he was as kind to Petronella as possible – he wasn't ruthless. Many men would have been much more ruthless.'

If Boris needed to be ruthless with anyone, it was surely with himself. He did not force himself to think through the consequences of having an affair. For him, and for his beloved wife and children, those consequences were likely to be even more severe than normal, because of the publicity which his adventures might attract.

Boris's gift for unclarity, and for avoiding inconvenient questions, instead gave Petronella the idea that he was more committed to her than he really was. As a male friend in whom she confided said: 'Boris certainly gave the impression that especially if she got pregnant there would be a future.'

Boris was wrong to start the affair, but it would be wrong to judge him too harshly for doing so. The pleasures of self-righteousness are repellent. Which of us, if we had had Boris's opportunities, and had found Petronella attractive, would have refrained from having a fling with her? He was only doing what any number of other men, including any number of other politicians and journalists, have done now and in the past. Once we start to demand a higher standard of sexual morality from politicians than from the rest of society, we imply that we want to be governed by politicians who are uninterested in sex. Yet politicians tend, with some exceptions, to have an above-average interest in sex.

One of Boris's lovers mentioned his predilection for canoodling in the back of taxis, which she thought was unwise as he doesn't tip much. Another woman, at whom Boris began to make a pass when left alone for five minutes with her, sought to explain, for the benefit of her husband, the way in which he is attractive: 'He's the male equivalent of a blonde with big tits. He's a powerful blond, he's quite funny and he's easy and he'd be in love with you for a bit. Then he'd piss off.'

Boris's writing is suffused with sexual imagery. He sees sex almost everywhere. After describing the 'pair of "acoustic couplers", a bit like a rubber fetish bra', which journalists were using in 1987 to transmit copy down a telephone line, he continued: 'No one who has done it can forget the semi-sexual sense of release when the electronic moaning and squeaking indicated that the article had arrived.' On riding to hounds for the first time in February 2005, as a guest of Charles Moore and the East Sussex and Romney Marsh hunt, he remarked on 'the weird semi-sexual relation with the horse'. He wrote of the women who tried a food writer's horrible recipes: 'They loved his "I eat anything" approach, with its flagrant sexual message.'

Life itself is often compared by Boris to a virility test. After mentioning the popularity of Ann Widdecombe as a speaker to Conservative audiences, and the difficulty of addressing people 'who have known the ecstasy of Widdecombe', he goes on: 'I imagine it is like being asked to make love to a woman who has just achieved bliss in the arms of Errol Flynn, or Robin Cook, or someone.'

Boris has also mentioned hearing his daughter play the James Blunt song which goes, 'You're beautiful', and describes how Blunt has no chance of getting the woman he has seen.

Boris had some blunt advice for Blunt: 'Come on, man: stop being so indescribably wet. If she's so beautiful, stop standing there in your T-shirt and floppy fringe, and hush your hopeless falsetto crooning. Go out and get her, is my advice.'

This captures something essential about Boris and women. If he sees an attractive woman, his instinct is to try to make a connection with her. A woman described being noticed by Boris in the deep-freeze section of the Holloway Road branch of Waitrose. Boris was with Marina, who was looking harassed, and their children, who were all in the trolley. The woman had her hand on a bag of frozen peas when she felt herself being watched. Whatever she leaned over, Boris leaned over. For the next few minutes, whichever aisle she was in, it seemed Boris was at the end.

Another woman, whom we shall call X, said: 'When Boris is taking no notice of you, you don't exist. He just seemed rather a juvenile kind of a guy. But when he turns it on, he becomes immensely charming and you feel very flattered to be noticed by him. It's digital – like a switch – I suppose that's what charm is like.'

The Englishman in love can be a sadly ineffectual figure, as the beautiful Canadian Leah McLaren complained in a cover piece published by Boris in the *Spectator* on 27 July 2002. But Boris was not like that. His pursuit of X could not have been more ardent, though his ardour, she thought, was in part an expression of the great strain under which he was operating: 'It's stress, it's pressure. If he's low and wants to cheer himself up I can get twenty text messages. And proposals of marriage. Phone calls in the middle of the night if he's feeling low. I've probably had 100 proposals in total over the year. He does believe it in the moment he says it, because it's the way to win the game. There's nothing he wouldn't do, nothing he wouldn't say, to get me.'

It follows that if Boris makes you a proposal of marriage, you ought not to take it seriously. He may mean it in that instant, rather as a journalist may believe some nonsense he is writing. But Boris is not the sort of literal-minded character who can be pinned down by a literal-minded analysis. He is more fluid, more passionate and more imaginative than a pedant could begin to conceive. Accuracy does not matter in the slightest to him.

Boris also takes a cavalier attitude to mere morality. The knowledge that he is being sincere is good enough for him. He wants everyone to have a good time, is seldom if ever censorious about other people's behaviour, and considers it distinctly uncalled for when they blame him. As X put it: 'He doesn't think he's a bad person. If you tell him, "You're sleeping with Petronella – you're betraying Marina," he doesn't have it in him to blame himself. I think the deal is basically that he's ruled by his feelings. The moment he feels not totally fired up and in love with someone, he needs that fix again. He has what Aristotle calls an incontinent personality.'

The Puritan element in British life is alien to Boris, and also to Petronella. They share an instinct not to do what they are told. The older woman already quoted above said: 'Boris shouldn't have started it – and he did start it – I think he absolutely went for her . . . He's very undisciplined, emotionally. He needs to be reassured, rather surprisingly . . . The reason he's so appealing is he's got this extraordinary energy, which brings with it a certain extra sexual energy. Like Lloyd George. It's wrong, bad and terribly hurtful. Nor do I think he can be excused by saying he's got more energy than other people. But he has. He's so ebullient it's bound to spill over in other directions. I think it's true to say he never intended to leave his wife. A slightly mitigating thing. Not much.'

Petronella's older friend contemplated her verdict on Boris: 'He's just larger than life – he's just got an incredible, cunning charm – there's enough genuine apologetic stuff – enough genuine remorse. He's a much more cunning man than perhaps people think. A Houdini of moral dilemmas.'

Other people in the office could see that Boris and Petronella's relationship was more ardent than is usually the case. Screaming matches occurred between them, and Petronella would weep, and Boris would make it up with her by sending her flowers. But staff at the *Spectator* did not realise their colleagues were having an affair until a taxi driver brought in a tape one day which Boris had left behind in a cab.

The tape was of Petronella singing songs from *La Bohème*, and
Boris and Petronella had asked the driver to play it while they
canoodled in the back. Not the least striking aspect of this story
was the fact that they had left the tape behind. They were already
displaying a very high degree of carelessness. This was something
which came naturally to them. Like Boris, Petronella is the sort
of person who forgets to take her passport to the airport.

The affair began to be talked about. Some have said that
Conrad Black and Barbara Amiel promoted Boris's affair with
Petronella, which they regarded with proprietorial pride as 'their
adultery'. But Black told me: 'I did take it upon myself to say to
Boris that he should bear in mind that his wife as I understood
it was a divorce specialist.' Black also remembered saying to
Boris: 'I don't care if you're charged with bigamy, but Boris, for
the sake of that great cause which unites people up and down
the land of "let's make Boris a greater figure", you'd better be a
little careful.'

According to Black, Boris reacted with 'a complete motion
scenario, like a cartoon, moving every joint and limb at the same
time. I said, "Look, I will not raise it again. It's not a question of
morals – that's not my business."'

While talking to me about Petronella, Black wished to check
if his use of idiomatic English was correct. 'Tell me if I'm mis-
using this phrase,' he demanded, before saying: 'I can understand
the temptation when working at close quarters with Petronella
to give her a seeing-to.'

Sarah Sands, who was at that time deputy editor of the *Daily
Telegraph*, sent Boris a veiled warning, with James Fenton's harrowing poem, 'The Mistake', which she thought described all
too accurately where Boris was going wrong. Nicholas Garland,
the *Telegraph*'s political cartoonist, had shown her the poem. As
Sands said with a smile: 'I've always tried to save Boris from himself. My message to him was that he was risking what was
important by not choosing.'

Sands is a friend of Marina, whom she knew as a child, when their fathers moved in the same circles at the BBC. She remarked laughingly that while she had a friend in journalism, Melanie McDonagh, who believed in the stoning of adulterers, 'mine is more a nice, bourgeois matron's view of life, that men must behave'.

Once the affair was being talked about, it began, still worse, to be written about. Peter McKay started alluding to it in his Ephraim Hardcastle column in the *Daily Mail*. Columns of this sort thrive on some regular characters whose latest extraordinary exploits can be chronicled, and Boris became one of Ephraim's. A sort of teasing persecution began, which was all the more damaging for being based on fact.

As early as 8 February 2002, Ephraim wrote: 'Father of four Boris may be influenced unduly in his libertarian attitudes to sex by freethinking Petronella Wyatt, daughter of the late Tote boss Lord (Woodrow) Wyatt, with whom he works closely at the *Spectator*.'

On 30 May 2002 Ephraim did a piece about Petronella's thirty-fourth birthday party: 'Those invited included Miss Wyatt's editor/mentor at the *Spectator*, Tory MP Boris Johnson. The conspiratorial pair consult so often on work matters that there was a management inquiry into their sky-high mobile phone bills.'

Ephraim acknowledged that Boris was in the ascendant, reporting on 20 June: 'Custard-haired Tory MP Boris Johnson was 38 yesterday and is considered by friends to be well on track to achieve his ambition of being editor of the *Daily Telegraph* and Tory prime minister.'

On 27 September, Ephraim told the world that Petronella had said she was 'smartly but not revealingly dressed' when her 'clip-on silver and diamanté earrings' were seized by muggers in Kensington as she waited for a taxi: 'Be that as it may – saucy Miss Wyatt sometimes resembles a knife-thrower's glamorous assistant in a Continental circus – where was her mentor Boris Johnson, the Tory MP who edits the *Spectator*, when the attack took place?'

Petronella, according to a friend, 'was very annoyed and terrified' by Ephraim's coverage, because she didn't want news of the affair to get into the papers, 'which would make life very difficult for everyone'.

Members of Boris's staff were more and more often asked by *Daily Mail* readers what exactly was going on. Matthew Pencharz, who was working in Boris's office at the Commons, said: 'It tended to be the parents of friends. They loved Boris and they would all ask about it. I would say, "I know nothing. I don't know anything." But we all knew.'

McKay is unrepentant about the references he made to Boris's 'mentoring' of Petronella: 'I thought it would be a friendly warning to Boris that people were talking about it. Boris just seemed to be encouraged by it. I think Boris, like a lot of men, believed it was right to lie about sex. To give him his due, he never stopped my invitation to the *Spectator* summer party.'

Petronella had by this time started working for McKay at the *Daily Mail*. He pointed out that she is half-Hungarian, and suggested that a meeting of 'the wild east' had taken place between her and Boris. In McKay's opinion, if Boris had not been married, Petronella would have made a marvellous wife for him: 'She loves entertaining and she sings beautifully. She's very, very loyal. She's never said a single disloyal thing about Boris.'

Several times Petronella broke off the affair. On one occasion she even went to America for three months, and got engaged to an American, but the engagement did not last. To her mother's despair, she refused to marry anyone with whom she was not very much in love. Her mother had arrived in England at the age of eighteen as a refugee from Hungary, having lost everything, and took the pragmatic view that it was unnecessary to be in love with someone in order to marry them.

Petronella was a bit vague and forgetful about contraception, and early in 2003 she found herself pregnant by Boris. According to Fop, she told Boris immediately: 'He was never nasty about it. He said to her, "It's your decision. Whatever you do you have my full support." Many men in that situation would have gone and ordered her to have an abortion. He was very considerate.'

A woman friend of Boris said of Petronella: 'She told him that she was on the pill.'

Boris had much trouble with Petronella's mother, Verushka, who rang him all the time to tell him: 'You said you'd marry my daughter.' Verushka would not stop interfering and Boris felt unable to point out that Petronella was now a grown-up woman and should be allowed to lead her own life.

An agonising position now existed. Petronella's friends thought he was keeping her hanging on. She was under the impression he had said he was going to leave his wife, and Boris was under the impression he had not said this. He was protective of her, and was bad at breaking off the affair, or at keeping it broken off, because when he felt lonely he would ring her up. Petronella wanted a child with him, but at the same time was terrified of the consequences of having one. This impasse could not last for ever, yet went on a long time, threatening sorrow and even disaster for Boris and those closest to him.

19

Sellotaping Everything Together

LIKE MOST EDITORS, BORIS SOMETIMES FUNKED DEALING WITH problems to which there was no obvious solution, and he had more than half a mind to the political opinions of his proprietor, Conrad Black. But he was also out in front of the rest of his staff, scouting out new possibilities, seeing if he could pull off that surprise interview with Robert Mugabe, exploring anti-Americanism as well as paying lip-service to the neo-con line.

There were hawkish pro-Israeli pieces in the *Spectator*, of a kind that would have pleased Black, but Boris also published the pro-Palestinian pieces of Emma Williams, wife of his old friend Andrew Gilmour, who was by now working for the United Nations in Jerusalem. Boris's own report on the battle between George Bush and John Kerry to become President of the United States included a masterly put-down to both candidates: 'We don't have much of a choice in this election: between a man who inspires not much confidence and a man who inspires fractionally less.'

One of the most disagreeable tasks for an editor is to sack contributors who he thinks are not doing well enough. It was said that Boris took Susanna Gross, the *Spectator*'s bridge columnist, out to lunch in order to sack her, but slept with her instead.

'Who told you that?' Susanna said, looking fierce, when I had lunch with her.

'Well, I don't remember,' I said. 'I mean, as far as I know, it's what everyone in London thinks. Not that I go out much.'

'I'm outraged by the idea that he was going to sack me,' Susanna said. 'He certainly was not going to sack me. He was meant to be having lunch with me to tell me off because my *Spectator* column was always late, but he didn't even mention it, because he hates confrontation. We had such fun that we had a series of little lunches.'

I remarked in a mild tone that her bridge column was said, in the early days, to contain a lot of typographical errors, especially when Mark Amory, the books editor, who is also an expert bridge player, was not around to cast an eye over it, but she replied with indignation: 'Every bridge column has a lot of typos and it was teething problems in the first two months. I haven't had a typo for years.'

Susanna is a handsome woman in her thirties. She is literary editor of the *Mail on Sunday* and the daughter of Miriam and John Gross, who are eminent in literary London. She was so enraged by the thought that her bridge column could have been thought dispensable that I began to fear our lunch would be a failure. But I was eventually able to bring the conversation back to the altogether less controversial question of whether she and Boris had had an affair.

'No,' Susanna said. 'We had a flirtation but we didn't have an affair. Our non-affair was a few lunches. He was often dashing across town on his bike, so someone like Mary Wakefield [a member of the *Spectator*'s staff] thought he was having an affair. I like Mary Wakefield, but she's very mischievous.'

'Why was there no affair?' I asked, for I had been counting on Susanna to bulk out my as-yet rather meagre researches in this field.

'First of all because I was then with [the actor] Neil Pearson,'

Susanna said, 'and secondly because Boris was married with a mistress and with a crush on Mary Wakefield. Boris's wife had a crush on Neil, which completed the circle.'

'But could there have been an affair, had you and Boris both been free?' I asked, since she did not seem to resent this line of questioning. 'No,' she replied. 'I don't fancy him. He's too self-deprecating. I like a man to be a bit of a bastard. Also going about on his bike all day. Too sweaty. And also I was madly in love with my boyfriend – a very handsome actor.'

Susanna had something else she wanted to impart: 'I do think it's important to say in the middle of this that Boris and his wife are terribly happy. He loves her and she obviously loves him and thinks he's a wonderful father. They obviously still have in every way a very full marriage. He obviously loves having children. I think he'd be happy for his wife to have more children. The thing about Boris is that ideally he'd like more than one wife.'

Boris has an immensely strong but also rather extendable idea of family. He is in many ways a homely man, who after a meeting in some distant town prefers to drive back through the night to his wife and children than stay alone in a hotel. But like many enterprising men, he is attracted by the idea of maintaining more than one establishment. When he wrote about Jimmy Goldsmith, he referred in an admiring tone to the tycoon's 'three concurrent families' and eight children.

Susanna mentioned several times how cross she was with Boris for generally being late for lunch: 'When he was late for me the other day I was so angry – it's like training a pet – I saw him on his bike coming up to Soho House and I called him on his mobile and said: "There's no point coming in." He's the most good-natured man I've ever met. You can get as angry as you like with him.'

In the autumn of 2003, Boris brought out his second book, *Lend Me Your Ears*, billed as 'The Essential Boris Johnson'. It was a

500-page collection of his journalism, but did not include some of his most interesting work, including his defence of Darius Guppy and his attack on *Have I Got News For You*.

Lynn Barber, who used the book as the peg for an interview in the *Observer*, admitted that she had surrendered to his charm after only five minutes in his company. But she wondered, as so many others have, what Boris's sticking points are, what principles he would go to the barricades for, what he would consider a resigning matter. Boris tugged his hair, snorted and groaned: 'Uh. Ah. Ha. Mwa. I'm a bit of an optimist so it doesn't tend to occur to me to resign. I mean there are honourable people around who would seize opportunities to resign, but I tend to think of a way of Sellotaping everything together and quietly finding a way through, if I can.'

Sellotape is useful stuff, but not all that robust. Boris was ludicrously busy, and it is tempting to suggest that he came unstuck because he had taken on more commitments than he could possibly satisfy.

Boris's column in the *Telegraph* continued after he became editor of the *Spectator*. The lateness of his copy drove some of his colleagues into paroxysms of rage. In the opinion of Charles Moore, the then editor of the *Telegraph*, 'Extreme unpunctuality is always a sign of selfishness.' He added that Boris was 'not horrible, but selfish'.

When a television programme was made about Boris, Charles said you could use of him the words used by David Niven of Errol Flynn: 'You knew where you were with Errol Flynn. He always let you down.'

Moore realised as soon as he had said this that it would be taken out of context. He had been asked what Conrad Black thought of Boris, and had replied that sometimes when Conrad thought of Boris, he was reminded of David Niven on Errol Flynn.

Boris also wrote about cars for *GQ*. Ann Sindall, his secretary, said: 'The car articles – so much work goes in to doing them. These guys at *GQ* deliver these cars. They leave them at his house and think he'll drive them to Henley. They get towed away and taken to the pound. I tell them they've got to get them from the pound. He came in once and said, "I can't find the car." I said, "What colour was it?" He said, "It's red or purple or green."'

Sindall once rang Paul Henderson at *GQ* and told him: 'If you're daft enough to give the guy an expensive car, go and find it yourself!'

Boris tended to miss the session at which he would have been shown by the delivery driver how to use the car. Sindall said: 'The thing is he's so busy sometimes I'll have Mary Wakefield outside the *Spectator* offices learning how to use the car. He'll ring me and ask, "How do I open the door?"'

Wakefield confirmed this account: 'He called me all through Saturday to get me to talk him through it, because he hadn't concentrated and couldn't work out how to open the door from the inside. He must have been stuck inside it. You had to turn a little dial to open the door.'

Boris loves driving fast cars – he mentions in a 2005 *Spectator* article that he has driven at 160mph on the M40 – and quite often describes them in sexual terms. He discussed a new Bentley in terms of penis size. He would sometimes be summoned to attend a 'bonding session' with other Tory MPs, and on these occasions it would amuse Ann Sindall to ensure that he arrived in a particularly expensive car.

But despite all the confusion behind the scenes, Boris was still the coming man. In October 2003, 'G2', the second section of the *Guardian*, appeared with a large, unnamed picture of Boris on his bike, and the headline, 'Only one man can save the Tories'. A month later Michael Howard made Boris a vice-chairman of the Conservative Party with special responsibility for campaigning. Boris's gift for cheering up the rank and file had been recognised. His talents were apparently so big that he could not be ignored.

Further promotion was not long in coming. In May 2004, Howard made Boris shadow arts minister. It was a minor post, which did not carry membership of the shadow Cabinet, but Boris made the most of it. Within minutes, as the following day's *Guardian* reported, he had issued a six-point programme:

> Day one and I have a six-point programme. I haven't cleared this with anybody, but here's what I think.
>
> On coming to power I am going to institute a Windows spell-check in English so that schoolchildren in this country no longer feel they have got it wrong when they spell words correctly.
>
> The Greeks are going to be given an indistinguishable replica of all the Parthenon marbles, done in the most beautiful marble dust to end this acrimonious dispute between our great nations.
>
> I am going to open up the bandwidth, so there is much more freedom on the radio stations. I am going to reduce some of the stuff allocated to the Pentagon, so you can get the Rolling Stones in Oxfordshire. I am fed up with just listening to treacly old Magic.
>
> Fourth? I can't remember what point four is. Ah, yes. We are going to convene a summit with Damien Hirst and the rest of the gang at which they are going to explain to the nation what it all means. Let us have a national 'mission to explain' by the Saatchi mob, which will be massively popular.
>
> We're going to have a national poetry Olympiad to restore rhyme and scansion. There will be some sort of stoop of wine for the winning prize.
>
> Point six is to move away from Labour's grim, utilitarian approach to culture. I took particular exception to Charles

Clarke's attack on the Classics. If we can't study ancient languages, culture and art, we are deracinating ourselves.

Boris sportingly agreed to take part in an arts quiz devised by the *Daily Telegraph*, in which he scored only seven and a half out of twenty. Afterwards he said: 'I did terribly. My feelings of inadequacy and humility have been totally reinforced. But ask me again after I have done a year in the job, and I'd like to think I'd get them all right.'

No Labour minister dared take part in this quiz.

Eighteen days after his appointment, Boris made his first appearance at the Dispatch Box as a shadow minister. I was privileged to watch this event for the *Daily Telegraph*, and reported:

He wore a baggy light-grey suit in which he looked as if he had often fallen asleep as he worked on his question, and his pallor was such that one could guess he had not been out of doors for the past eighteen days . . . From the press gallery it was possible to note that Johnson had covered an entire A4 sheet of paper in messy handwriting, and as culture questions proceeded, he could be seen adding what looked like whole new paragraphs to his already lengthy question.

Some of his fans began to fear he might have over-prepared himself.

At last, when the tension had become almost unbearable, the Speaker called Johnson to speak.

He sprang to the Dispatch Box and started to flay the Government for allowing so many playing fields to be built over.

Last year, he pointed out, the Government had condemned no fewer than 404 playing fields to 'total extinction', and 'given the decline of contact sport in part due to litigation . . . will the minister, apart from encouraging people to run round concrete roads', arrange an annual meeting 'to arrest the decline of school playing fields?'

It was a magnificent question. In a desperate attempt to derail Johnson, Labour MPs started shouting 'too long', but he was unstoppable.

The belief that Boris would go higher was widely shared. Toby Young bet Dominic Lawson £1,000 that Boris would be Prime Minister within ten years. Young has since said that he was 'slightly in his cups' when he made this wager, but at the time Boris had such an extraordinary gift for making news that anything seemed possible. On Thursday 3 June 2004, the *Spectator* appeared on the streets of London with a political column in which Peter Oborne discussed the enmity between Tony Blair and Gordon Brown:

> The underlying tension came to the surface last week in a most unexpected way. Boris Johnson, editor of this magazine, was sitting stationary astride his bicycle in Pall Mall, waiting for the traffic lights to turn green. Suddenly he found that he was not alone. Jonathan Powell, Downing Street Chief of Staff and Tony Blair's most senior adviser, had drawn up alongside. Johnson raised the subject of relations between No. 10 and the Treasury. Powell cast his eyes heavenward. 'It's a Shakespearean tragedy,' declared Powell. 'Gordon Brown is like the guy who thinks he's going to be king but never gets it. He's never going to be Prime Minister.'

Friday's papers reported Downing Street's reaction to this story. In George Jones's account in the *Daily Telegraph*, Blair's official spokesman admitted that Powell and Boris had met, but insisted Powell had not said that Brown would not become

Prime Minister: 'There was some light-hearted banter on Pall Mall but the last person Jonathan would confide his innermost thoughts to is Boris.'

Jones quoted Boris, who said Powell's memory 'must be playing him false'. Boris insisted the account which appeared in the *Spectator* was 100 per cent accurate: 'I'm absolutely certain – I went away and wrote it down afterwards. I have absolutely no doubt whatsoever.'

But Powell's partner, Sarah Helm, told me that 100 per cent accuracy was the last thing Boris could claim: 'There was an element of truth in it. There was a mention of Macbeth, but most of it was Boris telling a good story. Boris's question – "So you don't think Brown will ever become Labour leader?" – was put into Jonathan's mouth. It was a fantastic, Boris-esque example of a story being half-way there but not standing up.'

As with so many of Boris's stories, one could say that while the details were dubious, the general drift was right. Jones quoted an 'authoritative source' who described the atmosphere between the Blair and Brown camps as 'poisonous'. Boris had managed, with his mention of 'a Shakespearean tragedy', to dramatise something that unquestionably existed.

Ginny Dougary, who interviewed Boris not long after the Powell story, asked him whether he felt it was dishonourable to repeat what Powell had told him. Boris said: 'I did have a few qualms actually, to be honest. But I thought it was a jolly interesting story.'

What were his qualms? 'Well, that we were there in the fraternity of cyclists and [very big sigh] there you go, anyway, it's done.' Dougary, by the way, joined Boris's huge fan club: 'I would defy anyone to spend an hour in his presence and not be charmed . . . Boris for Prime Minister.'

Boris only took up cycling in London in 1999, but he was by now perhaps the most famous cyclist in Britain. He declared in a column that he was proud to be a member of 'that hated minority that rides a bicycle' and would defend his right to 'use my bike as my office'. He made these defiant remarks after he was upbraided by a woman in Islington for talking on his mobile while cycling. Boris had emerged as an outspoken champion of the right to use a mobile phone while on his bike: 'Just as I will never vote to ban hunting, so I will never vote to abolish the freeborn Englishman's time-hallowed and immemorial custom, dating back as far as 1990 or so, of cycling while talking on a mobile.'

In March 2006, Boris came off his bike for the third time in seven years, and was treated at Guy's & St Thomas' Hospital for an injured arm. In a short piece for the next day's *Guardian*, he said that he had been going at 'a responsible speed' towards 'a traffic light which was irrefutably green' when a group of French tourists started to cross the road. Boris shouted 'Ho!' and tried to weave around a large Frenchman who leapt directly into his path.

Boris identified 'the catatonically oblivious pedestrian, in particular the foreign tourist who thinks the traffic is coming the other way,' as the greatest threat to cyclists. This produced a letter from a *Guardian* reader, Andrew Stilwell, who said: 'If Boris Johnson casts his mind back to autumn 2005, he may just recall bicycling at top speed through a red light at the intersection of Bloomsbury Way and Bury Place as I was attempting to cross the road. I managed to avoid an afternoon at Guy's & St Thomas', but it was a close thing.'

When an interviewer remarked to him that 'cyclists drive other commuters ballistic', Boris replied: 'They're jealous. It's sheer jealousy at the way we pass them with ease and grace while they are stuck in queues.'

Cycling had several attractions for Boris. It was energetic, dangerous and anarchic: for most of the time, nobody controls the London cyclist and he or she decides from one moment to the

20

The Calm Before the Storm

A FRENCHMAN, LA ROCHEFOUCAULD, SAID THERE IS something not displeasing to us in the misfortune of our best friends, but this elegant formula does not do justice to the British press. Our newspapers cannot bear it when someone is too successful. As soon as they have created a hero, they try to drag him back down into the mud.

In July 2004, Tom Baldwin, a political reporter on *The Times*, wrote: 'I don't know when I really started hating Boris Johnson, but I will try to tell you why.' Baldwin considered various reasons for hating Boris before saying it was none of those: 'No, *the* reason has something to do with him being perfectly pleasant to just about everybody and just about everybody apparently thinking he's great . . . I hate him because he's been built up and not yet knocked down. He has defied the usual laws of gravity.'

Boris was ripe for shaking, but was not the first person at the *Spectator* to get done over. The hounds of Grub Street first fastened their jaws around some of his colleagues. Within the space of a few months, the magazine acquired a reputation as a hotbed of illicit liaisons and became known to a wider audience as the *Sextator*.

It was possible, with the benefit of hindsight, to see the signs of strain building up months before. An editorial conference I attended on the morning of Thursday 27 November 2003, just after Conrad Black's troubles had burst upon an astonished world, indicated a degree of tension, even of hysteria.

Boris began by saying something about 'the magazine's future' – i.e., whether it would be bought by someone else because of Black's difficulties. In answer to this disturbing question, Boris said: 'I don't know.'

Christopher Fildes, the *Spectator's* long-serving City columnist and a member of its board, said: 'I'd like to add my don't know to your don't know.'

Boris asked Fildes if Black would go to prison. Fildes said he thought not, as the problem was not fraud, but confusion between Black's private and public companies, leading to money getting into the wrong pocket. He said how sorry he was about Black, as he was a very fine proprietor.

Immediately after this conference, when Boris had left the room for a moment and Kimberly Fortier, the magazine's American publisher, had come in, a spectacular row broke out. Rod Liddle, the magazine's associate editor, who had been brought on to the magazine by Boris in 2002 after being sacked as editor of BBC Radio's *Today* programme, generally looked as if he had spent the night clubbing before crashing out for an hour or two on a park bench, but this morning seemed in an even rougher state than normal. He had almost lost his voice and was trying to get out of speaking at a debate organised that evening by Kimberly. After he lit a cigarette, the following dialogue took place:

KIMBERLY: 'You shouldn't smoke!'
LIDDLE: 'Don't you fucking well tell me how to live my life!'
KIMBERLY: 'If you've got bronchitis, you shouldn't smoke. I'm telling you that as a friend.'

LIDDLE: 'I'm not fucking speaking! I can't fucking speak!'
BORIS [re-entering the room] 'Pax vobiscum! Hey, hey, it's
    Thanksgiving! Peace!'
KIMBERLY: 'I'd rather be at home cooking the turkey.'
MARY WAKEFIELD [leaving the room]: 'I don't mind the row,
    it's the reconciliation scene I can't stomach.'

Next Thursday there was another row. The magazine had appeared that morning on the newsstands with a small but significant error. It carried the price for the Christmas double issue, which is twice the normal price, and Kimberly was frantic, convinced that we would lose 20 per cent of our newsstand sales. In what struck the editorial staff as a waste of our time, she brought in one of her staff to give us a lecture about late deadlines.

Boris, to his credit, threw Kimberly and her sidekick out of the room, after which for good measure he threw out a Channel 4 film crew who were filming the proceedings. He then readmitted the film crew, on condition that they did not show his row with Kimberly.

I rather liked Kimberly, and respected her ability to sell advertising, but she could get extremely cross with people. For most of the time, she was friendly to me, while also indicating that I was the kind of bumbling no-hoper who could never be of any interest to her. There were only two occasions when I incurred her wrath, both of which cast some light on Boris.

The first was after I had written a self-pitying piece for the *Daily Telegraph* in which I complained that my wife, Sally, wanted me to help look after our three small children. This article included an exchange in which Sally threatened to go back to work, to which I replied: 'Oh darling, you'd just be one of those horrid driven women.'

While writing this article I consulted Boris, who agreed that it was jolly inconvenient having a wife who went out to work. Boris has an acute sense of what can and can't be said, but it is clear that he very much regrets the rise of the career woman, at least in so far as it affects the home comforts of the career man. He offered me the following quote for my article, on condition that I did not mention him by name: 'Nobody takes any interest in whether you have any socks or indeed pants. My wife buys herself pyjamas, but she never buys any for me. I've totally run out.'

I put in this lament by a neglected man without saying who had uttered it, but Marina immediately spotted that it came from Boris, and teased both me and him about it the next time I bumped into them at a party. Her laughing reaction made me think how lucky Boris was to be married to her. Boris doesn't fall in love with horrible women, and in Marina he had found someone who could see the funny side even of male whingeing.

Kimberly, however, was not amused. She assumed, wrongly, that the article was about herself, and flew into a rage. The following Thursday she caught me on the stairs and told me that if I wanted a wife who stayed at home, I had no business wasting my time hanging about at the *Spectator* and should go off to the City and earn some real money.

The second time I irritated Kimberly was when I wrote an editorial for the *Spectator* attacking David Blunkett, the Home Secretary, for destroying our ancient liberties. Kimberly intercepted me on the stairs and said 'I didn't realise you were so nasty', while I wondered why she had taken the trouble to read such an unglamorous part of the magazine by ten o'clock on a Thursday morning. If anyone had put it to me that Kimberly was having an affair with Blunkett, I would have given an incredulous laugh.

In July 2004, Rod Liddle, the magazine's associate editor, was revealed to be having an affair with Alicia Munckton, the amiable young woman who answered the telephone at the reception desk on the ground floor.

Boris was highly amused by the exposure of the affair.

According to Liddle, 'Boris broke off discussing my next article to howl with laughter.' But Liddle's wife, Rachel Royce, cut up rough, and wrote at least a dozen articles denouncing him. She called his behaviour a 'classic philandering-husband-meets-muppet story' and said that having won ten tons of horse manure in a raffle, she would arrange for it to be delivered to the *Spectator*.

One could see why Royce felt furious. She and Liddle had lived together for eleven years but had only got married in January 2004, by which time, unknown to her, he was already seeing Munckton, a blonde who was twenty-one years younger than him. Worse than these admittedly provoking details, Liddle and Royce had two young sons.

So as usual in these cases, two stories ran in parallel: public soap opera and private agony. Liddle admitted in an interview with Cassandra Jardine in the *Daily Telegraph* that he was worried about his boys: 'I wish I saw more of them . . . It's scary to see how it affects them. I can't excuse my behaviour. It is tempting to say these things happen, but they don't unless you allow them to.'

The Liddle story was soon overtaken by the astonishing news that the Home Secretary was having an affair with the publisher of the *Spectator*. The story of Blunkett and Kimberly's affair broke in August 2004.

Boris himself still seemed in pretty good nick. On 14 September 2004 the launch party for his thriller, *Seventy-Two Virgins*, was held at the Travellers' Club in Pall Mall. The book, about a group of Islamic terrorists who seize the President of the United States while he is giving a speech at Westminster, is not a masterpiece, but it was still an amazing effort by such a busy man. It included a flirtation with anti-Americanism, and showed some sympathy and insight into a great diversity of characters, including William Eric Kinloch Onyeama, a traffic warden of kingly

West African lineage whose first three names are the same as the first three names of Sir Eric Anderson, Boris's old headmaster at Eton.

Quentin Letts, in a review for the *Evening Standard*, wrote: 'The Tory MP in the book is terrified that a sex-related indiscretion of his is about to be exposed in the *Daily Mirror*. It is interesting that Johnson should write so convincingly about a politician's fear of scandal.'

In the book itself, Boris's MP character, Roger Barlow, says after finding no revelations about himself in a tabloid newspaper: 'He felt like laughing at his own egocentricity. There was something prurient about the way he wanted to read about his own destruction.'

When Sue Lawley interviewed Boris on *Desert Island Discs*, she asked him about the book: 'Well as if you hadn't got enough on your plate you published a novel last autumn, didn't you, *Seventy-Two Virgins*, about a home-grown terrorist attack on London. It was chillingly prescient.'

BORIS: 'Eerily prescient. Uncannily. Four suicide bombers, travelling from the north [as was to happen in London in July 2005], and the heroine was called Cameron.'

LAWLEY: 'Yes, that's true, I hadn't thought about that.'

BORIS: 'Right name, wrong sex.'

LAWLEY: 'But it was weird.'

BORIS: 'It was weird.'

LAWLEY: 'But even weirder, actually, we have to say, it's a comic novel.'

BORIS: 'It is, it is meant to be a comic novel, yes, parts of it.'

LAWLEY: 'Well, it is quite comic and there's this chap called Roger Barlow who's sort of a bumbling Tory MP who rides a bicycle.'

BORIS: 'Yes, I know, but that's been grossly exaggerated. He sort of fades from the scene a bit.'

LAWLEY: 'He doesn't. He crops up, I've read it.'

BORIS: 'Gosh, have you? You're incredibly kind.'

LAWLEY: 'And he's – you know what I'm going to say next, don't you – excessively exercised as to whether the tabloids are going to find out whether he's having an extra-marital affair.'

BORIS: 'I don't think you've read the novel with quite the attention it deserves, Sue.'

LAWLEY: 'Possibly not.'

BORIS: 'I think you need to go back, because otherwise people are going to come away with the wrong idea. I'm going to insist on this point. That's not what he's worried about. What he's done, if you remember, is he's invested unwisely in a – is it called lingerie? Lingerie – he's invested in . . .'

Barlow has lost £20,000 by investing in a lingerie shop called Eulalie. This revelation occurs at the very end of the book, for the rest of which we has been led to believe that the MP has been having an affair.

When P. G. Wodehouse ridiculed, in the figure of Roderick Spode, a fascist leader, he gave the would-be dictator a dark secret, which was to be the proprietor of a lingerie shop called Eulalie. Boris was following one of his literary idols. In the sunlit world of Wodehouse, Bertie Wooster can get into any number of scrapes, but is always rescued in the end, whether by Jeeves or by the self-defeating machinations of his foes or even, occasionally, by his own unexpected resourcefulness.

As the action in *Seventy-Two Virgins* reaches its climax, Boris allows Roger Barlow to get hold of a weapon and administer the *coup de grâce* to the chief terrorist: 'Then Roger drew back his arm with a wristy motion he had first learned as a child when thwacking the tops of the thistles in the meadow, and hit him very hard, on the base of the skull.'

There are thistles at Nethercote, the Johnson farm on Exmoor, which Boris had thwacked as a boy. He was drawing himself as the have-a-go hero who saves the free world. The book was a fantasy where an absurd and minor figure suddenly comes good.

At the start of September 2004, *Vanity Fair* magazine billed Boris as 'the Tory MP who could one day be Britain's Prime Minister'. It published an admiring profile of him by Michael Wolff, who ended by comparing him to two actors who went into politics: 'He is, it occurs to me, as he woos and charms and radiates good humor, Ronald Reagan. And Arnold Schwarzenegger . . . He is, I find, inspirational.'

No other British MP could have been compared to Reagan or Schwarzenegger. Only Boris was in a position to make the leap from celebrity, or ham actor, to serious politician. The public was willing him on, for it loves such implausible transformations, but the leader of Boris's party was about to cut this maverick exhibitionist down to size.

21

Operation Scouse-grovel

WITHIN A MONTH OF *VANITY FAIR*'S PAEAN OF PRAISE, the storm started to break over Boris. The Liddle and Kimberly scandals can be seen in retrospect as the first flashes of thunder and lightning, heralding mortal danger for the man billed as the next Prime Minister but three.

The first bolt of lightning struck him in a most confusing and unexpected way. Many people will recall that Boris had to go on a mission to apologise to the people of Liverpool, without being able to remember exactly what he said about them that was so offensive. But even at the time it was hard to tell what exactly had gone wrong, especially from the brief phrases in the offending article which were quoted over and over again in other accounts of the row.

On Thursday 14 October 2004 the *Spectator* appeared with an editorial about the reaction to the murder of Ken Bigley, a British hostage who had been working in Iraq but came from Liverpool. The article criticised 'the mawkish sentimentality of a society that has become hooked on grief and likes to wallow in a sense of vicarious victimhood', and went on:

> The extreme reaction to Mr Bigley's murder is fed by the
> fact that he was a Liverpudlian. Liverpool is a handsome

city with a tribal sense of community. A combination of economic misfortune – its docks were, fundamentally, on the wrong side of England when Britain entered what is now the European Union – and an excessive predilection for welfarism have created a peculiar, and deeply unattractive, psyche among many Liverpudlians. They see themselves whenever possible as victims, and resent their victim status; yet at the same time they wallow in it. Part of this flawed psychological state is that they cannot accept that they might have made any contribution to their misfortunes, but seek rather to blame someone else for it, thereby deepening their sense of shared tribal grievance against the rest of society. The deaths of more than 50 Liverpool football supporters at Hillsborough in 1989 was undoubtedly a greater tragedy than the single death, however horrible, of Mr Bigley; but that is no excuse for Liverpool's failure to acknowledge, even to this day, the part played in the disaster by drunken fans at the back of the crowd who mindlessly tried to fight their way into the ground that Saturday afternoon. The police became a convenient scapegoat, and the *Sun* newspaper a whipping-boy for daring, albeit in a tasteless fashion, to hint at the wider causes of the incident.

It is not Boris's style to be wilfully abusive: on the rare occasions when he attacks people, he does it in a good-humoured tone. The author of the piece was Simon Heffer, whose original draft was nastier about Bigley himself. Stuart Reid, the *Spectator's* deputy editor, removed these taunts, by comparison with which the remaining insults thrown at Liverpudlians seemed so mild as to be harmless.

But the leader provoked what Boris himself described, in an article a few days later for the *Liverpool Daily Post*, as 'one of those sudden media firestorms: the cameras on the doorstep, the phone ringing off the hook, the endless requests for interviews, the shouted abuse'.

Some of this protest was genuine, but some was concocted by those who saw an opportunity to embarrass the Conservative leader Michael Howard or the party in general. It was, to say the least, extremely unfortunate that the article had grossly under-stated the death toll at the Hillsborough disaster, in which 96 people died, and had blamed drunken fans at the back of the crowd, when this cause was specifically ruled out by the inquiry report.

When Howard, a passionate supporter of Liverpool Football Club, was first asked to disown the piece, he thought a clarifica-tion issued by Boris might suffice. But it proved impossible for Howard's staff to agree a form of words with Boris, who was worried he would be disowning something in his own magazine. Heffer told Boris 'to tell Howard that I wrote it – I offered to own up – but Boris to his credit said no'.

As the story ran out of control, Howard was lobbied by people from Liverpool Football Club and by Tory candidates in the north-west. He was warned that when he attended a forth-coming Liverpool game, he would be booed, and on Saturday – two days after the offending piece had appeared on the streets of London – he ordered Boris to go to the city to apologise.

Boris was in two minds about whether to go. In retrospect, it seems clear that he should have refused Howard's order. The most handsome way for Boris to demonstrate his own inde-pendence, and the independence of the *Spectator*, would have been to resign his front-bench post, apologise for the errors of fact in the editorial, and make his own arrangements for any visit he might or might not make to Liverpool.

But he reluctantly agreed to Howard's request, having failed to realise (as Boris put it in the following week's *Spectator*) that 'Michael's brilliant spin-doctors would present this as some sort of disciplinary procedure, in which the ideal headline was intended to be: "Shamed Tory buffoon Johnson in Liverpool grovel – Iron Mike gets tough".'

Howard is in many ways a delightful man, but he also has a ferocious temper, and he cannot bear indiscipline among his sub-ordinates. He got his way over the visit to Liverpool, but he and his staff grossly underestimated Boris's star appeal. As one of Howard's people put it, 'Boris was the story and we weren't pre-pared for that.'

The mission was conceived in such a way as to invite ridicule. Conservative Campaign Headquarters, which we shall call by its traditional name of Central Office as that was how most Tories still referred to it, was put in charge of the arrangements. It was decided that Boris should talk only to the Liverpool media, and not the national media. This was an untenable idea, for anyone who had given the matter a moment's dispassionate thought would have realised that the scores of journalists and photogra-phers who were dispatched from London to cover Boris's trip were hardly going to accept that they could not see this national figure for themselves. Many of these correspondents already knew Boris quite well, and all of them realised they would be treated by their offices as total incompetents if they failed to find him.

Boris himself warned at a meeting two days before the trip that Central Office was getting over-involved, and suggested that it would be better to go up and do a press conference with everyone who wanted to see him. But Howard's people wanted to control everything, and insisted on treating the trip as an expedition into cannibal country. As one of them put it, 'We couldn't send him on his own. He would have been eaten alive.'

Another member of the team said: 'We booked him in under a false name at some hotel, which was probably in retrospect a mistake. Everybody felt it was a complete nightmare from start to finish. I've blotted most of it from my memory, I'm happy to say. They felt it needed large men to head up there because of expected trouble. They were going round the office the previous week saying, "You're large, you're large." Richard Shackleton, Nick Carter and Matt Cumani are all a good six-foot-plus, and the fourth member of the party, Ramesh Chhabra, is quite beefy. They were selected for their ability to take part in a rugby scrum.'

It must be said that not everyone took quite such a dim view of Boris's behaviour as Central Office did. It was quite common to hear people say that they agreed with him about Liverpool, and even in the city itself there did not seem to be many people who were thirsting to tear him limb from limb. In the press, too, he had eloquent supporters, including Michael Gove, whose defence of Boris appeared in *The Times* on Tuesday 19 October 2004:

If we Britons love our shambolic bumblers, then we must expect them, sometimes, to bumble into something of a shambles ... Alongside the disciplined ranks of parliamentary infantry, we need a few Cossacks, whose dazzling swordplay may not always hit the target, and may even cause the odd self-inflicted wound, but whose dash, verve and sheer élan help to lend the cause colour ... For many contemporary Britons, part of the problem with Parliament is its crushing of individuality. A culture that seems to value the robotic on-messageness of a Hoon or Milburn over the freshness of a Boris must have something wrong with it. More than that, Boris himself seems to recognise, whether intuitively or through observation, that celebrity now plays the role in politics that possession of an aristocratic name or a distinguished war record used to perform. It gives you a right to be heard. Celebrity allows you into people's lives and homes, where they give you permission to share your views, in a way that others are denied ... So I for one am happy to say: let us acknowledge that his weaknesses as much as his strengths are all too visible, but let us cherish this free spirit while we still have him – the MP for Henley, the People's Boris.

Boris's four minders set to work to carry out the insane strategy of keeping him away from most of the press, and from just about the entire population of Liverpool. Shackleton and Chhabra formed the advance party, which went up a day early and carried out a reconnaissance of the places Boris would visit, including the Liverpool Institute for the Performing Arts.

Carter and Cumani had the job of escorting Boris to Liverpool on the evening of 19 October 2004. It was reported in the *Evening Standard* in London that journalists were staking out the stations, Euston and Lime Street, which Boris would use if he travelled from London to Liverpool by train. The airports from which one might fly to Liverpool were also being watched. The Conservatives therefore hired what one of Boris's minders called 'this enormous fuck-off top-of-the-range Range Rover, black with tinted glass, a monstrous brute. It couldn't have been more indiscreet. We took this brute up to Boris's house off the Holloway Road and drove round the block a couple of times just to make sure it wasn't staked out. One of us walked up and down his road, and knocked on his door. Boris went upstairs to pack his things, and at about 8 p.m. we set off. We had various plans in case we were followed. We were going to go to the House of Commons, drop Boris off with one of us at St Stephen's Entrance, walk him through the underpass and to Portcullis House and pick him up in the Range Rover there.'

But the Range Rover was not followed and they started the long drive to Liverpool. Boris sat in the back, either editing the *Spectator* or sleeping. According to one of his minders, Boris's mood varied between 'this is all an incredible pain in the arse and I'm hating every minute of it' and 'the schoolboyish sense that it was all a jolly wheeze'.

At two in the morning they arrived at a hotel in the Sefton district of Liverpool which belonged to a chain with which the Conservative Party had a corporate account. In the minder's opinion it was 'a pretty sleazy dive and freezing cold'. The rooms were booked in the name of Birkenshaw, but according to the minder, this was not an assumed name for Boris, but the real name of the man at Central Office who dealt with such matters.

The big story at breakfast time on local television was 'where is Boris Johnson – please phone in'. The hunt was on. Quentin Letts of the *Daily Mail* managed to contact Boris on his mobile phone: 'He was finishing off a newspaper column. Where the heck was he? "I don't know where I am," he blustered. "Can't talk, man. Gotta go!" Click, brrrrrrrr, went the receiver.'

Boris went for an early-morning breath of air in Sefton Park, where he met a jogger, who according to Boris said: 'Welcome to Liverpool. Never mind the bollocks.' Boris also did a quick exclusive interview with the evening *Echo*, which was sworn to secrecy.

His minders left him for a couple of hours at the hotel and did a final recce. It had been agreed that a 'pool' of twelve journalists would be allowed to follow Boris. One of the minders takes up the tale:

At this point we go into the dream sequence. What happened was so surreal, the picture goes a bit shimmery about the edges. I had to pick up the pooled hacks in a pub car park in Sefton and take them to the Liverpool Institute for the Performing Arts. It was a bit like taking a school outing. I called the register, someone distracted me and an extra person was smuggled in. I had twelve journalists with mobiles. It was just impossible. The first event was a photo call with Boris at the Institute. I got them there and we waited for him. Then the awful news came down my mobile that Boris was basically throwing a strop and they were going to be ten to fifteen minutes late. Boris told them: 'This is all a farce. This is going wrong. I know how to look after myself.' This was where the plan just fell apart. I don't know if you've seen the film *Zulu*, but it was a bit like that, when the British at Rorke's Drift suddenly see the Zulu *impi* coming over the brow of the hill. This army, this *impi* of hacks, with tripods and notebooks instead of assegais and shields, poured down the hill in a torrent. I was the only advance man there. I was swept aside. There was nothing I could do. Sixty seconds later Boris sweeps up in Matt Cumani's car, preceded by four police officers in a police Range Rover. Boris met the director of the Institute. There were shouts of 'Boris, have you come up here to apologise?' It was just bedlam after that. How were we going to separate the people in the pool from the rest of this Zulu army? I hadn't a bloody clue who was who. The antipathy towards us from the non-pool people was immense. At the bronze gates into the Institute we were vetting people and people were saying: 'Do you know who I am? How dare you keep *The Times* out?' All the time various broadcasters were ringing and asking how to get hold of Boris. The press office at Conservative HQ was also ringing and saying, 'This looks awful,' so I said to them, 'How do you think I feel?'

A press officer who had been left behind in London says: 'Those of us who were mercifully not sent on the mission but were watching the television in the office – our hands were wringing in total despair as it went from one catastrophe to another.'

According to Simon Hoggart, whose sketch of the occasion appeared beneath a large picture of the back of Boris's head on the front page of the next day's *Guardian*, the man at the eye of the storm 'performed rather well'.

Boris apologised for the hurt he had caused, and for the error made about the Hillsborough disaster. But he stood by the 'thrust' of the piece: 'It would be mad to say that I had undergone a pre-frontal lobotomy and everything I said last week was no longer operative.'

One of the minders takes up the tale: 'We were there for a good hour, with Boris watching various sorts of dancing shows, and then we slipped out the back, Matt brought his car round and we went to our next assignment, which was BBC Merseyside. Boris was being fairly game about it. He was going to do a phone-in and was going to abjectly apologise for his comments, or at least for Simon Heffer's comments. As we got there Kevin Bouquet was doing his piece to camera for the one o'clock news and Boris walked across behind him and said, "I never said that." The whole place descended into total confusion and laughter. The BBC thought it was so good they wanted it done again. Boris went and did his phone-in and a huge row erupted because George Eustice had promised Channel 4 they could go in and film the phone-in, and the BBC said they wanted to do that. We managed to resolve that.'

But Boris was still defying his leader by saying things like: 'Michael Howard was completely wrong to say that the article was "nonsense from beginning to end". I don't think he can have read it properly.'

Someone from Conservative HQ rang up one of Boris's minders to observe: 'It's all going horribly wrong, you prat. Get a grip on it.' Another apparatchik from Tory HQ actually rang a minder to say that Boris had got his lines wrong, and must be told to say the right lines.

Worse was to follow. Paul Bigley, the brother of the murdered hostage, phoned the radio programme to tell Boris: 'You're a self-centred, pompous twit; even your body language on TV is wrong. You don't look right, never mind act right. Get out of public life!'

Boris tried to apologise, but Bigley went on: 'Get out of private [sic] life, and leave us alone!'

Shortly before Boris left the phone-in, one of his minders found a woman dressed in pink lying in wait for him in the BBC car park.

Minder: 'Who are you?'

Woman: 'I want to talk to Boris Johnson. I'm a professional griever.'

Minder: 'What do you want to talk to him about?'

Woman: 'Alder Hey hospital. I want him to apologise for Alder Hey hospital.' The distressing case of Alder Hey hospital involved the retention of parts of dead children without their parents' consent.

The minder described what happened next: 'I wondered if BBC security could remove this woman, but they could not. We had to bring Boris past her. She pushed in. The television cameras pounced. Boris said: "Oh well, that's very interesting. I will report back to Michael Howard and he will write to you." The woman said: "I want a reply this afternoon." Then Boris went after her with a kind of strangling motion.'

The minder took more phone calls from Conservative HQ: 'This looks terrible.'

Minder to HQ: 'Well, what do you want me to do about it? Start assaulting the woman?'

According to the minder, 'Boris is beginning to get a bit pissed-off at this point.'

The *Spectator* sent over a copy of Boris's piece for that week's issue to the minder's BlackBerry. He found that Boris had written:

What makes Operation Scouse-grovel even more depressing is that I am attacked by my own troops for embarking upon it. In the journalistic equivalent of the fragging that GIs used to perform upon their officer, Stephen Glover, our own media correspondent, has said that in coming to Liverpool I am letting down the *Spectator*. He claims in Tuesday's *Daily Mail* that in going to apologise, at the behest of Michael Howard, the Tory leader, I am acting like a whipped cur . . . He ends his piece with words of dark foreboding about the freedom of the press.

The first thing to say is that Glover's piece shows, of course, the fearless independence of all *Spectator* columnists. Not only does he beat up Michael Howard and the Tory party, he also administers a resounding kicking to his own editor – with whom he had lunch less than a week ago, at which companionable and bibulous ceremony he requested and was granted a sizeable rise! That's the spirit, Glover! If that isn't freedom of the press, I don't know what is.

Boris rejected the idea that Johnson the politician was betraying Johnson the journalist: 'Johnson the politician apologises for and refuses to apologise for exactly the same things as Johnson the journalist.'

As the minder read this unrepentant piece, he thought 'Oh my God', but he also found that 'by that stage I was past caring'. On they went to the Granada studios, a huge round of local ITN interviews, and a photo call by the Albert Dock. They were supposed to go on to yet another radio station, but decided they had had enough, so Boris did that interview by telephone. They later learned that the station had been going to present Boris with an enormous humble pie.

The minders drove Boris to Speke airport and he flew back to London alone. One of the minders said: 'By that stage he looked like a wrung-out flannel. He really had been through the mill. We went back to the hotel, and those who weren't driving had stiff double whiskies. Then we drove back down in the huge Range Rover. We were laughing like lunatics at that stage. We were laughing so hard that we missed the turning from the M62 on to the M6. It was like the aftermath of the Charge of the Light Brigade – the survivors coming out of the valley of death. The usual debriefing meeting never happened. The idea was so flawed that the execution was a total irrelevance. The story played very big on the rolling news channels, but on the BBC *News at Ten* that night it had boiled down to only twenty or thirty seconds. But there was a certain *Schadenfreude* among elements of the parliamentary party, that Boris had been made to look a complete and utter chump.'

Susanna Gross said: 'He came and joined me and some friends for dinner on the night he came back from Liverpool. He was very annoyed with Howard, but as usual unbelievably good-natured. Boris just wanted to meet someone for a drink to unwind.'

Boris's attack on Liverpool gave him cult hero status among football supporters whose teams were playing Liverpool. Patrick Hennessy heard Chelsea fans chanting 'There's only one Boris Johnson' at the final of the Carling Cup in February 2005 at the Millennium Stadium in Cardiff.

Howard's people were not the only ones to have adopted an impossible plan. Boris had also adopted a career plan which could not long survive contact with reality. The Liverpool débâcle exposed the impossible contradiction between editing the *Spectator* and being a front-bench spokesman. When Sue Lawley interviewed Boris on *Desert Island Discs*, the following exchange took place:

LAWLEY: 'Well, let's move on to the Ken Bigley affair.'
BORIS: 'Why do we have to move on to that?'
LAWLEY: 'Because it does absolutely exemplify the dilemma, doesn't it.'
BORIS: 'Oh yes, good point.'
LAWLEY: 'Between the journalism and the politics. There

you are. You have to decide in that moment whether you're going to toe the party line because you're a front-bencher, or whether you're going to say what you really think, and you chose in favour of saying what you really think. In other words the paper won over the party. Is that fair?'

BORIS: 'Yes, what happened was that we had a very, very vigorous editorial which made some points about the culture of sentimentality, I'm racking my memory now . . . and that was what the editorial was meant to be all about.'

LAWLEY: 'Did you write it?'

BORIS: 'I take full responsibility for that editorial.'

LAWLEY: 'Did you write it?'

BORIS: 'I commissioned it, I edited it and I carried the can for it.'

LAWLEY: 'Ah, but you didn't write it.'

BORIS: 'And whether I wrote it or not is completely immaterial, Sue, because I'm the editor.'

LAWLEY: 'Of course, no, no, no, that's quite right.'

BORIS: 'And editors are responsible for whatever appears in the editorial columns.'

LAWLEY: 'But it would be quite interesting to know if you actually wrote it.'

BORIS: 'It would be. It would be. Er, but, I take full responsibility and I did, I went on this pilgrimage of penitence to Liverpool . . . to clarify and to apologise for the factual error which was related to the number of casualties at Hillsborough . . .'

LAWLEY: 'There were a lot of people who thought you just shouldn't have gone. You should just have resigned from the front bench. Do you think you should?'

BORIS: 'I think probably, yes, probably. Well, no, what I should have done, what I should have done is I should have resigned from the front bench and apologised for those things that we got wrong.'

Alan Watkins, one of the great political columnists of modern times, condemned both Howard and Boris. Watkins was at one time the *Spectator*'s political columnist, but was by now writing for the *Independent on Sunday*, where he observed that since the mid-1950s, when Ian Gilmour acquired it, the *Spectator* has been the most stimulating of all the weeklies:

> Its editors have included, if Mr Howard will forgive me, three Conservative politicians of greater ability, intelligence and distinction than he possesses himself: Gilmour, Iain Macleod and Nigel Lawson. Who, not to put too fine a point on it, does this pipsqueak think he is, issuing orders to the editor of a great journal?

Watkins thought Howard had made 'an outrageous demand':

> But once he had, it was Mr Johnson's clear duty to reject it, if necessary in the most forceful language.
>
> If Mr Howard had then dismissed him from his front bench, Mr Johnson should have taken it on the chin. As it was, he chose to place his own political career or the interests of the Conservative Party or both above his duty as an editor. I do not want to make heavy weather about this, but he has let down his leader-writer, his staff, his contributors, his readers and, not least, himself . . . He has tried to ride two horses and has, I am afraid, succeeded in falling off both of them.

Many people agreed with Watkins. Boris's star was no longer in the ascendant. Gwen Halley, in the *Sunday Independent* in Ireland, attacked Boris's claim that there are two Boris Johnsons,

Johnson the politician and Johnson the editor: 'There are two
Boris Johnsons all right: the Public Boris and the Real Boris.
Charmingly sloppy and self-deprecating on the outside, arrogant
and deeply driven on the inside. Boris Johnson has his nose in
the bountiful trough of public life. The image of bonhomie he
projects is a high art that will survive long after his comparably
paltry achievements in journalism and politics are forgotten . . .
like all babies – real or fake – Boris is indulged by those around
him. Spoilt babies become spoilt adults, manipulative and
morally degenerate.'

Yet it can also be argued that like many of the setbacks in
Boris's career, the Liverpool débâcle did him no permanent
damage. It amused a great number of people and made him even
more famous. To subvert Howard's control freakery from the
inside was perhaps more fun, and was certainly more trouble for
the Tory leader, than a gentlemanly decision to resign from the
shadow team would have been.

The story has a happy coda. Little more than a year later, on 2
December 2005, a party was held at Westminster to launch the
all-party parliamentary group to support Liverpool in its role as
the 2008 European Capital of Culture.

George Howarth, the Labour MP for Knowsley North and
Sefton East, who set up the group, invited Boris to become one
of its founder members, and Boris accepted this public gesture of
forgiveness.

As Mr Howarth said, 'The people of Merseyside are nothing
if not generous,' to which Boris replied: 'The quality of Mersey
is not strained.'

There was a general air of contentment as Boris mingled with
the dignitaries who had travelled from Liverpool to the reception. The Bishop of Liverpool, James Jones, told me he could
confirm 'out of personal experience' that Liverpool is 'a very
forgiving city'.

Not that Boris was about to yield any more ground than he had yielded at the time. He avoided answering questions about the original row by saying: 'You'll have to ask Michael Howard what I was apologising for.'

A beaming Howard arrived at the reception. It was only four days before he handed over the leadership of the Conservative Party to his successor, David Cameron, and he looked demob-happy. Howard was in no mood to dwell on his difficulties with Boris, and instead said: 'The difference between London and Liverpool is this. If you get into a lift in London, you will get out and no one will have said a word to each other. If you get into a lift in Liverpool, you can almost guarantee to come out laughing.'

Boris came out laughing from his contact with Liverpool, and did so by declaring a boundless affection for the place rather than by grovelling.

On 26 January 2006, when Boris appeared on the *Richard and Judy* show on television to publicise his programmes about the Romans, Richard Madeley took the chance to raise the Liverpool visit, and asked what Boris thought of Howard's order to go there: 'Were you actually furious about that? Why didn't you tell him to sod off?'

Boris replied: 'Because I thought it would be rude . . . It was fine . . . I love Liverpool. You can't get too much of it.'

22

The Pyramid of Piffle

AS THE LIVERPOOL STORM BROKE OVER BORIS, HIS private life also reached a crisis. On the day before he set out for the city, Petronella aborted the second child she had conceived by him. In normal circumstances, this miserable event would probably have remained private, but for Boris the circumstances were not normal. He was by now so celebrated that news about him was at a very high premium, and on Sunday 7 November 2004 the story of the abortion broke in the press.

It should be said that Petronella rather than Boris reached the decision to have an abortion, and her friends are adamant that she has never sought to blame him. Fop, the close friend of Petronella quoted earlier, said, 'Nobody forced her into it. She didn't want to be a single mother, and she thought it would cause immense complications.'

The older woman friend of Petronella, also quoted earlier, tried to defend Boris: 'I think Boris didn't want Petronella to have an abortion. This is a way in which Boris is not a horrible man. Petronella wanted Boris to marry her, obviously. I think he was very upset by the abortion. I think he would have stood by her financially, visited the child, et cetera, if she had gone ahead.

He would think it was his responsibility if she had had a child. I don't think he would have chucked her.'

But many people, including many of Boris's friends, were indignant on Marina's behalf and distressed by the abortion. As one man put it: 'All that abortion stuff – it just didn't look good – it was horrible.'

Some of Boris's friends thought he was secretly glad to have the whole situation resolved. One woman said: 'I think Boris doesn't like hurting people and he'd got himself in a position where someone had to be hurt, and he couldn't do it because he's a big softy. He was paralysed. In a way the awful scandal when it came out was his way out, and I think there was a bit of him that was relieved. It took it out of his hands.'

This woman added: 'I think the public humiliation has been terrible for him. But let's not blow this out of proportion. Lots of men have affairs.' She expressed the hope that he would be able to restore his reputation: 'If he's given a shadow post I hope he can prove himself reliable.'

The private pressure on Boris, and on those near to him, was enormous, but to this was added a tidal wave of publicity which threatened his political career. Rival newspapers acted as a pack of hounds, each leaping at their common quarry, each drawing blood, and each emboldened by the others to fresh frenzies of aggression. Boris now lost his head and committed a very foolish error.

The *Sunday Mirror* of 7 November broke the story of the abortion, carried out on 18 October at the Portland Hospital in London, but without naming either Petronella or Boris. Meanwhile the *Sunday Express* said Boris was about to resign his post as shadow arts spokesman, 'amid rumours of a crisis in his private life', and referred to his 'close relationship' with Petronella. But it was the *Mail on Sunday* which did the fatal damage to Boris, or gave him the chance to do the fatal damage to himself.

Simon Walters, the Political Editor of the *Mail on Sunday*, has a formidable record of breaking big stories, and unlike his rivals he managed to get through to Boris and extract a comment from him. Walters' story appeared under the headline 'Boris, Petsy and a "pyramid of piffle"', with large photographs of both Boris and Petronella. The piece opened with Boris's famous, and disastrous, denial: 'I have not had an affair with Petronella. It is complete balderdash. It is an inverted pyramid of piffle. It is all completely untrue and ludicrous conjecture. I am amazed people can write this drivel.'

Boris had denied something which was known to be true. One can see why he did this. He reckons it is nobody's damn business who he sleeps with, so he is entitled to lie about it. He is convinced that his private life has no bearing on his fitness for high office, and believes that the press and public are motivated by a disgusting jealousy of his sexual conquests.

We know this is what Boris thinks, for he stated his case in a passionate defence of the right of politicians to lie about their private lives, published in the *Daily Telegraph* in January 1998. The piece takes the form of a defence of President Bill Clinton, who was under fire for having denied having 'sexual relations' with Monica Lewinsky when it was pretty clear that some kind of sex had taken place.

Boris observes that Lewinsky herself is not blameless. He suggests she may be lying, and accuses her of trying to seduce the President:

> It seems at least conceivable that she is lying her head off, a star-struck booby trapped in a fantasy malevolently encouraged by others ... Some have implied that the President coerced Miss Lewinsky. What tosh. The more footage we see of the pair together, the more obvious it is that she transpires at every pore with lust to be noticed by the 'big he', as she calls him. The more we learn about how

she used her Blue Pass to hang around outside the Oval Office in a low-cut dress, the more one is inclined to sympathise with Clinton's predicament.

Boris took the unfashionable view that Clinton was Lewinsky's victim. He saw how vulnerable a powerful man could be to this sort of harassment, and he sympathised with the powerful man. But much more significantly, Boris tackled head-on the claim that 'it's not the sex' but 'the *lying*' which is so objectionable in such cases. According to our hero: 'It was a lie about sex, the kind of lie we try to avoid, but which we would all admit is sometimes justifiable, even, God knows, desirable.'

Boris has no time for the notion that a man who lies about sex is untrustworthy:

> Extra-marital sex is said to be of immediate political relevance, and not just a matter for the couple concerned, because it is said to expose a basic treacherousness, 'If-a-chap-can-lie-to-his-wife . . .' etc. Oh really? Is Gladstone to be condemned, because of what we now know about his weird work with prostitutes? Was Thomas Jefferson a failure as a President, because he had an affair with a slave-girl? Does it really *matter* what Palmerston got up to with women in Hyde Park?

Nor does Boris accept the idea that politicians should 'set an example' and help to uphold the institution of marriage, so that children do not grow up without fathers, which makes them more likely to turn to lives of delinquency and crime:

> Does anyone think a bunch of uniformly virtuous politicians would make the slightest difference? Of course they wouldn't. The decay of marriage, the rise in illegitimacy, are far more directly traceable to female emancipation,

unemployment and the vast welfare state, which so often supplants the role of the husband. The press wilfully muddles the issue, feeding on public prurience and jealousy.

We come to the heart of Boris's counter-attack against people who expose the affairs of politicians, including the late Robin Cook, who was found while Foreign Secretary to be having an affair with his secretary. The repellent motives of prurience and jealousy are at work:

Yes, jealousy. We know why these politicians are so attractive to young interns. It is because they have power, and *we* gave them that power. We want to delimit the consequences of electing them, to stop them enjoying the attentions of the likes of Miss Lewinsky; and how snivelling and short-sighted that attitude is.

We believe it is our democratic right to insist that Clinton and Cook have no mistresses, when it is nothing whatever to do with us. So politics is trivialised and turned into hell for so many of its practitioners.

Politics had become hell for Boris, but he made matters worse by claiming that the allegations were 'an inverted pyramid of piffle'. This bizarre phrase had already been used by Boris in a completely different context in a piece in the *Daily Telegraph* on 19 July 2001, and he may well have used it before then, for like most performers he constantly recycles his material, and finds certain phrases almost irresistible.

Boris's straight denial of the affair, to which the inverted pyramid was added as a flourish, gave the tabloids a perfect excuse to intrude on his private life. They could embark on a self-righteous mission to prove Boris a liar.

What should Boris have said? There was no good reply to give when the press started asking him about Petronella and her abortion, but the least bad response would have been: 'I don't answer questions about my private life.' This would have had the additional merit of being true, for the real meaning of the piffle quote, as a member of Boris's family explained to me during the writing of this book, was: 'Go away, it's got nothing to do with you.'

A version of this defence was successfully employed by David Cameron during the Tory leadership campaign, when he refused in a calm and amiable tone to say whether he had ever taken drugs. Most people believed he had every right to say this, and after blustering about it for a week or so, and ordering him to come clean, even papers like the *Daily Mail* were obliged to fall silent. To this day, we do not know about Cameron and drugs, which helps his friends to believe whatever they like on this controversial topic, while his enemies cannot drag him down by showing that he has lied.

Part of Boris's difficulty was that the papers already knew an awful lot about him, and he did not even know how they had discovered some of the worst bits. When the story of the abortion broke, a friend of both Boris and Petronella says: 'He was suspicious. He didn't understand how this came out. How did they know about the abortion? He wanted to know how they knew. He was really scared that Petronella had something to do with it. He wanted to be reassured that she had nothing to do with it, but he couldn't speak to her. But poor Petronella. The whole thing was horrible – really horrible to be in love with someone who was married – really horrible.'

Boris was one of the great loves of Petronella's life, but she was now cut off from him in the house in St John's Wood, just north of Lord's cricket ground, where she lives with her mother. She was offered a variety of safe havens by her friends, but chose to stay there. It is a fine, detached house, standing in its own garden, which is itself separated from the road by a reasonably high wall. Trees help to screen it from view. But a friend of Petronella – the same Fop quoted before – said: 'It was horrible having the press camped outside her home, and the inaccuracies and lies written about the affair were horrible too. Petronella was very upset by a horrible article by Amanda Platell which accused her of sleeping with Boris because he was going to be Prime Minister. So much rubbish was written. Petronella bears no grudge at all against Boris, but she hated the way the affair ended with the press and all that. She had people standing outside the house with cameras all the time. She couldn't go out, and she couldn't ring Boris because she knew he was being watched too. All that she wanted was to be left alone. And then journalists were ringing up pretending to be other people.'

Verushka Wyatt at first went along with Boris's denial. In Monday's *Daily Mail* she said her daughter had a 'close relationship' with Boris, 'but that is all'.

According to Lady Wyatt: 'She has not had an affair with him. She has not been pregnant by him nor had an abortion. She has not been pregnant at all. She is in a stable relationship with someone else but I am not going to talk about that.'

Boris hates rows and confrontations, and may have harboured hopes, as one of his closest friends put it, 'that everyone would be frightfully civilised and Marina would just accept the situation. I do think he thought he could have two wives and two establishments and get away with it. I think that is what he wanted to do.'

But he now had to make a choice between Marina and Petronella. He could no longer go on having both of them.

As Fop said of Marina: 'Obviously she gave Boris an ultimatum. At that point Petronella was just terrified. She didn't want to see Boris because she so hated the press intrusion. All that concerned her was to be left alone.'

The news itself was not news to Marina. She had known about Boris's affair with Petronella for some time and she now took the view that it had been grossly exaggerated by the press.

She does not talk to journalists, and knew it would be a hope-less task to try to correct the inaccuracies in their stories, but she could not help feeling annoyed by the implication that she was a push-over. She reckoned Boris did not have an easy time with her. She also felt he treated her fine and that while the Petronella thing was unfortunate, it was not as bad as people made out. It was something which had happened, as she found when friends commiserated with her, to a surprising number of people.

But she was also very angry with her husband for seeing Petronella again a couple of times quite recently, and she threw him out of the house. Many others were distressed on Marina's behalf. A friend of Boris's mother said: 'How could Boris do the same thing to his wife that his father did to his mother? I don't think he enjoyed that moment when he was a boy.'

Another woman who knew Boris when he was growing up said: 'We don't think Boris is as funny as he thinks he is. His thing is to gloss over all the real damage and pain he's caused to people. His thing is to be like a little boy – a forty-year-old man being more irresponsible than a well-brought-up teenager.' She blamed Stanley for setting a bad example: 'I'm saying that Boris got the idea you could walk all over females and didn't have to take their feelings into account.'

But once one starts passing the blame back down the gener-ations, where is one to stop? Stanley's own father was no model of rectitude, while Ali Kemal, Stanley's grandfather, somehow lost contact with his children in England; an interruption with which the First World War, in which Turkey joined the German side, must have had something to do.

On being thrown out of the family home, Boris took refuge with Justin Rushbrooke, a friend since Balliol, who was 'very happy to help – if he hadn't rung me to say "Can I come?", I'd have rung him.' Rushbrooke is married to Nell Butler, daughter of Lord Butler, the former Cabinet Secretary and present Master

of University College, Oxford. The couple were living with
their children in Albert Street, Camden Town, in north London,
and the tabloid press soon discovered that Boris was living with
them.

Rushbrooke may have been an idle undergraduate, but by this
time he had qualified as a barrister and was working at 5
Raymond Buildings in Gray's Inn, a chambers which has abbre-
viated itself to the more groovy '5RB'. He specialises in media
law with a particular emphasis on defamation, breach of confidence and privacy, and described the period Boris spent staying
with them: 'I don't know if you've ever had representatives of
the press besieging your house but it's actually quite an unpleasant experience. Boris did tell them to bog off outside our house,
which was quite commendable. Considering it can't have been
very pleasant, he took the whole thing in reasonably good part.'

Meanwhile Rushbrooke resisted the temptation to tell the
press: 'Do you realise I'm a barrister specialising in privacy law?'
The furthest he went was to say to one reporter, 'Do you know
you're invading my privacy?'

The press printed pictures which showed that Boris had worn
the same clothes for four days running. In one photograph
(reproduced as Plate 29) he can be seen on the doorstep with the
unidentified figure of Rushbrooke, wearing a red dressing-gown,
who is pointing and appears quite cross. 'It looks,' Rushbrooke
said, 'as if I'm engaged in a contretemps, but the truth is much
more mundane. Boris has spotted the *News of the World* paparazzi
mobile parked about fifty yards away, which is clearly likely to
have long lenses there, but equally Boris didn't have a parking
permit for his car, which on the dot of 8.30 was going to get
clamped. I also had a terrible hangover. I thought I should offer
a bit of moral support.'

What made the whole situation more complicated was that
Rushbrooke and his wife knew Marina very well. Rushbrooke
had met Marina before she even started going out with Boris.

This enabled Rushbrooke to tell Marina to tell Boris that 'the next time he came to stay he mustn't leave beer and coffee cups lying around. He was no better at clearing up in our house than in his own. But he was pretty self-sufficient in most respects. He used to go off running in the morning. He remains a prolific reader and when venturing down to the basement we would find three different books, all of which he was reading.'

Another old friend wrote a letter to Boris at this time. Darius Guppy told him: 'You must remember from our classical education and our love of the Greeks that family is everything.' Guppy received no reply, and hoped that Boris had not found his advice impertinent.

But the fact that he had gone to stay with friends of Marina, and not with friends of Petronella, was indicative of where Boris's deepest loyalties lay. Many wives would have been so furious with a husband who behaved like Boris that they would have hurled him into outer darkness and given him no way back. Marina, in her fond and cool-headed way, had been wiser than that.

23

Toff Fired

FOR SIX DAYS BORIS'S FATE HUNG IN THE BALANCE. IT was not known whether he would be taken back by Marina, or whether he would be sacked from his front-bench post by Michael Howard, or even whether he would survive as editor of the *Spectator*.

On Thursday 11 November 2004, as luck would have it, Howard was presenting the awards at the *Spectator* Parliamentarian of the Year lunch held in the ballroom at Claridge's. I went that morning to the *Spectator* and after the morning conference had a word alone with Boris.

He said with deep feeling: 'I'm getting a bit fed up with it. Obviously I've been very selfish and stupid, but it's not me . . . There were things in the papers yesterday . . .'

There certainly were some fairly appalling things in the papers. Rachel Royce, the ex-wife of Rod Liddle, had expressed her sympathy for Marina in an excruciating piece in the *Daily Mail* headlined 'Confessions of an (ex) *Spectator* wife'. Royce described how she and Marina had struggled after a full day's work to get to a party at the *Spectator* 'full of glamour girls half my age who'd had hours to pamper themselves and would now be batting their carefully curled eyelashes at the paunchy,

egotistical males strutting round the room like peacocks'.
According to Royce,

> Men like Boris, with their power and celebrity, are so
> puffed up on their own egos they end up living in a parallel
> universe, where they think they can do what they please.
>
> Once they shut their front doors behind them in the
> morning, it's as though their homes disappear into the
> ether. Ties of loyalty to the women who have borne their
> children simply evaporate . . . They honestly feel they are at
> the centre of some mini-universe and they think no one
> else is as funny or clever as themselves.

If Royce had been feeling more charitable, she might have
realised how bad this was for Boris. Marina saw him surrounded
by predatory women, and knew how distorting their flattery
could be.

Boris was certainly suffering that Thursday morning from the
knowledge of the pain which people near to him were experi-
encing. He was also trying to think what to say in his speech at
the awards, while at the same time coping with Kimberly
Fortier, the publisher of the *Spectator*, who was refusing to release
the names of the winners to the *Evening Standard*.

The usual arrangement was to release the winners' names to
'Londoner's Diary' on the *Evening Standard*, for use in the edition
of the paper which appeared on the streets at two in the afternoon. This was clearly in the interests of the *Spectator*, which
gained extra publicity for the awards without breaking the sus-
pense of the lunch.

But Kimberly was refusing to release the names to 'Londoner's
Diary' because she was angry about the things it had written
about her affair with David Blunkett. Boris assured Sebastian
Shakespeare, editor of the Diary, that Ann Sindall would phone
the names of the winners over, whereupon Kimberly, who was

not actually in the building but had somehow got wind of this arrangement, began to harass Boris. This extra complication prompted the editor to say, in a voice of agony: 'It doesn't make life any easier.'

Cars had been booked to take people from the *Spectator* to Claridge's, but Boris biked there. Pictures of him wheeling his bike along the pavement outside the hotel appeared in the next day's papers.

Politicians and journalists filled the ballroom at Claridge's with a buzz of laughter and conversation. We sat at large, round tables and lunch was served quite fast so that those MPs who needed to get back to Westminster would not be detained for long. Those of us who were drinking could drink as much as we liked. Kimberly had entered the hotel by some sort of back entrance. A place was laid for Petronella, but she had not turned up.

Much of the talk was about Boris and his prospects of survival. I found myself sitting next to Paul Johnson – no relation of the editor, but a *Spectator* columnist since the days of Alexander Chancellor – who said of Boris: 'Fortunately for him, he's a very hard man not to like.'

Towards the end of lunch, Boris and Michael Howard mounted a small stage at one side of the room. Boris began by twitting his party leader: 'We at the *Spectator* know that sometimes it can be a very, very difficult burden on members of the Tory front bench to agree with every word we write.'

Then it was Howard's turn, and the ingenious and playful manner in which he discharged his task caused general hilarity: 'These are the *Spectator*'s awards and the *Spectator* is an incomparable magazine. There is nothing like the *Spectator* for stirring up and stimulating political controversy. Indeed in all senses of the word it could best be described as political Viagra [laughter]. And I must [prolonged laughter], I must take this opportunity of congratulating Boris on the tremendous enthusiasm with which you have approached your various front-bench duties. I had no idea when I appointed you as shadow minister for culture, media and sport that you would take to the task with quite such aplomb. You were keen to make your mark with the city of culture [i.e. Liverpool]. You wanted them to get to know you better. And you succeeded beyond my wildest dreams . . . All I can say is Boris . . . keep it up!'

The audience loved this, but Boris did not, and could be heard saying: 'I don't know how he's allowed to get away with this. Absolutely outrageous.'

It appeared, however, that Howard had decided to treat his shadow minister's exploits as a joke, rather than a hanging offence. Boris's punishment was to be laughed at in public, which was not pleasant, but seemed to put him in the clear as far as keeping his shadow post was concerned.

But relations between Boris and Howard were much worse than they appeared. Boris had indicated to Howard, after the Liverpool débâcle but before the Petronella affair broke, that he wished to resign from the shadow team. Given that Howard had only promoted Boris in May, this must have seemed both ungrateful and unserious to the Tory leader and his circle. But to Marina, it now seemed that Howard was fanning the flames of the Petronella affair as a means of getting rid of her husband, and she instinctively sided with Boris, who was certainly not inclined to resign under pressure. Nor did Boris consider that he had lied either to Howard or to Howard's aides. He reckoned that Howard could quite easily have stood by him, and had failed to do so.

Two days later, Howard sacked Boris. The *News of the World* claimed the credit, if that is the word. It splashed on its front page with the headline, 'Bonking Boris Made Me Pregnant'. According to a friend of Petronella, she 'loathed' this headline, because it made it seem as if she had herself spoken to the paper, which the rest of the story demonstrated she most certainly had not.

A second headline in smaller type announced: 'Liar FIRED after Tory chief sees *News of the World* evidence'. The newspaper gave the following account of Boris's Saturday afternoon sacking:

At **16.20**, when we put our revelations to him, he snapped: 'What I will say to you is, "Publish and be damned!"'

But by **16.30**, when Tory leader Michael Howard was informed of our story, it was Boris who was damned.

At **18.30** Mr Howard ordered him to be officially removed from his posts as shadow arts minister and vice-chairman of the Conservative Party – one of the fastest political sackings in history.

The *News of the World*'s 'revelations' were far skimpier than its presentation of them suggested, but both here and in Simon Walters' front-page piece in the *Mail on Sunday*, Verushka Wyatt had ceased to back Boris's version of events. The *Mail on Sunday* said Lady Wyatt had confirmed to the paper that Petronella did become pregnant by Boris and did have an abortion.

A close friend of Petronella is at pains to defend Lady Wyatt: 'A lot of people think her mother spilled the beans on Boris deliberately, but what happened was that a good friend who happened to be a journalist told her it would go no further, and then she started talking, and it appeared in the paper. Lady Wyatt is quite naïve about journalists. Some articles said it was the mother's revenge on Boris, but she adores him. Still does.'

Other papers were obliged to follow the story. Patrick Hennessy, who overlapped with Boris at school and university and was now Political Editor of the *Sunday Telegraph*, remembered: 'We got word that he was being sacked. I rang him at about 8 p.m. and he was very, very upset – really genuinely upset. What he really wanted to know was how the *News of the World* was playing it. I said if I could find out I'd ring him back. When the story was read over to him there was some phrase in it about "the snooty toff" and Boris replied: "Bloody hell, that's outrageous, I'm not a snooty toff.""

The phrase used by the paper was 'the snooty mop-haired toff'. Its story ended:

> Speaking through the letter box at a pal's house last night, Boris said: 'I am sorry this decision has been taken in response to stories about my private life.
>
> 'I am looking forward to helping promote a new Conservative policy on the arts, if only from the back benches, and I will continue to do my utmost to serve the people of Henley and south Oxfordshire. I am now going to have a stiff drink.'

One of Boris's warmest admirers said: 'I think Michael Howard wanted to get rid of him anyway. That's what I later heard from other Conservatives. I don't think Howard ever liked Boris, and I think he annoyed the Whips by not turning up for various things, and of course there's a lot of jealousy.'

Howard ran a tight ship, and sacked two Conservative candidates during the 2005 General Election campaign. He believed in discipline, and was harsh to anyone who gave so much as the appearance of indiscipline. That was the way Howard was, and it left no room for someone like Boris. But one should add that such rigid party management made a poor impression on many voters, and was one reason why Howard proved unable to extend Tory support beyond its core vote. His treatment of Boris indicated his limitations. For all his gifts, Howard was too narrow for the nation to take him to their hearts.

But the whole affair looked much, much worse for Boris. Few people doubted that he had suffered a very severe and perhaps terminal setback. The general line in the press was that Boris had been sacked for lying to Howard. The *Observer* said Boris was 'facing the end of what promised to be a coruscating political career, not to mention his editorship of a national magazine'.

Yasmin Alibhai-Brown, in the next day's *Evening Standard*, had no sympathy for Boris and expressed outrage on Marina's behalf:

> This scandalous behaviour of Boris's, you imagine, must leave her both deeply hurt and seething. Only those who have been through it can understand the unspeakable anguish, what it feels like to be deceived so totally, to be humiliated and lied to, to be treated with such indifference by your husband and his lover, and, in this case, in public . . .
>
> How do women like Petronella forgive themselves for wrecking the lives of so many people? . . . We take infidelity too lightly and forgive lying cads too easily, especially if they are charmers like Boris Johnson, charmers who come to believe it is their right to betray the mothers of their children and their lovers.

But at least Boris was back at home, as he showed the world when he emerged for a jog at 7.30 on the morning of Monday 15 November in his son's ski hat (generally, but incorrectly, described in the press as a 'bandana'). He told the press: 'I advise you all very strongly, go for a run, get some exercise, and have a beautiful day.'

On returning home, Boris found the door of his own house locked, and was asked as he waited to be let in if he felt unfairly treated, to which he replied in the words of Voltaire's Dr Pangloss: 'All is for the best in the best of all possible worlds.'

Boris was also asked if he had misled Howard and replied: 'No, I certainly didn't. Will you kindly hop it?'

The graver problem for Boris was not Howard, who was not going to be around for long, but other Tory MPs who were by now both jealous of his fame, and sceptical about his reliability.

24

Theatricals

BORIS HAD COME DOWN TO EARTH WITH A BUMP AND nothing about his position looked very secure. On 15 November 2004 it was announced that Andrew Neil had been brought in as chief executive of the *Spectator*, which had by now passed, like the *Telegraph*, into the ownership of the Barclay brothers. Neil was close to the new owners, but this former editor of the *Sunday Times* was not someone whom one would expect to be in sympathy either with Boris or with the *Spectator*.

Michael Portillo took the chance, in the *Sunday Times* of 21 November 2004, to launch a sublimely self-important attack on Boris:

> When I first met Boris Johnson, I marked him down as unserious. He came to interview me as Defence Secretary and arrived forty-five minutes late. Apparently, experienced political journalist that he was, he had thought the ministry was in Victoria Street, not in Whitehall. He had the decency to look flushed and sweaty, but also gave the impression that I should find his shambolic performance endearing. I pretended to do so.

Portillo contemplated Boris's prospects, now that he was known to have had an affair with Petronella: 'If this were France, Johnson's prestige as a politician would have soared for attracting such a mistress and we might be talking of him as a future leader of his party. Being Britain, his celebrity has increased and his earning potential with it, but his political career is over.'

If only Boris had taken Portillo's advice:

Nearly four years ago, when he had entered Parliament, I knew he was clever and discovered he had the right ideas (to my mind) about reshaping the Tory party. He wanted to be a future leader and of course he was highly media savvy. I advised him to focus on Parliament, stop being funny and resign from editing the *Spectator*.

I can see why he rejected my suggestions. His journalism and television work have brought him money and fame. Devoting himself instead to mastering a shadow spokesman's brief would have been tedious and impoverishing. But if he calculated that he could leap from celebrity to leading the party he was wrong. His success had created too many jealousies among MPs and the buffoonery had gone beyond the point of recall.

Portillo ended his piece by predicting future greatness for a man who had acted as one of Boris's stooges at Oxford, but was not yet even a Tory MP:

Like Johnson he is a journalist, but unlike him he would never be late for a meeting. His name is Michael Gove, who long ago wrote a kindly biography of me. He survived that lapse of judgment and climbed the ladder. He has given up the prospect of editing *The Times* to become a humble backbencher in a party whose fortunes are at a low ebb. That is what I call serious.

The pressure on Boris and Petronella was soon relieved by new revelations about Kimberly and Blunkett. On 28 November 2004, the *Sunday Telegraph* reported that 'open war' had broken out between them, with Blunkett accused of 'fast-tracking' a visa for her Filipina nanny. Thanks to the collapse of his relationship with Kimberly, Blunkett was now on the downward path which led on 15 December to his resignation as Home Secretary.

When Kimberly found out about Petronella's affair with Boris she took a high moral tone about it, so now that Kimberly's own affair had become public, Petronella 'laughed like a drain'. She also wrote a piece in which she described introducing Blunkett to Kimberly Fortier three years before at Wheeler's fish restaurant in St James's, and how Kimberly flirted like mad with him, saying she had always wondered what it was like to sleep with a blind man: 'Mr Blunkett and I ate dover sole. Miss Fortier ate Mr Blunkett.'

Boris remained capable of marvellous ebullience. One of his friends was surprised to hear him say, in a buoyant tone, that things could be patched up at home without undue difficulty: 'Put on a good Christmas and it'll all be all right.'

On 16 December 2004, I sat opposite him at the *Spectator*'s Christmas lunch, held in a cellar at Berry Bros & Rudd, the grand wine merchants in St James's. Boris started his speech: 'It has been a difficult and turbulent year, in the immortal phrase of Norman Lamont.'

The reference was to Black Wednesday, 16 September 1992, when Lamont as Chancellor tried and failed to defend the pound's place in the Exchange Rate Mechanism against a wave of speculation. Lamont at one point raised interest rates to 15 per cent, and later emerged from the Treasury to say, 'This has been a very difficult and turbulent day.' Boris quotes this in the introduction to his book of collected journalism. Unlike many men who want to be successful, he also enjoys the comedy of failure.

In his Christmas address to the troops, Boris refused to be

downhearted: 'In spite of all our efforts to shake off readers . . . they continue to subscribe to us in ever greater numbers.' After some classical references – to Odysseus' dog and Caligula's horse – Boris described a visit to the *Spectator* by a girl from the magazine *Dazed and Confused* who expected to find 'people shagging in the toilets' but instead discovered it to be 'a place of monastic seclusion'.

Boris as usual thanked every one of the staff by name, including the humblest people in the advertising and circulation departments – a list of fifty or more people drawn up by Ann Sindall.

'Penultimately,' Boris said, 'I want to thank Ann Sindall, the be-all and Sindall.'

But Boris ended with a generous reference to Kimberly, who was at that point heavily pregnant with her second child and had been taken to hospital. Boris proposed a toast to 'absent friends and those who have done so much, now languishing in their hospital beds. I miss her, this is not a popular view, I miss her dynamism.'

One could say Boris was having it both ways. He got a big laugh for 'this is not a popular view'. But he was also behaving towards Kimberly with far greater charity than most of her colleagues did.

At the General Election in the spring of 2005, another Johnson took the field. Boris's father Stanley had got himself selected as the Tory parliamentary candidate in Teignbridge, a constituency in south Devon which had fallen into Liberal Democrat hands. Boris said: 'Never in history, as far as I know, has a father followed his son into Parliament. Our party cares about the older generation.'

There was some confusion among members of the public between the two Johnsons. Stanley was sometimes asked: 'Is it true that Boris Johnson is your father?'

Boris took time off from his campaign in Henley to try to help Stanley. He went down to speak for him in Dawlish (Stanley: '"How many other languages can he speak?" a Polish friend of mine asked') and on 22 April 2005 I saw father and son campaigning together in the small coastal town of Teignmouth.

Boris arrived from the constituency of North Devon, where he had campaigned earlier that day on behalf of Orlando Fraser, grandson of his grandparents' great friends Lord and Lady Longford. Boris was wearing a suit with no tie and a modest blue rosette, while Stanley's rosette was a good six inches across.

Stanley persuaded him to do a short walkabout in the rain, for the benefit of the considerable number of journalists who had come to watch. Boris was not keen and said: 'Sod the press.' A few minutes later he denied point-blank to me that he had said this.

We piled in to the Dairymaid restaurant, where I had earlier lunched with Quentin Letts of the *Daily Mail* and Valerie Grove of *The Times*. Boris said: 'So sorry to barge in. We're surrounded by the media.'

Boris and Stanley sat down on either side of two waitresses who were having their own lunch – it was about 2.15 in the afternoon. There was much laughter. Boris said as he left: 'Look, I'm so sorry to have troubled you.'

His apologetic manner, and the way in which he dissociated himself from the mob of reporters and photographers, helped to defuse any possible irritation, but did not always lead to promises of support. In Luders Patisserie, the woman behind the counter told Boris that she used to be a Conservative, 'but I would never vote Conservative again. Because of the Conservatives we lost our house, our business, everything.'

At the Carlton Theatre, a disappointingly small audience of forty-seven mostly Tory voters had come to hear Boris and Stanley, who competed to cap each other's jokes. The Johnsons were asked if it could really be right to send 50 per cent of school leavers to university – the target set by the Labour

Government. Stanley used this an occasion to mention that five of his children went to Oxford, and one to Cambridge.

Boris denounced 'these loony degrees in windsurfing from Bangor University', whereupon Stanley broke in: 'They also surf who only stand and wait.'

In a sketch for the *Daily Telegraph*, I quoted Boris's attack on 'loony degrees', which produced the following response in the paper's letters column from Dr David Roberts, Registrar of the University of Wales, Bangor: 'There are no such degrees, of course, at Bangor. What the university does have is an internationally renowned School of Ocean Sciences.'

A woman in the theatre said: 'I think if Boris were Tory leader they would get in without any trouble whatever.'

We drove through the rain to Newton Abbot, where Boris and Stanley played squash. Stanley wanted this match in order to show that he was still fit enough to be an MP. The encounter was built up, for the benefit of the press, as the greatest sporting contest of the campaign. Boris, who looked thin and attractive, but a bit pissed-off, beat his father easily.

After the match, Stanley gave Lauren Booth – the half-sister of Cherie Blair – and myself a lift to the railway station. He was on friendly terms with Lauren, who was writing a piece for one of the Sunday papers, and as we pulled away from the squash courts he started broadcasting through the loudspeakers mounted on his Hyundai battle bus: 'This is Stanley Johnson, your Conservative candidate, with Lauren Booth.'

Lauren took the microphone from him and said: 'This is Lauren Booth. I will not be supporting Stanley Johnson but I like him.'

Stanley never tired of repeating another joke made during the campaign: 'I visited a retirement home in Newton Abbot and was pleased when one of the residents confided that she had been impressed by my running in the famous Newton Abbot pancake race on Shrove Tuesday.'

'"You were very good," the old lady said. "Are you a practised tosser?"'

This is not the kind of joke one is used to hearing from a Tory candidate, and it may not have amused everyone who heard it in Devon.

At the General Election on 5 May 2005, Boris held Henley with an increased majority of 12,793 over the Liberal Democrats, while Stanley lost in Teignbridge to the Lib Dems by 6,215 votes.

The man sitting beside me as Boris and Stanley performed in the Carlton Theatre had said: 'A theatre's the right place for these two.'

The same thought, at least as far as Boris was concerned, struck a number of people, including two of Boris's old friends from Oxford, Toby Young and Lloyd Evans, both of whom he employed to write theatre reviews and other pieces for the *Spectator*.

Young and Evans composed a play, *Who's the Daddy?*, which was put on at the King's Head Theatre in Islington in July 2005. The play was set at the *Spectator* and revolved around three couples: Boris and Petronella, Blunkett and Kimberly, Liddle and a young woman at the magazine who turned out to be an undercover reporter. The set included a picture of Margaret Thatcher which pulled down into a bed.

When the authors informed Boris about the play, he wrote back to them: 'I always knew my life would be turned into a farce. I'm glad that the script has been entrusted to two such eminent men of letters.'

Young wrote in the programme that they had both known Boris since they were all at Oxford in the mid-1980s, and asked: 'Could we justify stitching up our old mate?' He went on:

After much deliberation, the only argument we found halfway convincing was that Boris's status as a public figure had, to a certain extent, eroded the protection he was entitled to as a friend . . . As aspiring satirical playwrights, what sort of precedent would we be setting if we decided it would be wrong to take the piss out of a public personality just because he happened to be an acquaintance of ours? . . . Ultimately, the reason Lloyd and I decided to go ahead with *Who's the Daddy?* is because we felt that if we're serious about wanting to be writers – whether of plays, books or theatre criticism – the writing must come first: it must trump all other considerations. That may sound harsh, but it's a feeling that any writer with a sense of vocation will recognise. In your soul, you know you'll never be any good unless you're willing to sacrifice more or less everything in order to produce the best work you can.

This 'sell your own grandmother' approach recalled the worst excesses of Oxford journalism. The play contained many good lines, but was somehow joyless in its lack of charity. We saw Boris lying to Marina (by telephone) and screwing Petronella, while a Chilean cook attempted to get his visa extended by giving Blunkett a blow-job while pretending to be Kimberly. Tim Hudson played Boris and was good at conveying some of his heart. There were cruel caricatures of Kimberly and Liddle.

Boris did not come to see the play, but felt deeply hurt by it. He took to telephoning Young, begging him to scrap the projected transfer to the West End (which in the end never came off) and telling him that his life had become 'purgatory'. Yet he gave no public expression to his distress, and did not sack either Evans or Young. A couple of months later, when there was some question of both Boris and Young appearing on the television show *I'm a Celebrity, Get Me Out of Here*, Boris did allow himself to say: 'I can't think of anything worse than being trapped in the jungle with Toby Young.'

There were several other plays about Kimberly, Blunkett, Boris and co., including *A Very Social Secretary* by Alistair Beaton, shown on television in October 2005. But no fictional version of Boris's adventures has yet been more than a pale echo of the reality.

25

Overtaken by Cameron

THE RISE OF DAVID CAMERON WAS ASTONISHINGLY SWIFT.
He is two years younger than Boris, and although he came into
Parliament at the same time, was much less well known. After
Michael Howard led the Tories to their third General Election
defeat in a row in May 2005, and announced that he would be
stepping down, several months elapsed before the rules for
choosing his successor were settled, and during this period David
Davis was the firm favourite to succeed him.

Cameron only emerged as a serious contender for the leadership on 29 September, when he launched his campaign. Boris
attended this event, which had the feel of a small but fashionable
wedding, thrown by grand people but in such a way as to make
everyone welcome.

The journalists had come straight on from David Davis's
launch, which was larger, but felt like a gathering of golf club
bores. Cameron seemed full of promise, while Davis gave the
impression of being a dull man who was unlikely to transcend his
own limitations.

The following week, at the Conservative Party Conference in
Blackpool, Cameron delivered the same kind of promising
speech as at his launch, including many of the same lines, but to

a far larger audience. Davis failed by comparison, and although Kenneth Clarke and Malcolm Rifkind spoke well, they could not match Cameron's momentum.

On the last day of the conference, Boris used his *Telegraph* column to announce to a wider public his support for Cameron. He began by saying: 'Over the past few months I have lost count of the number of people who have asked me – satirically – why I am not standing in the current Tory leadership contest.'

Boris was not in a position to stand because he would have enjoyed virtually no support among MPs, and most of the people around Michael Howard had switched to Cameron. Howard himself preserved an appearance of scrupulous neutrality, but was reckoned to favour Cameron, whom he had promoted to the shadow Cabinet. Cameron looked new, but he was also the Establishment candidate, while the disappointed men in their fifties who felt unjustly ignored by Howard tended to cluster around Davis. There was not enough room for a third candidate, as Kenneth Clarke and several other aspirants were soon to discover.

The new leader was elected by the whole party, an arrangement which might have favoured Boris. But although he was immensely popular in the wider party, and had been assiduous in visiting constituency associations, the events of the last autumn, culminating in his sacking, made too many people fear he might turn into a liability. Boris had been given his chance to show what he could do as an apparatchik, but it was not in his nature to display the self-effacing steadiness and common prudence which were required. He was also very inexperienced. But so too was Cameron. As a public speaker, and also as a television performer, Cameron was much less experienced than Boris, at least as far as high-profile events and programmes were concerned.

The parallels between the two men were very close. Cameron is from a grander family, with aristocratic connections stretching back into the Middle Ages, but as far as most people were concerned, they were equally privileged, for they had both been to Eton. This presented them with a problem which has perplexed Etonians ever since three of their number – Eden, Macmillan and Douglas-Home – succeeded each other as Prime Minister, only for the last to be narrowly defeated in 1964 by Harold Wilson, who mocked his aristocratic lineage.

How could an Old Etonian succeed in such an egalitarian, or at least pseudo-egalitarian, age? The next six leaders of the Tory party – Heath, Thatcher, Major, Hague, Duncan Smith and Howard – were all from relatively humble backgrounds, and when Douglas Hurd, like Boris a scholar of Eton, stood for the leadership, he made a fool of himself by pretending to be humbler than he was. When Hurd said he was not really a toff, he sounded as if he was denying his own background, even though in traditional terms what he said was true.

Boris seemed brilliantly placed to crack this Etonian problem. Far from denying his toffishness, he played up to it in such an amusing way that hardly anyone held it against him. He was at once gloriously traditional, and gloriously capable, unlike Douglas-Home and Hurd, of communicating with people via television. In class terms, Boris also carried less baggage than Cameron, who had married an upper-class wife and was a member of White's club.

Yet Boris had been sidelined, and tactful, charming, self-possessed Cameron had come through. Boris now had the wit to back him wholeheartedly, and urged his colleagues in Parliament to back him too, 'for the entirely cynical and self-serving reason that he is not only the best candidate, but that he is going to win'.

Part of the charm of politics is its unexpectedness, but it must have been a bitter blow to Boris to see Cameron overtake him. A trace of disappointment appeared in one line of Boris's 'I'm backing Cameron' piece: 'I like his constant repetition of "we're

all in this together"; indeed, I am vain enough to have a feeling
that he nicked it from me.' But a woman who knows Boris well
said that he is too proud to feel any real sense of disappointment,
and is so confident of his own abilities that if he fails to become
Prime Minister, he will not consider it his fault but the fault of
everyone else in the party for failing to choose him as their
leader.

Only nine days before the result of the Tory leadership contest was declared, by which time it was clear that Cameron was
going to win, Boris made his appearance on *Desert Island Discs*.
Tom Stoppard has a character in *The Real Thing* who is about to
go on this programme and is worried that 'I don't like the pop
music which it's all right to like . . . *I* like Wayne Fontana and the
Mindbenders doing "Um Um Um Um Um Um".' But choos-
ing the music was the least of Boris's worries. As we have already
seen, Sue Lawley subjected him, under the guise of a friendly
chat, to a ruthless interrogation. When people interviewed Boris
for newspaper pieces, there was every chance he could win over
the interviewer and ensure that a reasonably favourable piece
appeared, with some of his prevarications and evasions omitted.
But in Lawley's cross-examination, his refusal to give straight
answers was exposed with terrible clarity. Boris sounded at times
like a cashiered major who is desperately trying to keep up
appearances. The conversation is punctuated by laughter –
Lawley is amused by him, and at times she sounds flirtatious –
but she is far too sharp to let him change the subject. One of
Boris's difficulties may have been that he was trying to sound
more serious, and less buffoonish, than he had in the past, in
order to show that he would be a fit member of Cameron's team.

Cameron's impending triumph, the speculation about what
post he would give Boris, and the awkward fact that Boris was
still editor of the *Spectator*, enabled Lawley to go for the jugular.
She confronted him with the choice he had been avoiding ever
since he was elected an MP:

LAWLEY: 'If you had to choose between journalism and politics, and you might, who knows, one day, have to do so, you'd choose politics, would you?'

BORIS: 'Yes, of course, but I don't think I'd abandon journalism.'

LAWLEY: 'You'd have to. I mean people have told you time and again you can't ride two horses. You've probably proved you can't ride two horses.'

BORIS: 'I think I have successfully ridden two horses for quite a long time, but I have to admit there have been moments when the distance between the two horses has grown terrifyingly wide.'

LAWLEY: 'Split you right down the middle.'

BORIS: 'And I did momentarily come off.'

LAWLEY: 'But if you had to choose, you would choose, would you, politics?'

BORIS: 'Yes, of course. I always wanted to do it. I always knew I was going to be an MP . . . I had a sense that this was the single most interesting job that one could do, it was the job that involved testing one to the greatest extent . . .'

LAWLEY: 'So political ambition there is. David Cameron, were he to get the leadership, do you think he'd get you back on to the front bench?'

BORIS: 'Well, I've no idea. I think it would be pretty bonkers of me now to outline a job request.'

LAWLEY: 'What do you think your area is?'

BORIS: 'What I would love to do, the thing that I, OK, I'll tell you, the thing I would love to do is something to do with agriculture, trade, world trade . . . But hey, it's not for me, I'll take anything.'

LAWLEY: 'Did you know him, because I mean he was at Eton and Oxford a couple of years behind you.'

BORIS: 'I do, I do, I did know him, I do, I remember him,

he was younger than me, I hope it wasn't one of the traumas I have to bear in my life, so we didn't know each other that well, but I certainly knew him. I haven't got a prayer of getting it, but, you know . . .'

LAWLEY: 'Have you got a prayer of becoming Prime Minister, because that's what you'd really like, isn't it . . . Was it your ex-mother-in-law who said, "Boris is very ambitious and always said he wanted to be Prime Minister"?'

BORIS: 'My ex-mother-in-law is in many ways a wonderful woman. Did I used to say that? Maybe I did. I suppose all politicians in the end are like kind of crazed wasps in a jam jar, each individually convinced that they're going to make it.'

As his first record, Boris chose 'Here Comes the Sun' by the Beatles. His second was the theme tune of *Test Match Special*, which brought 'very fond memories of playing cricket in the yard with my brothers, all of whom are better than me at cricket'.

Sue then probed Boris's ambition: 'You like testing yourself . . . You set your sights on things and go for it, because that's what gets you going.'

Boris replied: 'You've been more or less programmed to want to have these things. My silicon chip, my ambition silicon chip, has been programmed to try to scrabble my way up this *cursus honorum*, this ladder of things, and so you do feel a kind of sense, you've got to . . . I think British society is designed like that. Because what we need as a society, we need all these grasping hacks and politicos to compete with each other and to advertise their wares to the public, because if they don't they won't be doing their job of serving.'

We see Boris avoiding responsibility for his behaviour by developing a doctrine of necessity – he has been programmed to try to scrabble his way up – and also by saying that this is what the public needs. For his third record he chose a piece of Bach from *St Matthew's Passion* – the tune also for the hymn 'Hail to the Lord's Anointed' – which was followed by the Rolling Stones' 'Start Me Up', 'the most fantastic, vigorous introduction to a rock song you could possibly have – it may be corny but it's brilliant'. Record number five was Brahms, 'Variations on a Theme by Haydn', followed by the Van Morrison song mentioned in the passage about Boris's novel, after which the dialogue continued with Sue observing: 'I haven't read a profile written about you, Boris, in which the interviewer doesn't come out feeling that they've been, you know, very unfair to you, as they've sort of pointed out all these misdemeanours, and you've sort of batted it back.'

BORIS: 'Yes.'

LAWLEY: 'But they all say they've been charmed by you, and isn't that the fact really that the strongest weapon in your armoury is charm?'

BORIS: 'Well again, I mean, it's very, very sweet of you to say this, Sue, but what are these misdemeanours you keep talking about?'

LAWLEY: 'We don't want to go back over them, Boris. I mean, I've left quite a few out.'

BORIS: 'What do you, I mean, for the benefit of your listeners, I think there are far fewer misdemeanours than there are demeanours, or whatever.'

LAWLEY: 'All right. Mishaps, I think. Mishaps. But what I want to know is whether the charm, whether it's all a bit of a ruse, or maybe you've always used it as a bit of a ruse, you know, to sort of get you by.'

BORIS: 'I suppose that could be, could be something. I was very deaf as a child, and I attribute, I used to have grommets, you know what I mean by grommets, I had terrible glue ear and could basically hardly hear anything anyone was saying, and I think I must have developed then a certain sort of evasiveness, because often really I couldn't follow what was going on at all, and if you can sort of guess what's going on but you're not quite sure, it's often as well to be a little bit vague.'

LAWLEY: 'Yes, but you are at the same time a comic institution, and you cultivate that image, because you go on *Have I Got News For You*, or wherever you crop up, I mean, you are highly entertaining, and I suppose what I'm asking is a question you can't answer, which is whether you do that in a calculated way or whether that's just Boris.'

BORIS: 'Yuuuh. I think the profound truth of the matter is it would be very, very hard to do it any other way. I think if I made a huge effort always to have a snappy, inspiring soundbite on my lips, I think the sheer mental strain of that would be such that I would explode, and I think it's much easier therefore for me to try to play what shots I have as freely as I can. Does that make sense?'

LAWLEY: 'Yes it does, but of course what happens is maybe the really clever and thoughtful Boris gets lost and people forget he's there, and that's the danger, isn't it?'

BORIS: 'Yeah, well, we need, we need to go and find him, we need to go and chivvy him out, wherever he is lurking in there . . .'

LAWLEY: 'Does he crop up quite often?'

BORIS: 'He does.'

LAWLEY: 'He does, does he? He's in there?'

BORIS: 'Yeah. He's there all right.'

LAWLEY: 'Record number seven.'

BORIS: 'Right. Ah, this is fantastic. It is The Clash, "Pressure Drop", and the great thing about The

Clash, of course, was apart from anything else, Joe Strummer was towards the end an avid *Telegraph* reader and it was the highest moment in my journalistic career when Joe Strummer actually sent me a letter saying how much he'd admired a column I'd written, about hunting funnily enough, and he was a fantastic man, a great hero of mine, a good poet as well as a fantastic rock musician.'

The last record, after Boris had said how on his desert island he would have 'a very disciplined approach to rebuilding civilisation as fast and as quickly as I could', and he enjoys making things out of wood, and would 'try to get to the heart of things' in his writing, was the opening of the last movement of Beethoven's Fifth Symphony. Boris said if he could only take one of the records it would be the Brahms. He chose Homer as his book – 'I think I could use up a few decades quietly translating that' – and mustard – specifically Moutarde de Meaux – as his luxury: 'any kind of meat is more or less bearable with mustard'.

On Tuesday 6 December 2005, David Cameron became leader of the Conservative Party. The next day, Cameron shone on his first outing at Prime Minister's Questions.

Two days later Cameron announced the remainder of his shadow Cabinet, and Boris got nothing. This was a humiliation, for which his appointment the next day to the shadow higher education post was scant compensation. Cameron had given his colleague a highly appropriate portfolio, but had also cut him down to size, especially as Boris was on the same day obliged to resign the editorship of the *Spectator*. The Tory party was not going to risk another Liverpool.

Petronella was still in love with Boris, and kept in touch with him, but she also managed to joke about how she had backed the wrong horse in the Tory leadership stakes. In a *Spectator* Diary she recalled how she met the young David Cameron, who was working for the Wyatts' great friend Norman Lamont, at that time Chancellor of the Exchequer. It fell to Cameron to organise his boss's fiftieth birthday party, held at 11 Downing Street, at which Petronella had been asked to sing: Lamont was particularly keen on her 'Lilli Marlene'.

After her performance, Cameron asked her to dance, which he apparently did 'with the grace of Astaire and the manliness of Gene Kelly'. He asked her to a Tory winter ball, but one of them was forced to cancel, and soon after that he began going out with Samantha Sheffield, whom he was to marry. Petronella ended her account: 'As Professor Higgins says, "Damn, damn, damn!" Oh, why did I muff my chance to become the wife of the next Conservative Party leader and perhaps First Lady? I have always looked rather good in the pillbox hats worn by Jackie Kennedy.'

Boris delivered a farewell speech to the *Spectator*'s staff at the Christmas lunch, held on 15 December at Franco's restaurant in Jermyn Street. When he rose to his feet he said he would be as quick as possible: 'I have a terrible feeling that I'm going to dissolve into great floods of blubbing sentimentality, and that would not be true to the traditions of the *Spectator*.' Boris used an image about his colleagues at the magazine which he had already used in public: 'For most of my time here I have been propelled by your talents, as a fat German tourist may be transported by superior alpinists to the summit of Everest.'

Like much of what Boris says about himself, this is funny because it is so wildly wrong. It is true that he owed an enormous amount to his staff, and that he left the routine editorial work in their hands. But it would be absurd, and he knew it was absurd, to speak of himself as a passenger. If Boris was climbing Everest, he would probably be wearing the wrong gear, and would have forgotten to bring a number of essential items of kit. But he would not want for physical courage and his instinct would be to get to the top first. He would want to be the leader who reconnoitres a brilliant new route to the summit, not some gormless passenger.

As usual Boris thanked every member of staff by name for their efforts: 'You have made my life each day for the last six and a half years.' Kimberly was present, and he asked where the magazine would have been without her: 'We might have slunk along without anyone paying any attention at all without Kimberly Fortier.'

Boris recalled that when he took over as editor it was likened to putting 'a Ming vase in the hands of an ape'.

'I think I know who said it. I think the Ming vase is in pretty good shape.'

'Who said it?' people asked, turning to one another. Nobody seemed to know it was me, and I was too far away from Boris to see whether he looked in my direction. Ann Sindall, who was sitting beside me, was weeping.

Towards the end of his speech, Boris said that if anyone asked them to leave 56 Doughty Street he would urge them 'to chain yourselves to the railings'. He added that 'I know Kimberly will fight like the Hyrcan tiger she is.' Not long after, *Spectator* staff heard they would be moved from Doughty Street to new premises in Westminster.

Stuart Reid paid tribute to Boris: 'Boris is an impossible act to follow . . . Boris leaves the magazine in better shape than it has ever been. We must carry on as before.'

Boris: 'Hear, hear.'

Reid: 'Without Boris guiding us.'

Boris: 'Oh yes.'

Reid: 'The *Spectator* is given to us in trust. It is more than just a product and more than just a brand.'

On 28 February 2006, Boris acted as Cameron's warm-up man at Vinopolis, a wine emporium in south London where the Tory leader was launching a platitudinous document called 'Built to Last'. Cameron, whose third child, Arthur, had been born two weeks before, began by saying he'd been having a lot of strain and some sleepless nights, and that was just thinking about Boris's introduction.

The joke went down well, but also expressed the implicit rivalry between the two men. Boris quite plainly remained a star speaker, and one with the capacity to ridicule Cameron as a man devoted to a mindless doctrine of 'change'. Cameron in this period was rather obviously repeating himself, and people were beginning to question whether there was any substance to him, or whether he would turn out to be one of the great bores of today.

26

Roman Civilisation

BORIS SET ABOUT HIS DUTIES AS TORY SPOKESMAN ON higher education in a completely different manner to his debut less than two years before as arts spokesman. There was no spoof top-of-the-head manifesto, but instead a clear effort to be taken seriously.

On bumping into him in December 2005, soon after his appointment, I invited Boris to condemn Oxford University's plan to strip the colleges of the right to decide which students they admit. This sounded like an outrageous attempt to crush the colleges by subjecting them to a central management scheme. Yet Boris refused to dismiss the idea, and spoke well of Sir Tim Lankester, the President of Corpus Christi College, Oxford, who had chaired the working party which produced the proposals.

In his first appearance in the House of Commons in his new capacity, he called on the higher education minister, Bill Rammell, to dissociate himself from the deprecatory comments about medieval history made by Charles Clarke while Education Secretary.

Clarke had volunteered in 2003 that 'education for its own sake' was 'a bit dodgy', and that the study of medieval history was 'ornamental' and did not deserve taxpayers' money. Boris was incensed by these remarks. He was determined to defend the idea that the study of Latin, Greek, medieval history and other subjects which philistines might claim were of no practical value is worth it as an end in itself.

Not that Boris entirely abandoned his love of the frivolous. Early in 2006, after the rectorship of Edinburgh University had fallen vacant, he put in for it. But even here, he was at pains to emphasise that he was not simply trying to make some kind of joke: 'I am deadly serious about becoming rector of the University of Edinburgh. I believe I have a lot to offer as an ambassador for the students, the staff and the university.'

The rectorship has been held by eminent figures, including Gladstone, Churchill and Gordon Brown. The press reckoned Boris was the front-runner, and assumed he would have no difficulty beating the two other journalists in the race, Magnus Linklater and John Pilger.

But Boris's support for top-up fees provoked great hostility and prompted the Edinburgh University Students' Association, which has traditionally stayed out of elections for the rectorship, to launch an 'Anyone But Boris' campaign. Posters were distributed urging students to 'Practice Safe X – Don't Wake Up With a Dumb Blond Tomorrow'.

To most people's surprise, the election, held in mid-February 2006, was won by Mark Ballard, a 34-year-old Green member of the Scottish Parliament who had studied at Edinburgh University and of whom the students' association warmly approved. Linklater came second and Boris was only third. His campaign had been an unsatisfactory compromise: he could not give free play to his comic genius, nor could he match Ballard's earnestness.

Boris issued a statement: 'I salute the student body of Edinburgh and congratulate the new rector on his success. I am sure he will do the job in tremendous style. It has been a very enjoyable campaign fought with tact, honesty and discretion. I am sorry the student body came out against me, but democracy has triumphed. Given I am English, a Tory and broadly in favour of top-up fees, this was a commendable performance.'

In his first interview as higher education spokesman, Boris impressed Donald MacLeod, of the *Guardian*, by 'quoting accurately, and off the cuff, from a landmark decision on academic freedom in the US supreme court'.

Boris delivered the following message: 'If I want to do anything, I want to help vindicate academic freedom as enunciated by Justice Felix Frankfurter: the freedom to decide on academic grounds who should teach, what they should teach, how it should be taught and whom to admit. I think that's a very good definition of what we should be trying to do.'

But as MacLeod said, 'the note of gravitas is dissipated when he declares with feeling: "*Ich bin ein Frankfurter.*"'

Boris then clutched his head and said: 'It'll be the headline, won't it? Oh Christ.' It was the headline, but in the interview Boris rallied and declared: 'I don't mind if that's the headline. If it gets Frankfurter's definition of academic freedom into the public imagination, it's a small price to pay.'

The liberalism of Boris's outlook was confirmed by his comment on the less academic university courses which are nowadays on offer: 'My instincts are not to go around trying to exterminate Mickey Mouse courses. One man's Mickey Mouse course is another man's *literae humaniores*.' So there were no more jokes about wind-surfing, of the kind which had so infuriated the Registrar of Bangor University only nine months before, and there were no wild promises. When Boris was asked if a Conservative government would raise the £3,000 cap on fees, he replied: 'That's exactly the sort of question I prefer to shirk at this stage.'

MacLeod was impressed by Boris's capacity 'to do what most politicians find almost impossible these days: think aloud', and also that he seemed 'intent on bringing joy into the debate'. Boris told him: 'There are certain things I've discovered about higher education that have been fascinating. And the first and most important is that it's a huge success story . . . There are 91,000 EU students alone, heaven knows how many non-EU students. We've got campuses being inaugurated in China, we've got programmes in India.'

Later the same week, the *Times Higher Education Supplement* published an equally positive interview with Boris by Anna Fazackerley. She reported that 'Mr Johnson's willingness to make some noise about universities – at a time when they have all but disappeared from the political agenda – is already winning him important friends in the sector . . . An insider at Universities UK reports that the group's chief executive, Baroness Warwick, was seriously impressed with Mr Johnson at a recent meeting. No mean feat considering she is a Labour peer.' To the 'amazement' of Universities UK, Boris had 'obviously digested the large pile of paper' it had sent him, 'and is keen to devour more'.

Fazackerley concluded her piece with the words: 'It is clear that those expecting controversy will not have long to wait. Mr Johnson has arrived. Let the show begin.'

At the end of the *Guardian* interview, Boris suddenly remembered to plug his new book, *The Dream of Rome*, which was published at the start of February 2006, accompanied by a two-part television series on BBC2. During one of these programmes someone says to Boris, 'I can see you are fascinated by empire – you would like to be an emperor,' to which Boris replies, 'Well, I can think of worse fates.'

Charles Brand, who produced the series, said that as a presenter, Boris 'proved himself to be a complete natural', and also 'didn't show the ego that TV presenters usually show'. In these programmes, he was like the best kind of schoolmaster: entertaining, energetic and plainly inspired by a deep love of his

subject. He had visited some of the greatest Roman sites, and
made one want to visit them too. At the Pont du Gard, the
stupendous aqueduct which carried water to Nîmes, Boris
remarked: 'Now one thing you can say about the Romans. They
certainly were not cowboy plumbers.'

The Pont du Gard may have been started by the Emperor
Augustus' right-hand man, Marcus Vipsanius Agrippa, in 14 BC.
This was the cue for another joke: 'If Augustus had any kind of
logistical or military problem his first reaction, I imagine, was to
shout "Get Agrippa!"'

Boris interviewed scholars in French, Italian and German, and
gave us a few words of Latin without making us feel hopelessly
ignorant. Brand said the only problem they had was with Boris's
English, which was 'too erudite for the BBC2 audience'. At the
screening held in a Soho hotel before the programmes were
broadcast, Boris said: 'What you realise about TV is it's a piece
of cake to say something about ancient Rome. The tricky thing
is to walk in a straight line as you say it.'

But some viewers thought he mucked up the Roman history
by shoving in a strained comparison with the European Union.
My wife watched for about three minutes before saying: 'There's
such an ideological bent behind it, you can't believe a word of it.
I can't watch it. I think it's just bollocks.'

My own view is that educated people have for many centuries
allowed the ancient and modern worlds to intermingle and
inform each other, and Boris stands in this grand tradition. The
comparison with Rome does help to suggest why the European
Union has failed to command our loyalties. Rome had an
emperor, and an emperor cult, the EU does not. There is no
Caesar on the Euro, but instead what Boris called the 'evasive
symbolism' of 'bridges, culverts, drainage ditches'. Rome persuaded the people it conquered to want to be Roman citizens in
a way that Brussels has failed to persuade us to aspire to
European citizenship.

At the launch party held at Daunt Books in Marylebone High Street, Boris said, 'I occasionally wonder what people like me are doing in public life,' and answered: 'It is because we hope to become shadow spokesman for higher education.'

He described his latest work as 'what is in a not particularly hotly contested field my best book yet'. He was right. It is true that like much of Boris's writing, *The Dream of Rome* would be better if he had taken more trouble over it. Boris is not a scientific historian, someone who attempts to examine evidence in the most meticulous and fair-minded way. But if Boris had proceeded with that kind of care, he would never have got the book written at all.

And Boris as a historian still has great merits, and insights which would usually escape more professional scholars. Boris is a man for whom the past, and especially the classical past, is still alive. Like P. G. Wodehouse's work, his writing is filled with similes which would occur to nobody else. Boris said a statue of the Emperor Augustus with his arm aloft looked 'like Shane Warne doing his flipper'.

Boris also pointed out that in the dining-rooms of sophisticated Roman families one would find a marble portrait bust of the emperor, and remarked: 'Imagine the frisson of horror if you went out to dinner in Islington and looked up to see a marble rendition of Blair, or Thatcher, or even John Major. You'd think it was either a joke or a demented piece of idolatry.'

To the Romans, it was neither frivolous nor idolatrous to regard their emperor as a god. The early Christians were offensive to Rome, not because they had their own God, but because they insisted he was the only God, which meant they denied the divinity of the emperor. It is clear where Boris's sympathies lie: 'In their sophistication, their understanding of human nature, pain and pleasure, the Romans had a civilisation as exalted as anything we have seen.' Boris loves the glory-chasing, the ostentation and the 'ceaseless competition between macho males' in the Roman Empire: 'It was a world that believed above all in winners and losers, in death and glory.' The Romans had an amazing literature, they had no hang-ups about sex and they 'used the written word to celebrate innocent pleasures that were to become the subjects of Christian guilt and hysteria'.

The Christians were also deplorably meek, which is not a Roman virtue. In the last pages of his book, Boris says it is 'not fashionable these days to cite Edward Gibbon', before confessing that 'I cannot help feeling there is a grain of truth in the following mordant analysis', after which he gives us this account by Gibbon of why the Roman Empire declined:

> The clergy successfully preached the doctrines of patience and pusillanimity; the active virtues of society were discouraged, and the last remains of the military spirit were buried in the cloister: a large portion of public and private wealth was consecrated to the specious demands of charity and devotion; and the soldiers' pay was lavished on the useless multitudes of both sexes, who could only plead the merits of abstinence and chastity.

Abstinence and chastity count for nothing with Boris. He does not pretend that Christianity was wholly to blame for the decline and fall of the Roman Empire, or even the chief cause. But it is clear that he is inspired by the Romans, and even more by the Greeks, and repelled by the early Christians: 'In their suicidal behaviour, in their belief in an afterlife, and in their rejection of the values of the culture in which they found themselves, the early Christians evoke obvious comparisons with Islamic suicide bombers of today.'

When *Third Way*, a Christian magazine, interviewed Boris about his faith, he said: 'My family background is Muslim, Jewish and Christian, so I don't find it very easy to believe exclusively in any one particular monotheism. In fact, my children are a quarter Indian, so their ancestors adhere to a polytheistic faith. I'm a sort of – yeah, I'm Church of England all right, no question about it. I was confirmed in a Church of England church, but I don't kind of . . . Religion is a very private thing . . . Actually I once won the Wilder Divinity Prize, and the prep school scripture prize.'

Boris the politician has demonstrated how well equipped he is for the multicultural world of Muslims, Jews, Christians and Indian polytheists. But Boris the man has revealed virtually nothing of his own religion. Later in the same interview, Boris said that like the radio signal for a London channel in the Chiltern hills, out towards Oxford, his faith 'sort of comes and goes a bit'. This makes him sound like a Christian who is troubled by doubts.

But beneath a top-dressing of Anglicanism, Boris remains a whole-hearted pagan. He is a pre-Christian figure who lives in a classical world of gods and heroes. A close friend said: 'He believes in god-like forces all of which are watching him. Because he is Achilles, chosen by the gods, he's put through these trials. Everything is always about him, and nobody is better than him. He can betray other people. It's all part of his drama, his trial by fire. He's very superstitious. He's Achilles and the gods are watching him and he's destined for greatness. He has funny obsessive-compulsive things. He reads car number plates and thinks of the first thing they could stand for. So BWW stands for Boris Will Win.'

This mixture of the educated and the popular – of classical literature and car number plates – is part of the essence of Boris.

27

Coming Up on the Outside

BORIS'S EFFORTS TO PRESENT A MORE SERIOUS FACE TO the world were dealt a severe blow on 2 April 2006, when his old friends at the *News of the World* put him on the front cover again. The headline was 'Boris Cheats With a Blonde' and the story described how 'we caught the shadow minister enjoying a series of secret trysts with blonde beauty Anna Fazackerley, 29, at her London flat'.

The paper printed photographs of Boris leaving Anna's flat in the King's Road, Chelsea, on three occasions within ten days at the end of March. In one of the pictures Anna gazed fondly after him from the doorstep, while in another he waved at her from his bike as she left by taxi.

Boris wore a black beanie hat pulled low down over his fore-head, which covered his hair but did not for one moment disguise who he was. If anything the hat merely served to emphasise his identity. To people worried about Marina, this was one of the most hurtful aspects of his behaviour: the lack of trouble he had taken to hide his meetings with Anna. But when I tried to put this point to Boris, he seemed to think that he had nothing to conceal.

It is true that he could just have been discussing higher education policy with Anna, who after all had recently interviewed him on this very subject. One should also note that the *News of the World* offered, as so often, less evidence than its headline suggested, and was quite capable of completely misinterpreting what scraps of information its agents had managed to obtain.

The following Sunday, the newspaper claimed that on the Thursday after the first story appeared, Boris had shared a hotel room with Anna in Paris, on his way back from a trip to China. Quite friendly observers started to ask if he had gone mad. But the *News of the World* was wrong about Paris. If its reporters had troubled to discover from the hotel staff what the woman who left Boris's room at seven in the morning looked like, they would have learned that, unlike Anna, she was rather small and dark. She was in fact Boris's wife, Marina.

This ridiculous error cried out for correction. But the trouble about correcting errors is that you may end up implying that everything you do not correct is true. Marina accepted Boris's assurance that there had been no affair, but very reasonably decided not to get into an argument with such opponents.

It emerged from the *News of the World*'s coverage that Boris was still visiting Petronella as well as Anna. This was certainly not something on which Boris was going to comment. When Anna was asked if she would like to comment on her alleged affair with Boris, she said: 'Absolutely not.' Boris said: 'You're very kind. But no thank you. Absolutely not. No comment whatsoever. Thanks a lot. Bye.'

This was a vast improvement on his denial of his affair with Petronella, but the whole situation was still pretty horrible for Marina. The press descended on their house off the Holloway Road. Boris was at this point in China, on a fact-finding mission about higher education, and she found herself questioned by reporters in front of her children. She lodged a complaint with the Press Complaints Commission about this.

Marina otherwise maintained a dignified silence. So did her

parents, though her father told a reporter that the story was 'rubbish'. He was infuriated to find he had instead been quoted as saying, 'I think it's rubbish, but I don't know.' In private, the Wheelers took a very dim view both of Petronella, and of her mother, Verushka Wyatt, for trying to seduce Boris away from Marina.

Meanwhile a friend of the Wyatts said Petronella was very upset, and felt 'heartbroken and betrayed', when the news of Boris's alleged affair with Anna broke.

Some of the tabloids made half-hearted calls for David Cameron to sack Boris, which the Tory leader quite rightly rejected, for it would have been ridiculous to set a precedent for sacking someone simply because they were said to have committed adultery.

Ephraim Hardcastle, in the *Daily Mail*, wrote daily reports on Boris, whom he diagnosed as suffering from satyrism, or 'unusually strong sexual desires'. He went on: 'Boris must re-establish himself as a serious political player. Why not portray himself as a victim of sexual addiction and seek treatment? This route was chosen by Hollywood stars Michael Douglas, Rob Lowe and Billy Bob Thornton.'

Shortly before he was done over by the *News of the World*, Boris used his *Telegraph* column to mount a robust defence of Silvio Berlusconi, who was about to lose the Italian General Election. Boris hailed Berlusconi as 'a standing reproach to the parade of platitudinous Pooters that pass across the stage of international diplomacy'. He gave some examples of the Italian Prime Minister's wild and tasteless behaviour, and asked why so many Italians still liked him: 'The answer is that they like him not in spite of the gaffes, but because of the gaffes. It is Berlusconi's genius that he has become the only world leader in the great queue of grey-suited line-toers who can be consistently relied on to say something eye-popping.'

One can see the bare bones of a defence of Boris here. He is more fun than the grey and cautious hypocrites who surround him. His very errors make him loveable.

Sue Lawley suggested to Boris on *Desert Island Discs* that he liked taking risks:

> LAWLEY: 'Aren't you somebody who, I mean, what, you like to play with fire.'
>
> BORIS: 'Sue, you're brilliantly good, you're a brilliant interviewer, but in the immortal words of, of Sue Lawley, more music please.'
>
> LAWLEY: 'You do like playing with fire though, don't you. It's all part of being tested.'
>
> BORIS: 'Well. I see. This is your, this is your theory, is it? . . . Well, I suppose there might be an element of truth in that, but anyway. Not unnecessary risks, no.'

Lawley was right to detect a craving for danger in Boris. He would find a life without risk intolerably dull. But he also craves comfort and reassurance. Unlike many Englishmen of his class, he actually enjoys the company of women, and acknowledges his need of them. He has also shown time after time that embarrassments which would make many people go away and hide in a hole in the ground were not quite so mortifying to him.

Boris finds himself trapped in the role of celebrity. Without ever holding a political office of any significance, he has become more famous than most Cabinet ministers, but is also considered more irresponsible. There is a danger that he will turn into a kind of national treasure, to be wheeled out and laughed at on significant occasions, or occasions which television producers regard as significant.

One of his weaknesses is an excessive desire to be liked, and he will be hurt if he does not come across as likeable in this book. Another flaw is his inability, or obdurate unwillingness, to make choices which would entail a degree of self-sacrifice. Asked if he would like A or B, he generally gives no clear answer and tries to have both.

He distracts our attention from this evasiveness by telling very enjoyable jokes, which along with his Woosterish persona have made him one of the most popular performers of our times. But the jokes can also make him seem to serious-minded listeners as if he does not believe a word he is saying. If he used to appear more grown-up than his contemporaries, he may by now be striking some of them as a bit juvenile.

Prigs think he needs to learn to be 'serious', by which they mean as dull as they are, and he has recently responded by giving a nod or two in their direction. The problem is that when he adopts a serious tone, he can begin to sound a bit like Prince Charles. But he is not without a sense of prudence, and has for years refused many more invitations to take part in mad stunts than he has accepted. He made an effort, when he was appointed shadow higher education spokesman, to show what a sober fellow he can be, but slightly spoiled the effect by giving a jokey, off-the-cuff speech to an audience of higher education dignitaries at King's College, London, who were expecting a considered account of Conservative policy.

The vein of anarchy in his character, and his impulse to do the opposite of what he is told, make it very hard for him to obey rules which seem to him to be an infringement of his right to do as he pleases. As Martin Hammond said of him when he was still at school: 'Boris sometimes seems affronted when criticised for what amounts to a gross failure of responsibility . . . I think he honestly believes that it is churlish of us not to regard him as an exception, one who should be free of the network of obligation which binds everyone else.'

This determination to do things his own way, even if it means breaking the rules, is one of the most characteristic things about Boris. He was very successful as a journalist, but did not just grind his way on to become editor of the *Telegraph* or *The Times*. He started a parliamentary career which could easily end in failure, and when *Conservative Heartland* – a magazine for Tory party members – asked him in 2001 why he had taken this risk, he said he wanted to be where the action is, not just watching it, and went on: 'We all have tram tracks. All our lives . . . marriage, children . . . there is a lot to do, a lot going on . . . There comes a point where you've got to put the dynamite under your own tram tracks . . . derail yourself. See what happens.'

It is an extraordinary image. The last thing most people want to do is to derail themselves. Boris is braver and more optimistic, and finds stability more suffocating, than most of us do.

Before the 2006 World Cup, when he turned out for England in a charity football match against Germany, he conducted a rugby tackle on one of the German players. The video clip of this bizarre spectacle become one of the most popular things on the Internet. Boris had entertained people by doing something which nobody else would have dared to do, or even thought of doing.

That formula does not do justice to Boris's sex life, where he has done what many men have thought of doing. According to Balzac, men of all kinds, the distinguished man and the fool, desire both an ideal love and pleasure, 'which most often turns out to be a work in two volumes'. Boris has committed adultery, but when millions of other people have done likewise, it would be intolerably prudish and self-righteous to hold that this debarred him from high office. The recently published diaries of Duff Cooper, a distinguished Tory politician of the 1930s, show him committing adultery with a prodigious number of women, but this did not prevent him from taking the brave and correct decision to resign in 1938 in protest at Neville Chamberlain's appeasement policy.

For Boris, it is a drawback that Parliament has many rules and people get quite cross if you break them. As an MP, you are expected to show an extraordinary degree of patience. Unless you spend hour after hour sitting in the Commons Chamber, the Speaker will not call you in debates, and unless you do your bit in committee the Whips will not rate you either. Boris lacked the time and docility to put up with day after day of this drudgery.

So although he is a brilliant debater, he has not yet established himself as a parliamentary performer. He is not among the few dozen Tory MPs who regularly turn up and speak. Even when Boris comes to Prime Minister's Questions, a highlight of the week which he often skips, he tends to stand behind the seat occupied by the Serjeant at Arms, a long way from the Conservative Party leader, David Cameron. There is no disguising the fact that while in the summer of 2004 Boris was still the coming man, in the summer of 2006, when these words were written, he looked a bit out of it, and was not one of the talented young group which had formed around Cameron.

But Boris was never the kind of politician who could expect to get to the top by dint of slow, inside work. This does not mean he has no chance of fulfilling his ambition to become Prime Minister. Insiders can become boring, and dangerously cut off. They can fail to see which way the world is moving, and can lose what capacity they may once have had to communicate with the wider public.

Boris is the opposite. He is very quick to see which way the world is moving and brilliant at reaching the wider public. These gifts have made him a successful journalist and may yet be of service to him as a politician. If he can lend his voice to public discontents which the insiders have ignored, he will at first be dismissed by the party establishment as a mere maverick, troublemaker and populist, but may end by becoming the indispensable figure which it needs to show that it has responded to the public anger. Boris is willing to go out in all weathers and is likely to thrive best when times are worst. In the summer of 2006, he gave a fiery speech in the Commons, denouncing Britain's unequal extradition arrangements with America. One of Boris's own constituents was on the point of being extradited to Texas, and his anger at the unfairness of this proceeding came through loud and strong. It did not matter that Boris used one or two bizarre turns of phrase: his moral seriousness was unmistakable.

Yet even without wars, tumults and other great themes, Boris is likely to be needed by the cautious insiders, to demonstrate that they have some connection with Merry England. This is the generous conservatism for which he stands. He wants people to be free to enjoy themselves, does not rush to condemn anyone whose pleasures are not his own and sympathises with the little man who finds himself caught in an impossible position. While many politicians have the urge to perfect society, Boris believes in the imperfectability of mankind, and especially of himself. He does not seek to attain impossibly high standards, nor does he impose them on others. He is unpompous, which is yet another reason why people like him so much.

Hayek said in 1944, 'British strength, British character and British achievements are to a great extent the result of a cultivation of the spontaneous.' That is what makes Boris so British: his capacity for being spontaneous. He has never prepared himself properly, and this means his whole life has been a preparation for being unprepared. His real problem, an old friend of the family suggested, is to take himself seriously.

When he was worrying over lunch about this book, Boris leaned across the table and recited in heartfelt self-defence Othello's great last speech:

> Soft you, a word or two before you go.
> I have done the state some service, and they know't:
> No more of that. I pray you, in your letters,
> When you shall these unlucky deeds relate,

Speak of me as I am. Nothing extenuate,
Nor set down aught in malice. Then must you speak
Of one that loved not wisely, but too well;
Of one not easily jealous, but, being wrought,
Perplexed in the extreme; of one whose hand,
Like the base Indian, threw a pearl away
Richer than all his tribe; of one whose subdued eyes,
Albeit unused to the melting mood,
Drops tears as fast as the Arabian trees
Their medicinable gum. Set you down this,
And say besides that in Aleppo once,
Where a malignant and a turbaned Turk
Beat a Venetian and traduced the state,
I took by th'throat the circumcised dog
And smote him – thus!

With these words, Othello stabs himself, kisses the dead body of
Desdemona and dies. Boris is not Othello, and stern judges will
think it was preposterous of him to recite those lines. But part of
the charm of Boris is that he is willing to be preposterous. He
has already done the state some service by entertaining us, and
by popular demand he can still attain the highest office. In a
world where Reagan can become President, it is not preposterous to think of Boris as Prime Minister. His rivals envy the love
and admiration he evinces, while lamenting how unpopular our
political system has become. If they try to exclude Boris because
he is too colourful, too talented and too good at reaching the
people, they will not be forgiven.

Picture Credits

1, 2, 4, 7–13, 15–17: Private collection; 3: Sophie Baker; 5, 6: Micky Böl; 14: *Tatler*; 18, 24: Nigel Howard; 19: Dave Bennett/ Getty Images; 20, 21: *Spectator*; 22: John Taylor/Pressnet.co.uk; 23: Courtesy of Hat-Trick Productions; 25: Caroline Moore; 26: Christopher Furlong/Getty Images; 27: Simon Brown; 28: *Private Eye*; 29: *News of the World*; 30: Richard Austin/Rex Features; 31: Mike Walker/Rex Features; 32: David Hartley/ Rex Features

Index

Ackroyd, Peter, 132
Aitken, Jonathan, 122
Ali Kemal (great-grandfather),
  5–9, 216
Alibhai-Brown, Yasmin, 225
Amiel, Barbara, 89, 153, 158,
  159, 170
Amory, Mark, 175
Anderson, Sir Eric, 49–51, 104
Ashdown House preparatory
  school, 29–34
Asquith, Cyril, 58
Asquith, Herbert, 58
Atatürk, Kemal (Mustafa Kemal),
  6–7

Bailey, David, 79
Baldwin, Tom, 185
Ballard, Mark, 248
Balliol College (Oxford), 58–9
Barber, Lynn, 177
Barclay brothers, 153, 226
Barnes, Jonathan, 58–9, 60–2, 73
Barwick, Sandra, 131
Bayston, Chris, 53–4
Beaton, Alistair, 234
Belloc, Hilaire, 144
Berlaymont building (Brussels), 98
Berlusconi, Silvio, 257

Bernard, Daniel, 158, 159
Bernard, Jeffrey, 132
Biffen, John, 86, 87
Biffen, Lady, 86, 87
Bigley, Ken, 193–4, 201
Bigley, Paul, 201–2
Billington, Rachel, 13
Binyon, Michael, 100–1, 105–6
Black, Conrad, 33, 131, 153–6,
  160–1, 174, 186; and Boris,
  89, 151, 154–5, 156, 158, 159,
  170, 177; faces charges, 153,
  161, 186
Black Wednesday (1992), 228
Blackburn, Tony, 66
Blair, Tony, 49, 134, 147, 181
Blunkett, David, 188, 189, 220,
  228
Blunt, James, 167
Boden, Johnnie, 48
Booth, Lauren, 231
Bouquet, Kevin, 201
Boyle, Tom, 146
Brand, Charles, 250, 251
Breakfast With Frost (TV
  programme), 130
Brock, George, 90, 93–4, 100
Brown, Andrew, 132
Brown, Gordon, 181, 348

Brown, Tina, 82–3
Brussels: Boris as *Telegraph* correspondent, 97–106, 108
Bryant, John, 95
Budgen, Nick and Madeleine, 113
Bullingdon (Oxford dining club), 63–6
Bush, George W., 174
Butler, Lord (Robin) 216–17
Butler, Nell, 216

Cameron, David, 71, 208, 235–8, 244, 245–6, 257; and drugs issue, 214; elected leader of Conservative Party, 243; at Eton, 52; parallels between Boris and, 236–7; rivalry with Boris, 246
Campbell, Alastair, 147
Carroll, Walter, 54
Carter, Nick, 197
Cash, Bill, 37
Catholic Herald, 135
Chancellor, Alexander, 132
Channon, Olivia, 82–3
Channon, Paul, 83
Charteris, Lord (Martin), 45
Chhabra, Ramesh, 197, 198
Churchill, Sir Winston, 143
Circassians, 5
Clarke, Charles, 247
Clarke, Jeremy, 134
Clarke, Kenneth, 150, 236
Clarke, Susan, 137
Clinton, President Bill, 211–12, 213
Cluff, Algy, 158
Cobbett, William, 143–4
Collier, Stuart, 117, 118, 120, 121

Colson, Dan, 134, 156, 158, 160
Connock, Alexander, 74
Conservative Heartland, 260
Cook, Robin, 213
Cooper, Duff, 260
Cox, Meyrick, 31
Cumani, Matt, 197

Dacre, Paul, 155
Daily Mail: Ephraim Hardcastle column, 171–2, 257
Daily Mirror, 165
Daily Telegraph, 91, 119, 126, 160; Boris as chief political columnist, 124–5; Boris as leader-writer, 97; Boris's back-page interview in, 126; Boris's column in, 177, 236, 257
d'Ancona, Matthew, 144
Davis, David, 150, 235, 236
de Pfeffel, Baron, 10
Deedes, Bill, 127
Deedes, Jeremy, 119
Delors, Jacques, 99, 101, 103–4
Denmark; rejection of Maastricht Treaty, 104
Desert Island Discs (radio programme), 101–2, 157, 190–1, 204–6, 238–43, 258
Devonshire, Duchess of, 132–3
Disraeli, Benjamin, 143
Dixon, Hugh, 51–2
Dougary, Ginny, 182
Douglas-Home, Charlie, 88
Dream of Rome, The (Johnson), 250–3
Duncan, Andrew, 126
Duncan Smith, Iain, 128, 150–1, 237

Edinburgh University, 248
Edward II, King, 91–3, 94–5
Ehrman, Richard, 137
Ekserdjian, David, 57–8, 61
elections: (1997), 125; (2001), 144–5; (2005), 229, 232
English, Sir David, 155
Eton, 39–55
Eton College Chronicle, 46–7, 51, 52
European, 98
European Commission, 98, 99, 100
European Union, 100, 103; comparison with Rome, 251
euroscepticism, 103
Eustice, George, 201
Evans, Chris, 126–7
Evans, Lloyd, 59, 60, 72, 74–5, 232
Evening Standard, 122, 225

Fawcett, Beatrice (Bice) (née Lowe), 13
Fawcett, Edmund, 109–10
Fawcett, Henry, 12
Fawcett, Sir James, 2, 12–13
Fawcett, Millicent Garrett, 12
Fazackerley, Anna, 250, 255–6
Fearnley-Whittingstall, Hugh, 52, 79–80
Ferranti, Alexa de, 77
Fildes, Christopher, 186
Fitzgerald, Patrick, 161
Fleming, Ian, 57
Fletcher, Kim, 135
Fortier, Kimberly, 158, 186–8, 189, 220–1, 228, 229, 245
Fraser, Orlando, 230

Friends, Voters, Countrymen (Johnson), 142, 145–6

Garland, Nicholas, 170
Garside, Charles, 98
Gibbon, Edward, 253
Gill, A. A., 144
Gilmour, Andrew, 49, 53, 64– 5, 93, 112, 174
Gilmour, Sir Ian, 65, 131, 206
Glover, Stephen, 144
Goldsmith, Jimmy, 176
Goodall, Brenda, 73
Goodman, Paul, 138
Gove, Michael, 70, 80, 144, 197–8, 227
Gowrie, Lord, 87
GQ: car articles by Boris for, 177–8; interview with Boris, 130, 151
Grant, Charles, 101, 102–3, 105, 109–10
Griffin, Jasper, 60, 61, 84
Gross, Miriam, 88–9
Gross, Susanna, 174–6, 204
Guppy, Darius, 57, 62–3, 64, 74, 80, 117–23, 128, 142, 218

Hague, William, 150, 237
Halley, Gwen, 206–7
Hammond, Martin, 40–4, 45–6, 48–9, 53, 54–5, 259
Hards, Eleanor, 146
Hartley, Aidan, 74
Hastings, Max, 91, 97, 104, 119, 122, 154, 155
Hatfield, Penny, 52
Hattersley, Roy, 146

Have I Got News for You (TV programme), 127–9
Headmaster's Essay Society (Eton), 50
Healey, Denis, 58
Heath, Edward, 51, 58, 84, 237
Heffer, Simon, 194, 195, 201
Helm, Sarah, 98–9, 182
Henderson, Paul, 178
Henley constituency, 142, 144–5
Henley Standard, 146
Hennessy, Patrick, 39, 62, 65, 204, 223–4
Heseltine, Michael, 141, 142
Hesketh-Harvey, Kit, 159
Hill, Paul, 114
Hillsborough disaster, 194, 195
Hislop, Ian, 127–8, 129
Hoggart, Simon, 200
Howard, Michael, 69, 115, 178, 236, 237; and Liverpool débâcle, 195, 196, 201, 204, 206, 208; relationship with Boris, 222, 224; sacking of Boris as shadow arts minister, 222–3, 224; at *Spectator* awards lunch, 221–2; steps down as leader, 235
Howarth, George, 207
Howe, Sir Geoffrey, 102
Hudson, Tim, 233
Hurd, Douglas, 104, 237

Independent, 98
Ingrams, Richard, 132, 143–4
Israel, 71

Jenkin, Anne, 148
Jenkin, Bernard, 148

Jenkins, Roy, 58, 84
Jenkins, Simon, 26
Johnson, Allegra (née Mostyn-Owen) (first wife), xii, 112–13; admirers while at Oxford, 79–80; collapse of marriage to Boris and divorce, 107–10, 113, 114; courtship with Boris, 76–84; first meeting with Boris, 76–7; and Guppy, 80; joint article with Boris in *Sunday Telegraph*, 82–3; law studies, 97, 110–11; marriage to Boris, 85– 7, 89–90; parental background, 77–8; post-marriage relationship with Boris, 112–13, 114; works for *Evening Standard*, 83
Johnson, Boris
  Early Years: academic record, 30; at Ashdown House preparatory school, 29–34; birth and naming, 1–4; in Brussels, 26–7; childhood and competitive upbringing, 11–12, 16, 17–18, 19; deafness as a child, 11–12, 241–2; and divorce of parents, 35–6, 36–7, 39; at Eton, 39–55; and acting, 52–3; made captain of school, 46; piano-playing, 53–4; plays rugby, 48– 9; rebuke from Provost of Eton, 44–5; school reports, 40–6, 54–5; Wall Game, 46–8; wins scholarship, 31; writes for the *Chronicle*, 51, 52; love of Classics, 30–1, 40, 54; love of

reading, 27; at Oxford,
56–84; elected to the
Bullingdon, 63–4, 65–6;
embracing of SDP, 71;
friendship with Guppy, 62–3;
idleness charge, 61, 62;
journalism, 73–5; member of
Chapsoc, 66; plays rugby, 62;
politics and route to Oxford
Union presidency, 59–60,
68–73; wins classical
scholarship to, 54–5; places
lived at with parents, 11, 14,
16, 17–18, 26
**Journalistic and Writing
Career**, xii, 83; article
defending Clinton over
Lewinsky affair, 211–13;
article defending hunting,
25–6; at Oxford, 73–5;
attributes, 109; Commentator
of the Year (1997), 125; back-
page interview in *Telegraph*,
126; Brussels correspondent,
97–106, 108; car articles for
GQ, 177–8; as political
columnist on *Telegraph* after
returning from Brussels,
124–5; combining MP duties
with editorship of the
Spectator, 143–4, 153, 156–7,
158, 204–5, 206–7, 239;
Telegraph column, 177, 236,
257; editorial style and
strengths, 45, 133–4;
editorship of the *Spectator*, 33,
131–4, 139, 141, 143, 153,
156, 174; editorship of the
Tributary at Oxford, 74–5;

Friends, Voters, Countrymen,
142, 145–6; impact of 'Delors
Plan to Rule Europe' article,
103– 4; as leader-writer at
Telegraph, 97; leaves Brussels,
115–16; *Lend Me Your Ears*,
90–1, 126, 176–7; and Powell
story, 181–2; resigns
editorship of *Spectator* and
farewell speech to staff, 243,
244–5; sacking from *The
Times* over 'Edward II' article,
91–6; *Seventy-Two Virgins*, 89,
189–92; training with
Wolverhampton Express & Star,
89–90; wanting editorship of
Daily Telegraph, 160; working
for *The Times*, 88, 89–90;
writes political column in
Spectator, 125; writing
suffused with sexual imagery,
167
Personal Life: ability to make
people laugh, 32, 72, 75,
128–9, 158; affair with
Petronella Wyatt, xiv, 33,
162–6, 169– 73, 211–16;
alleged affair with Anna
Fazackerley, 255–6; ambition
and competitiveness of,
17–18, 57, 145, 240; ancestral
and parental background,
2–3, 5– 10, 11–16; appeal and
attraction of, 20, 165, 169,
262; attributes and qualities,
xvi, 49, 50, 261; aversion to
eggs, 12; birth of children,
115, 125; and car number
plates, 254; care for mother,

36; celebrity of, 258; character and mannerisms, 17, 37, 41, 60, 135–6, 155; charity football match against Germany, 260; charm and charisma of, 60, 72, 88, 158, 168, 169, 177, 241, 263; collapse of marriage to Allegra and divorce, 107–10, 113, 114; courtship of Allegra, 76–84; courtship of Marina, 111–12, 113; craving of action and danger, 139, 258; and cycling, 182–4; debating talents, 51, 72, 261; determination to do things his own way, 259–60; energy and vitality of, xvi, 50, 169; fails in bid for rectorship of Edinburgh University, 248–9; favourite food, 107; financial affairs, 138; and Guppy scandal, 117–23, 142; hair, 5, 39; insecurity and vulnerability of, 16, 17, 20; intellectual abilities, 27, 30, 41, 145; interview with *GQ*, 130, 151; love of children, 165, 176; love of driving fast cars, 178; marriage to Allegra, 85–7, 89–90; marriage to Marina, 114–15, 176; opposition to corporal punishment, 33; and painting, 19; profile of by *New York Times*, 157–8; recital of poetry, xiii, 105–6; and religion, 253–4; self-criticism, 126, 128–9; similarities with

father, 37, 38–9; as a speaker, 70; story of Petronella affair comes out, 209–16, 222–5; thrown out of house over Petronella affair, 216–18; weaknesses, 258–9; and women, 166–8, 258

Political Career: ambition to become Prime Minister, 143, 161, 261; as an MP, 149; and Cameron, 235–8, 245–6; candidate for Clwyd South, 125; combining of editorship of the *Spectator* with, 143–4, 153, 156–7, 158, 204–5, 206–7, 239; confrontation with Campbell, 147; election campaign (2005) and holding of seat with increased majority, 230–1, 232; first appearance at Dispatch Box as a shadow minister, 180–1; hit in the face with a bread roll, 146–7; holds Henley seat at 2001 election, 144–5; and Liverpool débâcle, 193–208; made vice-chairman of Conservative Party, 178–9; as a parliamentary performer, 261; popularity, 148, 151–2; relationship with Duncan Smith, 150–1; relationship with Howard, 222, 224; sacking of as shadow arts minister by Howard, 222–5; selected for Henley seat, 141–3; as shadow arts minister, 179–80; as shadow spokesman for higher education under Cameron, 243, 247–8, 249–50, 259

Television and Radio: appearance on *Desert Island Discs*, 101–2, 157, 190–1, 204–6, 238–43, 258; *Richard and Judy*, 208; *Have I Got News for You*, 127–9; presenter of Turkish exhibition at Royal Academy programme, 7; programmes appeared on, 130; series on Rome, 250–1

Johnson, Cassia Peaches (daughter), 125

Johnson, Charlotte (née Fawcett) (mother), xv, 87, 109; ancestral background, 12; and birth of Boris, 1–2; divorce, 35–6; married life, 1–4, 11–12, 14, 25; nervous breakdown, 27–8, 109; at Oxford, 11; and Parkinson's disease, 36; teaching of children herself, 19

Johnson, Frank, 88, 95, 97, 155–6, 158

Johnson, Irène ('Buster') (née Williams) (grandmother), 10, 23

Johnson, Jenny (Stanley's second wife), 18, 81

Johnson, Julia (Stanley's daughter by second wife), 18, 19

Johnson, Lara Lettice (daughter), 115, 125

Johnson, Leo (brother), 14, 32

Johnson, Margaret (wife of Ali Kemal), 8–9

Johnson, Marina (née Wheeler) (second wife), xv, 26–7, 188:

background, 111; and Boris's affair with Petronella, 215–16; and Boris's alleged affair with Anna Fazackerley, 256–7; courtship with Boris, 111–12, 113; marriage to Boris, 114–15, 176; throws Boris out of house, 216–17

Johnson, Milo Arthur (son), 125

Johnson, Paul, 221

Johnson, Rachel (sister), xv, 14, 17, 18, 23, 32, 33, 66–7, 81

Johnson, Stanley (father), 32, 87, 216; and birth of Boris, 1–2; divorce, 35; early married life, 1–4, 16; and environment, 38; *Gold Dust*, 14; humour of, 37–8; joins Foreign Office, 14; *Life Without Birth*, 14–15; meeting with author at Nethercote Cottage, 21–6; political career, 37–8; selected Tory candidate for Teighbridge but loses in election (2005), 229–32; similarities with Boris, 37, 38–9; wins Harkness Fellowship, 2; works for European Commission, 26

Johnson, Theodore Apollo (son), 125

Johnson, Wilfred (Osman Ali) (Johnny) (grandfather), 8, 10, 23, 24

Jones, James, 207

Jowett, Benjamin, 58

Kavanagh, Trevor, 139

Kennedy, Charles, 129

Kenny, Sir Anthony, 59, 84

Kerr, John, 105
Kerridge, Roy, 132
Kerry, John, 174
King, Martin Luther, 14
Kuneralp, Zeki, 9

Lamont, Norman, 228, 244
Lamy, Pascal, 99–100
Landale, James, 115–16
Lane, Tony, 146–7
Lankester, Sir Tim, 247
Lawley, Sue, 157, 190–1, 204–6,
    238–40, 240–3, 258
Lawson, Dominic, 125, 131, 181
Lawson, Nigel, 131
Layfield, Luke, 150
Lend Me Your Ears (Johnson),
    90–1, 126, 176–7
Lester, Lord, 13
Letts, Quentin, 190, 199
Lewinsky, Monica, 211–12
Lewis, John, 40
Liddle, Rod, 186–7, 188–9, 219
Linklater, Magnus, 248
Litwin, Boris, 2, 3–4
Liverpool débâcle, 193–208
Longford, Lord and Lady, 230
Lowe, Elias, 13
Lowe-Porter, Helen, 13
Lucas, Dr Colin, 92, 93–5
Luntz, Frank, 71–2

Maastricht Treaty, 103, 104
MacAlister, Katherine, 145
McDonagh, Melanie, 171
McKay, Peter, 171–2
McLaren, Leah, 168
MacLeod, Donald, 249–50
Macleod, Ian, 131

Macmillan, Harold, 58
Madeley, Richard, 208
Madrid summit, 101
Magdalen Women's Group, 63
Mail on Sunday, 210–11
Major, John, 113, 237
Malcolm-Smith, Sally, 113
Mandelson, Peter, 137–8
Mango, Andrew, 6
Mann, Thomas, 13
Mansell-Pleydell, Toby, 64
Marnham, Patrick, 132
Mercouri, Melina, 73
Merton, Paul, 128, 129
miners' strike (1984/85), 59–60
Moon, Tim, 31
Moore, Charles, xviii, 73, 104,
    126, 131, 132, 146, 156, 159,
    160, 177
Mostyn-Owen, Gaia, 78, 82
Mostyn-Owen, Willy, 77–8,
    82
Mount, Ferdinand, 132
Munckton, Alicia, 188, 189
Murdoch, Rupert, 162

Naipaul, Shiva, 132
Nath, Kabir, 53
Nationality Act (1981), 115
Neil, Andrew, 130, 226
Nethercote Cottage, 17–18, 21–6
New York Times: profile of Boris,
    157–8
Newland, Martin, 160
News of the World, 222, 255,
    256
Newsnight (TV programme),
    151
Norman, Jesse, 52–3

Oborne, Peter, 66, 133, 140, 147, 150, 181
O'Brien, Edna, 88
Observer, 224–5
Observer Food Monthly, 80
O'Meara, Sebastian, 81
Oxford Mail, 145
Oxford Myth, The (ed. R. Johnson), 66–7, 68, 74
Oxford Union, 68–73
Oxford University, 247; Boris at *see* Johnson, Boris: at Oxford

Parkinson (TV programme), 130
Paterson, Peter, 132
Patten, Chris, 16
Paxman, Jeremy, 146
Pearson, Neil, 175, 176
Peel, Sir John, 38
Pencharz, Matthew, 147, 148–9, 172
Peyam-i Sabah, 7
Pilger, John, 248
Platell, Amanda, 215
playing fields issue, 180–1
Political Society (Eton), 45, 51
Portillo, Michael, 150, 162–3, 226–7
Powell, Jonathan, 181–2
Pulay, Jessica, 72

Queen Mother, 147
Question Time (TV programme), 130

Radio Times, 126
Rammell, Bill, 247
Reid, Stuart, 134–6, 151, 157, 158, 194, 245

Rentoul, John, xviii
Richard and Judy (TV programme), 208
Richardson, Paul, 53
Risdon, Peter, 117
Roberts, Andrew, 151
Roberts, Dr David, 231
Rockefeller, John D., 14
Roman Empire, 251–3
Rome summit (1990), 102
Roosevelt, Franklin Delano, 154
Royce, Rachel, 189, 219–20
Rudd, Roland, 65
Rushbrooke, Justin, 62, 216–18
Rutland, Duke of, 37

Sabiha (second wife of Ali Kemal), 9
Sands, Philippe, 38, 112
Sands, Sarah, 159, 160, 170–1
Sayle, Murray, 132
Scargill, Arthur, 60
Scotsman, 151
Scriven, Marcus, 122–3
SDP, 59, 71
Seventy-Two Virgins (Johnson), 89, 189–92
Shackleton, Richard, 197, 198
Shakespeare, Sebastian, 220
Sheffield, Samantha, 244
Sieff, Teddy, 81
Sikorski, Radek, 64, 71, 79
Silvester, Christopher, 146
Sindall, Ann, 132, 136–9, 177–8, 229, 245
Singh, Dip *see* Wheeler, Dip
single currency issue, 101, 102
Smiley, Xan, 132

Spectator, 125, 128, 156, 206, 219–20, 228–9; Boris as editor, 33, 131–4, 139, 141, 143, 153, 156, 174; Boris's speech at Christmas lunch (2004), 228–9; circulation, 156; ownership of by Barclay brothers, 226; Parliamentarian of the Year awards lunch (2004), 219–22; reputation as a hotbed of illicit liaisons, 185–6, 188–9; resignation of by Boris and farewell speech to staff, 243, 244–5

Spencer, Charles (Viscount Althorp), xiv, 56, 62–3, 65, 66, 74, 119

Steiger, Anna, 85

Stilwell, Andrew, 183

Stothard, Peter, 91

Sunday Mirror, 210

Sunday Telegraph, 82, 103–4

Sunday Times, 144

Taki, 132

Taylor, Frank, 103

Tebbit, Norman, 158

Thatcher, Margaret, 65, 101, 102, 104, 112, 138, 237

Third Way, 253–4

Thomson, Alice, 144

Times Higher Education Supplement, 250

Times, The, 100; Boris works for, 88, 89–90; sacking of Boris over 'Edward II' article, 91–6

Top Gear (TV programme), 130

Tributary, 74

Universities UK, 250

Usborne, David, 98, 99, 100

Utley, T. E. (Peter), xii, 91

Van Oss, Oliver, 47

Vanity Fair, 192

Very Social Secretary, A (TV drama), 234

Wahl, Nick, 36

Wakefield, Mary, 175, 176, 178, 184

Wall Game (Eton), 46–7

Walters, Simon, 145, 211, 223

Warwick, Baroness, 250

Watkins, Alan, 206

Watson, Rory, 98

Waugh, Auberon, 20

Wellington, Duke of, 121

West, Richard, 132

Wheatcroft, Geoffrey, 132

Wheeler, Charles, xv, 111, 256

Wheeler, Dip, xv, 27, 111, 256

Wheeler, Marina *see* Johnson, Marina

Who's the Daddy? (play), 232–3

Widdecombe, Ann, 167

Williams, Clive, 29, 30–2, 35

Williams, Emma, 112, 174

Williams, Sir George, 10

Williams, Rowena, 32–3

Williams, Stanley, 10

Williamson, Billy, 29

Wilson, Charlie, 95–6

Wodehouse, P. G., 127, 191, 252

Wolff, Michael, 192

Wolverhampton Express & Star, 89

Worsthorne, Peregrine, 63
Wyatt, Petronella, xiv, 169–70,
243–4, 256; abortion, 209–10;
affair with Boris, 33, 162–6,
169–73, 215–16; and Boris's
alleged affair with Anna
Fazackerley, 257; and
Cameron, 244; story about

abortion and affair breaks in
press, 210–16, 222–5
Wyatt, Verushka, 162, 172, 173,
215, 223, 257
Wyatt, Woodrow, 156, 162, 163

Young, Toby, 56–7, 65, 66, 67,
74, 79, 95, 181, 232–3